SPARKNOTES®
ACT*
english &
reading
WORKBOOK

Spark Publishing
A Division of Barnes & Noble
120 Fifth Avenue
New York, NY 10011
www.sparknotes.com

Please submit changes or report errors to www.sparknotes.com/errors.

ISBN 13: 978-1-4114-9675-0
ISBN 10: 1-4114-9675-2

Printed and bound in Canada.

10 9 8 7 6 5 4 3 2 1

CONTENTS

The ACT
English &
Reading
Workbook

Overview of the ACT Reading Test 95

Review for the ACT Reading Test 102

Practice for the ACT Reading Test 129

Overview of the ACT Writing Test 168

Practice for the ACT Writing Test 191

INTRODUCTION

Welcome to the *SparkNotes ACT English & Reading Workbook*. No doubt you've bought this book because you need some extra practice for the English and Reading Tests. You've come to the right place. We created this workbook to give you targeted practice, as well as a thorough review of the topics covered by these two sections on the ACT.

This workbook comes equipped with specific test-taking strategies that will help you on the English and Reading Tests. Plus, we'll show you how to craft a "6" essay for the optional Writing Test. After learning our test-taking strategies and drilling yourself with 170 practice questions, you should be ready to ace the English and Reading Tests on the ACT. And after trying your hand at the two essay prompts we've included and reviewing the "3" and "4" essays we've reworked to a "6," you'll kick butt on the Writing Test too.

Let's begin by looking at the entire ACT. This chapter will explain all the topics the ACT covers, how it's formatted and organized, and how it's scored.

CONTENT AND STRUCTURE OF THE ACT

The writers of the ACT pride themselves on the regularity and predictability of their tests. They claim that every test has the same breakdown of question types. For example, every English Test contains ten punctuation questions, and every Math Test contains four trigonometry questions. The ACT writers believe that it is very important to maintain these numbers exactly. The numbers of questions will not vary.

The essential unchanging content of the ACT means you can be thoroughly prepared for the test. The ACT doesn't aim to trick you. The test writers are prepared to offer you exactly what type of information will be on the test and give you an opportunity to prepare for it. The exam will test your knowledge, and it makes sense that the best way to do that is to let you know precisely what will be covered and then see how well you can learn it. You won't be caught off guard by unfamiliar material on test day. Phew!

The ACT consists of four multiple-choice tests covering English, Math, Reading, and Science Reasoning. The optional writing section is tacked on to the very end of the test. These subject tests will always appear on the ACT in the order in which we just named them. The following provides a summary of the four sections and optional Writing Test:

- **The English Test (75 Questions, 45 Minutes).** The English Test contains five reading passages with grammatical and stylistic errors. Each passage is accompanied by fifteen questions. You are given 45 minutes to answer these 75 questions, which test your ability to make corrections. The English Test assesses your understanding of basic grammar, as well as your grasp of the tools and strategies a writer can use to put sentences together to form paragraphs and arguments.
- **The Math Test (60 Questions, 60 Minutes).** The Math Test covers six areas of high school math: pre-algebra, elementary algebra, intermediate algebra, coordinate geometry, plane geometry, and trigonometry. The majority of questions deal with pre-algebra, elementary algebra, and plane geometry, which are topics usually covered at the beginning of high school. The other three topics—intermediate algebra, coordinate

geometry, and trigonometry—constitute only 22 of the 60 questions on the test. You should learn these more difficult topics by the end of your junior year in high school. If you have not learned trigonometry by that time, don't sweat it: There are only four trig questions on the test, and four questions won't ruin your score. The Math Test differs from the other tests in two significant ways:

1. You're allowed to use a calculator.
2. There are five answer choices for each question, rather than four.

- **The Reading Test (40 Questions, 35 Minutes).** The Reading Test consists of four passages, each approximately 750 words long. The passages cover prose fiction, social science, humanities, and natural science. These passages always appear in the above order, and they are given equal weight in scoring. Each passage is accompanied by ten questions of varying levels of difficulty. Unlike the English and Math Tests, the Reading Test evaluates a set of skills you've acquired, rather than your mastery of the subjects you've learned. As the name of this test implies, these skills are your ability to read and to comprehend different types of passages.

- **The Science Reasoning Test (40 Questions, 35 Minutes).** Despite its intimidating name, Science Reasoning doesn't test your understanding of any scientific field. Instead, this test assesses your ability to "reason like a scientist" or to understand and analyze data. All of the information you need to know for the Science Reasoning Test will be presented in the questions. You just have to dig it out. The Science Reasoning Test consists of seven passages that contain a mixture of graphs, charts, and explanatory text. Each passage is followed by five to seven questions.

- **The Writing Test (1 Essay Question, 30 Minutes).** The Writing Test, which comes at the end of the exam, gives you 30 minutes to construct an essay based on a certain issue. The issue will be relevant to your life as a high school student. You can either choose to support the perspective given on the issue or provide a position based on your own experience with the question topic. Remember that the Writing Test is optional. Optional, you say? Yes, optional, but make sure you read the fine print closely: the 30-minute test is optional in the sense that institutions—colleges and universities—have the option of requiring it. The only way for you to get out of taking the Writing Test is to know well in advance that you won't be applying to a school that requires it for admission. However, you can take the Writing Test separately at a later time if you've already taken the ACT and want to apply to a school that requires a writing score. Note that if you do choose to take the Writing Test, your writing scores will be sent to all schools regardless of whether or not they require the Writing Test. Schools must specifically request not to be sent the writing scores, which is fairly unlikely. Either way, our chapter in this workbook will show you how to ace the Writing Test. Check it out after the Reading Test chapter.

ACT SCORING AND THE SCORE REPORT

The way the ACT is scored might be the most confusing aspect of the test. The number of scores a single ACT test produces is mind-boggling.

- First, you receive **four raw scores,** one for each subject test, in addition to **raw subscores** for subsections of the subject test (for example, Usage/Mechanics and Rhetorical Skills are the two subsections of the English Test).
- Those raw scores are converted into **four scaled scores** for the subject tests and **scaled subscores** for the subsections.
- The four scaled scores are averaged, producing the **Composite Score.**
- Finally, every single score is assigned a corresponding **percentile ranking,** indicating how you fared in comparison to other test-takers.

The two scores that will matter most to you and to colleges are the Composite Score and the overall percentile ranking. You will receive these two numbers, plus your scaled scores and subscores, in a score report about four to seven weeks after you take the test.

Raw Scores

Although you will never see a raw score on your score report, you should know how the raw score is computed. All raw scores are based on the number of questions you answered correctly. To compute the raw score of a subject test, simply count up the number of questions you answered correctly in that subject test. For each correct answer, you receive one point. Your raw score is the total number of points you receive. There are no point deductions for wrong answers.

Raw Subscores

Each subject test contains component subsections, each of which is assigned a raw subscore. For example, the English Test breaks down into Usage/Mechanics and Rhetorical Skills. Let's say you correctly answered 32 Usage/Mechanics questions and 21 Rhetorical Skills questions. Your raw score for those two subsections would be 32 and 21, respectively.

Scoring Practice Sets

This workbook is geared toward helping you find your strengths and weaknesses by taking the English and reading practice sets. Use the practice sets to figure out which areas you need a little more help in, then focus your study time on those. For example, if you find yourself answering more Usage questions correctly than Rhetorical Skills, you should devote more time to brushing up on Rhetorical Skills in the review section.

ACT Scores and the Optional Writing Test

The Writing Test is graded on a scale of 1 to 6. Two raters will grade your essay, and their scores will be added for a final subscore between 2–12. This subscore will then be combined with the English score to create a "Combined English/Writing score," on a 1–36 scale. This score, along with the Writing Test subscore, is listed on your score report in addition to the regular battery of scores. Also, the Writing Test answer sheet will be scanned and made available for download, so institutions will be able to read exactly what you wrote.

SPECIAL NOTE: If you take the Writing Test, all scores, including the Combined English/ Writing score and Writing subscore, will be sent to all the institutions you requested to receive your scores during the registration process. *This is regardless of whether or not those schools require the Writing Test.* A school must specifically request not to receive the results of the Writing Test or they will be sent to the school automatically.

Percentile Rankings

Percentile rankings indicate how you performed compared to the other students in the nation who took the same test you did. A percentile ranking of 75 means that 74 percent of test-takers scored worse than you and 25 percent scored the same or better.

The percentile rankings that matter most are the ones given for each subject test and the one accompanying the Composite Score (the following chart gives a sampling of percentile rankings and their corresponding Composite Scores). You will receive these percentiles on your score report.

The Composite Score

The Composite Score is the big one. It is the score your parents will tell their friends and the one your curious peers will want to know. More precisely, it is the average of your scaled scores for the four tests. So, if you got a 28 on the English Test, a 26 on the Math Test, a 32 on the Reading Test, and a 30 on the Science Reasoning Test, your Composite Score will be:

$$\frac{28+26+32+30}{4} = \frac{116}{4} = 29$$

On your score report, look for the Composite Score at the bottom of the page.

Correspondence of Composite Score, Percentile Rank & Correct Answers

The chart below shows a sample of Composite Scores and how they correspond to percentile rankings and percentages of questions answered correctly. This chart should give you some context for understanding the relative levels of achievement indicated by these Composite Scores:

Composite Score	ACT Approximate Percentile Rank	Approximate Percentage of Correct Answers
31	98%	89%
26	86%	76%
23	70%	66%
20	49%	55%
17	26%	44%

Who Receives the Scores? Not You.

That heading is a little misleading, but we thought we'd draw your attention to a bizarre aspect of the test. If you follow the ACT's registration instructions, you probably *won't* receive your score directly—your high school guidance counselor and any colleges you list (see the following section "Sending Scores to Colleges") will get it first, and then you must retrieve your score from your guidance counselor. But there are ways around this bureaucracy.

If you want to receive the report directly at home rather than through a third party at your high school, you can do one of two things:

1. Have your high school give the ACT test company permission to send your score to your home.
2. Leave the High School Code blank when you sign up for the test.

Option 2 is less complicated than Option 1, and there are no repercussions from leaving the code blank. Although ACT won't explicitly tell you about Option 2, it will work.

Early Score by Web

Now you are able to view your ACT score report 10 to 15 days after you take the test, and well before the 4 to 7 weeks it normally takes them to mail the scores to you. Simply log on to **actstudent.org** and locate Early Scores by Web. Of course there is a cost involved, as with most things related to the ACT, and satisfying your need to know will cost you $8. Note that it will cost $8 each time you view your scores, not a flat $8 fee, so make sure you print that score report page the first time you view it. Also, this feature is only available for national test dates.

Sending Scores to Colleges

In the moments before you take the ACT, the test administrators will give you a form allowing you to submit a list of up to six colleges that will receive your score directly from the company that makes the test. Don't submit a list unless you feel extremely confident that you will achieve your target score on the exam. After all, once you receive your score report and *know* you got the score you wanted, you can always order score reports to be sent to colleges. True, forwarding your scores costs a small fee after the first three reports, but the security it provides is worth it.

There is only one reason why you should opt to have your score sent directly to colleges. If you take the test near college application deadlines, you will probably have to choose this service to ensure that your scores arrive at the colleges on time.

Canceling the Score Report

If you choose to send your score report directly to colleges, but then have a really horrible day at the test center, don't panic. You have several days to cancel your score report. To do this, call ACT at (319) 337-1270. You have until noon, Central Standard Time, on the Thursday immediately following your test date to cancel your score.

Taking the ACT Twice (or Three Times)

If you have a really horrible day at the test center but you *didn't* choose to send your score report directly to colleges, don't cancel the report. No matter how many times you take the ACT, the colleges you apply to will see only one of your scores—the one you pick. If you don't score as well as you want to the first time, you can take the test again (and again and again) with impunity until you receive a score with which you are happy.

You have a good opportunity to improve your ACT score on the second try. More than half of second-time test-takers increase their scores. Taking the test a third or a fourth time probably won't make much difference in your score unless something went seriously awry on your previous tries.

WHAT AN ACT SCORE MEANS

You've taken the test and received your score; now what happens? If you're still in your junior year of high school, your ACT score can help you determine which colleges to apply to. Numerous publications each year publish reports on college profiles. Both these reports and your high school guidance counselor should help you determine your safety, 50/50, and reach schools, based on your ACT score, high school GPA, and other factors such as recommendations and extracurricular activities. While an applicant's total package is what counts, a good ACT score will never hurt your chances of getting into the schools you want. If you scored better than you expected, your score may help your applications at schools that you previously considered reaches.

How Your ACT Score Fits into Your Application Package

You may be wondering why a standardized test score matters in your college application. Let's compare two students, Megan and Chloe. Megan and Chloe are straight-A students at their respective high schools. These grades reflect the girls' relative standings at their schools (unless everyone at these two schools gets As), but how can college administrator Tim use these grades to compare Megan and Chloe? It seems like we're leading you to answer, "ACT scores!" Well, that's not entirely true. The truth is that Tim will look at a number of things to differentiate between the two girls. He'll carefully consider extracurricular activities, the girls' essays, and their recommendations. He'll also look at course descriptions to see whether Megan has long been acing Advanced Number Theory and Sanskrit while Chloe has been queen of her shop class.

So where does the ACT fit into this? Well, it's just another way of confirming relative standing among applicants. Tim may have access to course descriptions, but that curious college administrator is always on the lookout for other means of comparison. The ACT provides that means: It is a national standard by which colleges can evaluate applicants.

The ACT is merely one factor in your total application package, but it is an important factor that should not be overlooked or slighted. Although many schools hesitate to admit it, the fact is that your ACT score is one of the first things that stands out to someone reading your application. That person will eventually get around to reading teacher recommendations and your personal essay, but your ACT score is an easily digestible piece of information that will allow an admissions staff to form an early impression of your academic achievement. We're telling you this not to scare you, but to give you an honest assessment of what the ACT means to your college application.

That said, you should think of the ACT not as an adversary but as a tool that will help you get into college. For example, if Chloe is really a class-A student, but her high school doesn't give her the opportunity to extend her talents beyond shop class, the ACT provides an opportunity for her to show Tim she isn't a flake. If you approach the ACT pragmatically and don't hope for a knockout score you can't achieve, and if you study with some vigor, you can control your ACT destiny and get the score you need in order to get into the colleges of your choice.

WHEN TO TAKE THE TEST

Most people take the ACT at the end of junior year or the beginning of senior year. We recommend taking it at the end of junior year for a number of reasons:

1. Taking the test junior year will give you time to retake it if necessary.
2. You will have covered most of the material on the ACT by the end of junior year, and it will be fresh in your mind.
3. You are likely to forget some material during the summer before your senior year.

Ultimately, when you choose to take the test depends on only one thing: you. If you don't feel comfortable taking it junior year, spend some time during the summer reviewing and take the test during the fall of your senior year. If you are applying for regular admission to colleges, you will probably have a couple of test dates to chose from during your senior year, but take the earliest possible test if you are applying for early admission.

ACT Registration

To register for the ACT, you must first obtain an ACT registration packet. Your high school guidance counselor will probably have these packets available for you. If you can't get the packet through your high school, you can write or call the company that offers the ACT at:

> ACT Registration
> P.O. Box 414
> Iowa City, IA 52243-0414
> (319) 337-1270

You can also register for the test by visiting ACT's student website (**actstudent.org**) or, if your high school has it, by using ACT's software program College Connector. If you have taken the ACT within the last two years, you may reregister over the phone for an additional fee. You must make a VISA or Mastercard payment if you register on the Web, through College Connector, or by phone.

Regular, Late, and Standby Registration

There are three types of registration: regular, late, and standby.

-   Regular registration deadlines are approximately five weeks before the test date. The basic fee is $29 in the U.S. and $49 for students testing internationally. In addition to the basic fee, the Optional Writing Test is $14 for all students.
-   Late registration, which costs you an additional $19, ends three weeks before the test date.

The ACT registration packet will contain the exact dates for regular and late registration deadlines.

-   Standby registration is for those students who missed the late registration deadline and need to take the test by a certain date. Standby registration occurs on the day of the test. It costs an additional $39, and it does not guarantee you a seat or a test booklet. Standby registration is a last resort. If you must use standby registration, make sure to bring a completed registration folder, fee payment, and appropriate personal identification to the test center.

The ACT Admission Ticket

If you have registered for the ACT using regular or late registration, you will receive an admission ticket in the mail. This ticket will tell you when and where the test will be administered. It will also list the information you submitted to ACT, such as any colleges that will receive your score directly. You should read the admission ticket carefully to make sure there are no mistakes. If you find a mistake, follow the instructions on the back of the ticket for correcting information.

Test Dates

ACT test dates usually fall in October, December, February, April, and June. Certain states also have a September test date. Double-check your test dates by going to ACT's student website at **actstudent.org.**

GENERAL TEST-TAKING STRATEGIES

In this section, you'll learn how to take advantage of the ACT's structure to achieve the score you want. You'll learn basic rules for taking the ACT, as well as pacing and preparation strategies. These are the general test-taking strategies that you should use in all sections of the test, not just the English and Reading Tests. There are, of course, specific strategies for each of the individual tests. We'll cover the specific strategies for the English, Reading, and Writing Tests in this workbook.

SEVEN BASIC RULES FOR TAKING THE ACT

These seven rules apply to every section of the ACT. We list them here because you should always have these rules of test-taking in the back of your mind as you take the test. You don't need to focus on them obsessively, but you should be sure not to forget them. They will help you save time and cut down on careless errors.

1. **Know the instructions for each test.** Since you'll need all the time you can get, don't waste time reading the test instructions during the actual test. Read the instructions before taking each practice set so you'll have them memorized for the actual test.

2. **Use your test booklet as scratch paper.** Some students seem to think their test booklet has to look "pretty" at the end of the test. Don't be one of those students. A pristine test booklet is a wasted opportunity. In the Math Test, the ACT writers even give you "figuring" space for drawing diagrams and writing out solutions. You should write down all your work for math problems, in case you want to return to them later to complete the question or check your answer. The Math Test isn't the only place where you can benefit from marginal scribbling, though. Making margin notes alongside the Reading and Science Reasoning passages can help you stay on track when answering the subsequent questions. In addition, if you want to skip a question and come back to it later, you should make a distinctive mark next to it, so you won't miss it on your second pass through the questions.

3. **Answer the easy questions first.** This is a crucial strategy for the ACT. Since all questions within a subject test are worth the same number of points, there's no point in slaving away over a difficult question if doing so requires several minutes. In the same amount of time, you probably could have racked up points by answering a bunch of easy, less time-consuming questions.

   So, answer the easy and moderate questions first. That way you'll make sure that you get to see all the questions on the test that you have a good shot of getting right, while saving the leftover time for the difficult questions.

4. **Don't get bogged down by a hard question.** This rule may seem obvious, but many people have a hard time letting go of a question. If you've spent a significant amount of time on a problem (in ACT world, a minute and a half is a lot of time) and haven't gotten close to answering it, just let it go. Leaving a question unfinished may seem

like giving up or wasting time you've already spent, but you can come back to the problem after you've answered the easy ones. The time you spent on the problem earlier won't be wasted. When you come back to the problem, you'll already have done part of the work needed to solve it.

This strategy goes hand in hand with Rule 3. After all, the tough question that's chewing up your time isn't worth more to the computer grading your answer sheet than the easy questions nearby.

5. **Avoid carelessness.** There are two kinds of carelessness that threaten you as an ACT test-taker. The first kind is obvious: making mistakes because you are moving too quickly through the questions. Speeding through the test can result in misinterpreting a question or missing a crucial piece of information. You should always be aware of this kind of error because the ACT writers have written the test with speedy test-takers in mind: They often include tempting "partial answers" among the answer choices. A partial answer is the result of some, but not all, of the steps needed to solve a problem. If you rush through a question, you may mistake a partial answer for the real answer. Students often fall into the speeding trap when they become confused, since confusion brings nervousness and fear of falling behind. But those moments of confusion are precisely the moments when you should take a second to slow down. Take a deep breath, look at the question, and make a sober decision about whether or not you can answer it. If you can, dive back in. If you can't, skip the question and go on to the next one.

The second kind of carelessness arises from frustration or lack of confidence. Don't allow yourself to assume a defeatist attitude toward questions that appear to be complex. While some of these questions may actually be complex, some of them will be fairly simple questions disguised in complex-sounding terms. You should at least skim every question to see whether you have a feasible chance of answering it. Assuming you can't answer a question is like returning a present you've never even opened.

6. **Be careful bubbling in your answers.** Imagine this: You get all the right answers to the ACT questions, but you fill in all the wrong bubbles. The scoring computer doesn't care that you did the right work; all it cares about are the blackened bubbles on the answer sheet and the wrong answers that they indicate.

Protect yourself against this terrifying possibility with careful bubbling. An easy way to prevent slips on the ACT answer sheet is to pay attention to the letters being bubbled. Odd-numbered answers are lettered **A**, **B**, **C**, **D** (except on the Math Test, where they are **A**, **B**, **C**, **D**, **E**), and even-numbered answers are lettered **F**, **G**, **H**, **J** (except on the Math Test, where they are **F**, **G**, **H**, **J**, **K**).

You may also want to try bubbling in groups (five at a time or a page at a time) rather than answering one by one. Circle the answers in the test booklet as you go through the page, and then transfer the answers over to the answer sheet as a group. This method should increase your speed and accuracy in filling out the answer sheet. To further increase your accuracy, say the question number and the answer in your head as you fill out the grid: "Number 24, **F**. Number 25, **C**. Number 26, **J**."

7. **Always guess when you don't know the answer.** We will discuss guessing in the following section, "Understand 'Multiple Choice,'" but the basic rule is: always guess! You're much better off guessing than leaving an answer blank because there is no penalty for wrong answers.

UNDERSTAND "MULTIPLE CHOICE"

The multiple-choice format of the ACT should affect the way you approach the questions. In this section, we'll discuss exactly how.

Only the Answer Matters

A computer, not a person, will score your test. This computer does not care how you arrived at your answers; it cares only whether your answers are correct and readable in little oval form. The test booklet in which you worked out your answers gets thrown in the garbage, or, if your proctor is conscientious, into a recycling bin.

On the ACT, no one looks at your work. If you get a question right, it doesn't matter whether you did impeccable work. In fact, it doesn't even matter whether you knew the answer or guessed. The multiple-choice structure of the test is a message to you from the ACT creators: "We only care about your answers." Remember, the ACT is your tool to get into college, so treat it as a tool. It wants right answers? Give it right answers, as many as possible, using whatever strategies you can.

The Answers Are Right There

When you look at any ACT multiple-choice question, the answer is already right there in front of you. Of course, the ACT writers don't just *give* you the correct answer; they hide it among a bunch of incorrect answer choices. Your job on each question is to find the right answer. Because the answer is right there, begging to be found, you have two methods you can use to try to get the correct answer:

1. Look through the answer choices and pick out the one that is correct.
2. Look at the answer choices and eliminate wrong answers until there's only one answer left.

Both methods have their advantages: You are better off using option 1 in some situations and option 2 in others. In a perfect scenario in which you are sure how to answer a question, finding the right answer immediately is clearly better than chipping away at the wrong answers. Coming to a conclusion about a problem and then picking the single correct choice is a much simpler and quicker process than going through every answer choice and discarding the three or four that are wrong.

However, when you are unsure how to solve the problem, eliminating wrong answers becomes more attractive and appropriate. By focusing on the answers to problems that are giving you trouble, you might be able to use the answer choices to lead you in the right direction or to solve the problem through trial and error. You also might be able to eliminate answer choices through a variety of strategies (these strategies vary, as you'll see in the chapters devoted to question types). In some cases, you might be able to eliminate all the wrong answers. In others, you might only be able to eliminate one, which will still improve your odds when you attempt to guess.

Part of your preparation for the ACT should be to get some sense of when to use each strategy. Using the right strategy can increase your speed without affecting your accuracy, giving you more time to work on and answer as many questions as possible.

Guessing

We've said it once, but it's important enough to bear repetition: Whenever you can't answer a question on the ACT, you must guess. You are not penalized for getting a question wrong, so guessing can only help your score.

Random Guessing and Educated Guessing

There are actually two kinds of guesses: random and educated. Random guesser Charlie Franklin will always guess **C** or **F** because he really, really likes those letters. Using this method, Charlie has a pretty good chance of getting about 25 percent of the questions right, yielding a Composite Score of about 11. That's not too shabby, considering Charlie expended practically no intellectual energy beyond identifying **C** and **F** as the first letters of his first and last names.

But what about educated guesser Celia? Instead of immediately guessing on each question, she works to eliminate answers, always getting rid of two choices for each question. She then guesses between the remaining choices and has a 50 percent chance of getting the correct answer. Celia will therefore get about half of the questions on the test correct. Her Composite Score will be about a 19, which is an average score on the ACT.

The example of these two guessers should show you that while random guessing can help you, educated guessing can *really* help you. For example, let's say you know the correct answer for half of the questions and you guess randomly on the remaining half. Your score will probably be a 22—three points higher than the score you'd get leaving half of the answers blank. Now let's say you know the correct answer for half of the questions and you make educated guesses on the remaining half, narrowing the choices to two. You can probably score a 26 with this method, landing you in the 90th percentile of test-takers. This is a good score, and to get it you only need to be certain of half the answers.

"Always guess" really means "always eliminate as many answer choices as possible and then guess." Practice your guessing when you take the practice sets.

A Note to the Timid Guesser

Some students feel that guessing is like cheating. They believe that by guessing, they are getting points they don't really deserve. Such a belief might be noble, but it is also mistaken, for two reasons.

First, educated guessing is actually a form of partial credit on the ACT. Let's say you're taking the ACT and come upon a question you can't quite figure out. Yet while you aren't sure of the definite answer, you are sure that two of the answer choices *can't* be right. In other words, you can eliminate two of the four answer choices, leaving you with a one in two chance of guessing correctly between the remaining two answer choices. Now let's say someone else is taking the same test and gets to the same question. But this person is completely flummoxed. He can't eliminate *any* answer choices. When this person guesses, he has only a one in four chance of guessing correctly. Your extra knowledge, which allowed you to eliminate some answer choices, gives you better odds of getting this question right, exactly as extra knowledge should.

Second, the people who made the ACT thought very hard about how the scoring of the test should work. When they decided that they wouldn't include a penalty for wrong answers, they knew that the lack of a penalty would allow people to guess. In other words, they built the test with the specific understanding that people would guess on every question they couldn't answer. The test creators *planned* for you to guess. So go ahead and do it.

PACE YOURSELF

The ACT presents you with a ton of questions and, despite its three-hour length, not that much time to answer them. As you take the test, you will probably feel some pressure to answer quickly. As we've already discussed, getting bogged down on a single question is not a good thing. But rushing isn't any good either. In the end, there's no real difference between answering very few questions and answering lots of questions incorrectly: Both will lead to low scores. What you have to do is find a happy medium, a groove, a speed at which you can be both accurate and efficient, and get the score you want. Finding this pace is a tricky task, but it will come through practice and strategy.

Keep an Eye on the Clock

Because the ACT is a timed test, you should always be aware of the time. The proctor at the test center will strictly enforce the time limits for each subject test. Even if you have only one question left to answer, you won't be allowed to fill in that bubble.

As you take the test, watch the clock. You shouldn't be checking it every two minutes, since you will only waste time and give yourself a headache. But you should check occasionally to make sure you are on pace to achieve your target score.

SET A TARGET SCORE

The ACT is your tool to get into college. Therefore, a perfect score on the ACT is not a 36; it's the score that gets you into the colleges of your choice. Once you set a target score, your efforts should be directed toward achieving *that* score and not necessarily a 36.

In setting a target score, the first rule is to be honest and realistic. Base your target score on the schools you want to attend, and use the results from your practice tests to decide what's realistic. If you score a 20 on your first practice test, your target score probably should not be a 30. Instead, aim for a 23 or 24. Your scores will likely increase on your second test simply because you'll be more experienced than you were the first time, and then you can work on getting several extra problems right on each subject test. Adjust your pacing to the score you want, but also be honest with yourself about what pace you can maintain.

PREPARE

Preparation is the key to success on the ACT. When the ACT is lurking sometime far in the future, it can be difficult to motivate yourself to study. Establishing an organized study routine can help keep you on track as you approach the test date.

Setting Up a Study Schedule

Rather than simply telling yourself to study each week, you might want to write down an actual schedule, just as you have a schedule of classes at school. Keep this schedule where you'll see it every day, and consider showing it to a parent who will nag you incessantly when you don't follow it. (You might as well use your parents' nagging capabilities to your own advantage for once.) You should reward yourself for keeping to your schedule.

You should allot at least a few hours a week to studying, depending on how much time you have before the test date. If you start preparing six weeks in advance, you might consider studying one subject per week, with the last week left over for light review. Our chapters on the English and Reading Tests will give you a solid review of the material you need to know.

To complement your studying, take the practice sets in the weeks leading up to the test. If you're preparing for English one week, take the English practice sets to help focus your studying.

Test Day

You must bring the following items to the test center on the day of the test:

1. Your admission ticket.
2. Photo ID or a letter of identification.

Unless a test proctor recognizes you, you will not be allowed in the test room without appropriate identification. We also suggest that you bring the following:

3. Number Two pencils.
4. A calculator. You should bring the calculator you normally use (preferably with an extra battery). You don't want to get stuck searching frantically for the right buttons on an unfamiliar calculator.
5. A watch. Your test room may not have a clock, or the clock may not be visible from where you're sitting. Since the test proctors only call out the time five minutes before the end of each section, you have to rely on yourself to know how much time remains.
6. A snack, to keep up that energy.
7. Lucky clothes. Why not?

GET ONLINE

Last but not least, don't forget to visit us online. Go to **testprep.sparknotes.com** to take a free ACT diagnostic test. With the purchase of this workbook, we'll also give you free access to another full-length ACT practice test. If you need more practice, log on to the SparkNotes ACT website to take another test for $4.95. Our powerful test software will pinpoint your problem areas and help you overcome your weaknesses. Based on your diagnostic test, we will build you a personalized study plan that links to the ACT topics you need to review. We recommend that you take a practice test after you've finished the practice sets in this book. You should also take advantage of the message boards where you can chat about your anxieties and share study tips with fellow test-takers.

OVERVIEW OF THE ACT ENGLISH TEST

The ACT English Test assesses your knowledge of English grammar and writing. On the English Test, you will have 45 minutes to answer 75 questions. That may seem like a large number of questions and relatively little time, but the ACT English Test, more than any other ACT test, assesses what you already know, your knowledge of grammar and writing. Essentially, this means you can be completely prepared for the English Test if you study all the material it covers. This section will teach you exactly that material. After you've reviewed the material, quiz yourself on what you learned and take the English practice sets.

THE INSTRUCTIONS

Memorize the instructions for the English Test long before you arrive at the test center. In fact, your first step in preparing for the ACT should be learning the instructions for all four individual tests. On the actual test, the test instructions are time-consuming obstacles, which you can remove by learning them in advance. You can also benefit from them while you study because they contain valuable information about ACT questions and how to answer them.

Read through each set of instructions several times until you know them all like the back of your hand. The English Test instructions are particularly long, so you'll save yourself time on the test by learning them now.

DIRECTIONS: There are five passages on this test. You should read each passage once before answering the questions on it. In order to answer correctly, you may need to read several sentences beyond the question.

There are two question formats within the passages. In one format, you will find words and phrases that have been underlined and assigned numbers. These numbers will correspond with sets of alternative words/phrases, given in the right-hand column of the test booklet. From the sets of alternatives, choose the answer choice that works best in context, keeping in mind whether it employs standard written English, whether it gets across the idea of the section, and whether it suits the tone and style of the passage. You will usually be offered the option "NO CHANGE," which you should choose if you think the version found in the passage is best.

In the second format, you will see boxed numbers referring to sections of the passage or to the passage as a whole. In the right-hand column, you will be asked questions about or given alternatives for the sections marked by the boxes. Choose the answer choice that best answers the question or completes the section. After choosing your answer choice, fill in the corresponding bubble on the answer sheet.

These instructions will seem much clearer to you after you've seen the sample English Test questions in the following sections and practiced with the practice sets.

FORMAT OF THE ENGLISH TEST

The five passages on the English Test contain two question formats: underlines and boxes. Both the underlines and the boxes will be numbered so you can find the corresponding multiple-choice answers in the right-hand column of the test booklet.

Below you'll find a sample English Test paragraph, illustrating both question formats:

[1] That summer my parents <u>buy</u> me my first bike—my first true love. [2] One day, I crashed into a tree and broke my leg. [3] Unfortunately, my control of the bike was not as great as my enthusiasm for it. [4] I spent all my afternoons speeding around the neighborhood blocks. [18]

17. **A.** NO CHANGE
    B. bought
    C. have bought
    D. buys

18. Which of the following provides the most logical ordering of the sentences in paragraph 3?

    F. 3, 2, 1, 4
    G. 3, 1, 4, 2
    H. 1, 4, 3, 2
    J. 1, 4, 2, 3

Question 17 demonstrates the underline format on the English Test. In this example, the word "buy" is underlined and numbered 17, indicating that you can replace "buy" with **B**, **C**, or **D**, or keep it by selecting **A** ("NO CHANGE"). Decide which answer choice makes the sentence grammatically correct, and fill in the corresponding bubble on your answer sheet. (The correct answer is **B**.)

Question 18 is an example of a Rhetorical Skills question indicated by a boxed number. The boxed number indicates that the question will deal with a large section of the passage, not just a few words. This question asks you to reorganize the sentences of the paragraph in a logical manner. Once you've arrived at an answer, fill in the corresponding bubble on your answer sheet. (The correct answer to this question is **H**.)

Don't worry about the answers to these questions now. We'll deal with the specific question types and the grammar covered on the English Test later on in this chapter.

CONTENT OF THE ENGLISH TEST

There are actually two types of content on the English Test: the content of the passages and the content of the questions. Question content is the more important of the two.

When we say "the content of the passages," we mean the subjects covered by the five English Test passages. The passages usually cover a variety of subjects, ranging from historical discussions to personal narratives. Don't worry about passage content for now; it is important when answering certain Rhetorical Skills questions, which we'll discuss toward the end of this chapter, but the grammar of the passage is generally more important.

Question Types

There are two types of questions on the English Test: Usage/Mechanics and Rhetorical Skills. The majority of this section is devoted to explaining the question content on the English Test. For now, we'll give you a brief summary of the material.

Usage/Mechanics Questions

The 40 Usage/Mechanics questions on the test deal with the proper use of standard written English. You can think of them as the "technical" aspect of the test because they ask you to apply the rules of standard English to sections of the passages. Questions covering usage and mechanics are almost always presented as underlined sections of the passages.

Usage/Mechanics questions test your understanding of the following categories:

1. **Punctuation (10 questions):** Punctuation questions ask you to identify and correct any misplaced, misused, or missing punctuation marks. The punctuation marks most commonly tested on the ACT are, in order of decreasing frequency, commas, apostrophes, colons, and semicolons.

2. **Basic Grammar and Usage (12 questions):** Basic Grammar and Usage questions usually target a single incorrect word that violates the conventional rules of English grammar. These questions frequently test your knowledge of agreement issues and pronoun and verb forms and cases.

3. **Sentence Structure (18 questions):** Sentence Structure questions tend to deal with the sentence as a whole. They test you on clause relationships, parallelism, and placement of modifiers.

If some of these Usage/Mechanics issues sound unfamiliar or confusing to you, don't worry—later, in the review chapter, we'll review all of the material you need to know for these questions.

Rhetorical Skills Questions

The 35 Rhetorical Skills questions test your ability to refine written English. If the Usage/Mechanics questions are the technical aspect of the test, then the Rhetorical Skills questions are the intuitive aspect—but they require an intuition you can develop through practice. The boxes you encounter on the test will deal with Rhetorical Skills questions; some underlined sections may deal with Rhetorical Skills as well.

Rhetorical Skills questions break down into the following categories:

1. **Writing Strategy (12 questions):** Writing Strategy questions are concerned with a passage's effectiveness. These questions require that you understand the point, purpose, and tone of a passage. When answering these questions, you must decide the best way to support a point with evidence, to introduce and conclude paragraphs, to make a transition between paragraphs, or to phrase a statement.

2. **Organization (11 questions):** Organization questions can deal with individual sentences, individual paragraphs, or the passage as a whole. They will ask you either to restructure the passage or paragraph or to decide on the best placement of a word or phrase within a sentence.

3. **Style (12 questions):** Style questions focus on effective word choice. They will ask you to eliminate redundancy and to select the most appropriate word or phrase. In order to answer style questions correctly, you need to understand the tone of a passage, and you need to have a good eye for clear written English.

Because Rhetorical Skills questions require a sense of what constitutes good writing in English, they tend to be more difficult than Usage/Mechanics questions, which primarily require that you understand grammatical rules. This sense for good writing can be developed through review and practice.

Memorization and the Content of the English Test

The ACT writers emphasize that the English Test is not a test of memorization. It would be more accurate to say that the test does not *explicitly* test your memorization of rules of the English language.

You will not be tested on vocabulary on the English Test, but having a decent vocabulary is important in answering style and strategy questions. The questions often ask you to choose the most effective word or phrase. If you don't know what some of the words mean, you may not be able to make the right choice. Take note of these tricky words on the practice sets and look them up if necessary. It never hurts to expand your vocabulary!

Technically, the test does not ask you to memorize grammar rules, but it should be obvious that doing well on the test requires that you know the conventional rules of grammar. You won't be asked to state the definition of a gerund, but you'll be in trouble if you can't make your subjects and verbs agree or if you think a comma splice is something tasty in your spice rack.

Obviously, you need to understand grammatical rules for the English Test. While knowing these rules does not explicitly require memorization, most people begin to learn grammar by memorizing its rules.

STRATEGIES FOR THE ENGLISH TEST

Although the English Test is relatively straightforward, you should use certain strategies to improve your speed and efficiency and to avoid any traps the ACT writers may have included. This section covers both broad strategies for approaching the English Test, as well as specific tips for eliminating multiple-choice answers.

Skim the Entire Passage First

Don't immediately jump to the questions. Instead, first read quickly through the passage you're working on; then begin answering the accompanying questions.

While reading the passage once through before getting to the questions may seem like extra work, it will prevent you from making unnecessary errors. The ACT English Test instructions warn that you may need to read beyond a question in order to answer it correctly. Reading the entire passage will also help you with Rhetorical Skills questions by giving you an understanding of the passage's purpose, argument, and tone.

If you need further convincing, the following sample English Test question demonstrates why reading beyond the underlined section is necessary:

her dogs <u>has</u> sleek, brown hair
14

14. F. NO CHANGE
    G. are
    H. have
    J. do not have

Seems pretty easy, doesn't it? "Ah, a simple subject-verb agreement problem," you're probably thinking. "The answer, obviously, is **H**." But what if we show you the whole sentence?

The girl walking her dogs <u>has</u> sleek, brown hair 14	**14.**	**F.**	NO CHANGE
		G.	are
		H.	have
		J.	do not have

Reading the rest of the sentence reveals that the sleek, brown hair belongs to a girl rather than a pack of dogs. The question was about subject-verb agreement, but the words directly next to the underlined phrase misled you into thinking that the subject was "her dogs" and not "the girl." If you had read the passage first, you would have realized that the correct answer is **F**.

Admittedly, this example exaggerates the case for reading beyond the question, but it gets our point across. Ultimately, if you quickly read through the passage before tackling the questions, you'll avoid unnecessary mistakes without sacrificing much time.

Answer the Questions in Order

Answer English questions in the order in which they appear. The questions appear in a certain order for a reason: a question at the beginning deals with the beginning of the passage, a question in the middle deals with the middle of the passage, and so on. An organization question in the middle of a passage won't ask you to reorganize the entire passage or a faraway section of the passage. It will ask you to reorganize the material directly to the left of the question. Rhetorical Skills questions on the passage as a whole appear at the end of the passage, and what better time to answer those questions that deal with the entire passage than at the end? Make sure you follow this order on the practice sets.

Organization of Usage/Mechanics and Rhetorical Skills Questions

Questions on the English Test do not appear in order of difficulty. On many passages, you tend to see easy Usage/Mechanics questions near the beginning and relatively difficult Rhetorical Skills questions at the end, but there is no set rule about the order of their appearance.

Guess and Move On

If you come to a question you can't answer, you can either circle the question number so you can return later, or you can guess right away, leaving the question behind forever. On the English Test, and only on the English Test, we suggest guessing and moving on. As we stated earlier, the questions on the English Test assess what you already know rather than what you can figure out, so if you don't get the answer right off the bat (or a few seconds off the bat), you're not likely to get it by intense wriggling and head scratching. With that in mind, marking the question in order to come back later seems like a needless waste of time—you might as well take your shot right away and move on to more fruitful English territory.

Following this strategy, you should not move on to a new passage without answering all the questions from the previous one. Needless to say, if you follow our suggestion and guess when you don't know the answer, you won't encounter this problem. But if you do decide to return to a question you skipped, do so before moving on to the next passage; otherwise, you're likely to forget crucial details from the passage.

Eliminate Answer Choices

As discussed in the "General Test-Taking Strategies" section, educated guessing is always better than blind guessing. Whenever you guess, try first to eliminate some of the multiple-choice answers to improve your odds of guessing correctly. Take a look at these sample answers:

> **A.** When I swung the bat I knew, I had hit a home run.
> **B.** When I swung the bat, I knew I had hit a home run.
> **C.** When I swing the bat I will know I always hit a home run.
> **D.** When, I swung the bat I knew, I had hit a home run.

You can probably figure out from these answer choices that there is a comma placement error. **A**, **B**, and **D** all give versions of the same sentence with different comma placement. **C**, attempting to lure you off the right track, offers a comma-less version of the sentence with nonsensically altered verb tenses.

Can you eliminate any of these answer choices? Well, **C** looks like a prime candidate for elimination because it makes little sense. **D** also looks like it can go because of the comma placed after "When," which leaves the word dangling at the beginning of the sentence. If you can eliminate either or both of these, you greatly increase the chance that you'll pick the correct answer, which is **B**.

Eliminate Answer Choices with Multiple Errors

Quite often, you will encounter questions that involve more than one error. While these questions may seem harder to answer than single-error questions, you can benefit from the multiple errors when trying to eliminate answer choices: if you can't spot one error, you might spot the other.

Instead of tackling all the errors at once, you'll have an easier time picking them off one by one. Let's use the following example:

> **A.** Cathys' friends left they're bags in the room.
> **B.** Cathy's friends left there bags in the room.
> **C.** Cathys friends left their bags in the room.
> **D.** Cathy's friends left their bags in the room.

These sentences contain two variations. If you focus on Cathy and her friends, you realize that you should eliminate **A** and **C** for incorrect apostrophe placement. Now you've narrowed your options to **B** and **D**, which respectively use "there" and "their" as possessive pronouns. If you don't know the difference between the two, you have a 50 percent chance of guessing the right answer. If you do know the difference, you know that "there bags" is incorrect and that the correct answer is therefore **D**.

Beware of Distractors

Be wary of answer choices that try to trick you into overcorrecting the problem. These answer choices are called "distractors" and are meant to trip you up. You shouldn't be fooled into finding additional "errors" by an answer choice that has completely made over the original. The correct answer to a question is not necessarily the one that has changed the most elements of the underlined phrase.

Choose "NO CHANGE"

In fact, the correct answer to a question is not necessarily one that has changed anything at all. All Usage/Mechanics questions and some Rhetorical Skills questions offer you "NO CHANGE" as an answer choice. Do not overlook "NO CHANGE" as a possible answer to the problem. It is correct approximately 20 percent of the time it's offered.

If your gut tells you there's nothing wrong with the underlined phrase, don't change the phrase.

Don't Hesitate to Choose "OMIT"

You will often see the answer choice "OMIT the underlined portion." By choosing it, you can remove the entire underlined portion from the passage.

When an answer choice allows you to "OMIT the underlined portion," think hard about that option. "OMIT," when it appears as an answer, is correct approximately 25 percent of the time. We don't suggest that you go through the test ticking off "OMIT" for every possible question, but we do want you to consider it as an answer.

"OMIT" is an attractive (and often correct) answer because it eliminates redundant or irrelevant statements. For example:

The bag was free. I didn't have to pay for it. 21	21.	A. NO CHANGE
		B. I paid five dollars for it.
		C. I paid almost nothing for it.
		D. OMIT the underlined portion.

The ACT writers want your edits to make the passage as concise as possible. A statement like the one above should strike you as redundant because you clearly don't need to pay for something that's free—so why say the same thing twice? If you choose **A**, you keep the redundant sentence in the passage and get the answer wrong. **B** and **C** don't make much sense because they have you paying for the free bag. **D** is the correct answer because it omits an unnecessary statement. Without the second sentence, a reader still understands that the free bag didn't cost anything.

When deciding whether to omit, read the passage or sentence without the underlined portion and see whether the new version of the sentence makes as much, if not more, sense to you as the original. If it does, go ahead and choose "OMIT." If the passage or sentence loses something in the omission, then turn to the other answer choices.

REVIEW FOR THE ACT ENGLISH TEST

In this review, we will touch on the concepts most frequently tested on the English Test. As we discussed earlier, there are two question types that appear on the test: Usage/Mechanics and Rhetorical Skills. First, we'll review the topics you need to know for the Usage/Mechanics questions.

USAGE/MECHANICS

In order to do well on the English Test, you need to know the basic rules of grammar. Specifically, you need to know the rules of grammar most often tested by the ACT. This section will teach you the grammar you need to know for the test. These Usage/Mechanics topics are:

1. Punctuation
2. Basic Grammar and Usage
3. Sentence Structure

Punctuation

Punctuation shows you how to read and understand sentences. For instance, the period at the end of the last sentence indicated that the sentence had come to an end and that the next sentence would begin a new thought. We could go on and on like this, but you get the point.

The ACT English Test requires that you know the rules for the following types of punctuation:

1. Commas
2. Apostrophes
3. Semicolons
4. Colons
5. Parentheses and Dashes
6. Periods, Question Marks, and Exclamation Points

Not all of these punctuation types are tested on every English Test. However, you can definitely expect to find questions dealing with the first four items of the list on the English Test you take.

Commas   6 uses

Misplaced, misused, and missing commas are the most frequent punctuation offenders on the English Test. Commas can serve several functions within sentences.

Commas Separate Independent Clauses Joined by a Conjunction [fan boys]

An independent clause contains a subject and a verb (an independent clause can be as short as "I am" or "he read"), and it can function as a sentence on its own. When you see a conjunction (*and, but, for, or, nor, yet*) joining independent clauses, a comma should precede the conjunction. For example:

> Lesley wanted to sit outside, *but* it was raining.
>
> Henry could tie the shoe himself, *or* he could ask Amanda to tie his shoe.

In each example, the clauses on both sides of the comma could stand as sentences on their own. With the addition of the comma and conjunction, the two independent clauses become one sentence.

Commas Delineate a Series of Items

A series contains three or more items separated by commas. The items in a series can be either nouns (such as "dog") or verb phrases (such as "get in the car"). Commas are essentially the structural backbone of a series. For example:

> The hungry girl devoured *a chicken, two pounds of pasta, and a chocolate cake.*
>
> When he learned his girlfriend was coming over, Nathaniel *took a shower, brushed his teeth, and cleaned his room.*

The comma follows all but the last item in the series. When using a conjunction, such as *and* or *or,* at the end of the series, remember to precede it with a comma (". . . brushed his teeth, *and* cleaned his room").

Commas Separate Multiple Nonessential Adjectives Modifying a Noun [→ can switch around]

When two or more nonessential adjectives modify a noun, they should be separated by a comma. Of course, the key to figuring out whether there should be a comma separating two adjectives is being able to determine whether the adjectives are essential or nonessential. Luckily, there's a simple rule that can help you: the order of nonessential adjectives is interchangeable. For example:

> Rebecca's new dog has *long, silky* hair.
>
> The *loud, angry* protesters mobbed the building.

These two sentences would make equal sense if you switched the order of the adjectives: "Rebecca's new dog has *silky, long* hair" and "The *angry, loud* protesters mobbed the building."

[handwritten margin notes: list / nonessential description / dep. / 2 Coord.]

The case is different if you have an essential adjective modifying the noun. Essential adjectives specify the nouns they modify; they are bound to the noun, so that the noun loses meaning if separated from its adjective. A noun modified by an essential adjective should be treated as a single noun. If you come across two adjectives modifying a noun, and one is essential, you should *not* use a comma between them. For example:

> My mother hates *noisy electronic music.*

"Electronic music" functions as an indivisible noun; "electronic" specifies the type of music the mother hates. "Noisy" is a nonessential adjective modifying the noun "electronic music." Changing the order of "noisy" and "electronic" ("My mother hates electronic noisy music") would not make sense. If you can't change the order of two adjectives preceding a noun, you know the adjective nearest the noun is essential, so you should not use a comma.

Commas Set Off Dependent Phrases and Clauses from the Main Clause of a Sentence
Unlike independent clauses, dependent phrases and clauses are not sentences in themselves; rather, they serve to explain or embellish the main clause of a sentence. When they appear at the beginning of a sentence, they should be set off from the main clause by a comma. For example:

> *Scared of monsters,* Tina always checked under her bed before going to sleep.
>
> *After preparing an elaborate meal for herself,* Anne was too tired to eat.

The first example shows a dependent clause ("Scared of monsters") acting as an adjective modifying "Tina." The second example shows a dependent clause acting as an adverb. Since the adverbial clause is at the beginning of the sentence, it needs to be set off from the main clause by a comma. Adverbial clauses should also be set off by commas if they appear in the middle of a sentence. However, if an adverbial clause appears at the end of a sentence, you do not need to use a comma. For example:

> Anne was too tired to eat *after preparing an elaborate meal for herself.*

Commas Set Off Nonessential Phrases and Clauses
Nonessential phrases are like nonessential adjectives in that they embellish nouns without specifying them. Nonessential phrases should be set off from the rest of the sentence by commas. For example:

> Everyone voted Carrie, *who is the most popular girl in our class,* prom queen.
>
> The decrepit street sign, *which had stood in our town since 1799,* finally fell down.

When you use nonessential phrases like the two above, you assume that "Carrie" and "the decrepit street sign" do not need any further identification. If you remove the nonessential phrases, you should still be able to understand the sentences.

Restrictive phrases, on the other hand, are not set off by commas because they are necessary to understand the modified noun and the sentence as a whole. For example:

The girl *who is sick* missed three days of school.

The dog *that ate the rotten steak* fell down and died.

If you removed the restrictive phrases ("who is sick" and "that ate the rotten steak") from these sentences, you would be left wondering "which girl?" and "which dog?" These restrictive phrases are used to identify exactly which girl missed school and exactly which dog died. Setting off "who is sick" in commas would assume that the girl's identity is never in doubt; there is only one girl who possibly could have missed school. In this case, we know the identity of the girl only because the restrictive phrase specifies "the girl who is sick."

Commas Set Off Appositives → *descriptor phrase, nonessential additional info*

Appositives are similar to nonessential phrases. An appositive is a phrase that renames or restates the modified noun, usually enhancing it with additional information. For example:

Everyone voted Carrie, *the most popular girl in school*, prom queen.

The dog, *a Yorkshire Terrier*, barked at all the neighbors.

In these two examples, "the most popular girl in school" and "a Yorkshire Terrier" are appositives used to explain the nouns they modify. You should be able to draw an imaginary equal sign between the noun and the appositive modifying it: Carrie = the most popular girl in school, the dog = a Yorkshire Terrier. Because they are equal, you should be able to swap them and retain the meaning of the sentence: "Everyone voted the most popular girl in school, Carrie, prom queen."

Apostrophes

Apostrophes are the second most commonly tested punctuation mark on the English Test. Apostrophes primarily indicate possession, but they also take the place of omitted letters in contractions (for example, "was not" becomes "wasn't" and "it is" becomes "it's"). You will be tested chiefly on your knowledge of the apostrophe's possessive function.

The Possessive and Singular Nouns

A singular noun (for example: "Simon," "the dog," "the bottle") can be made possessive by adding an apostrophe followed by an "s." For example:

Simon's teacher was in the room.

My mom forgot the *dog's* food.

We removed the *bottle's* label.   *bottles'* (handwritten)

The apostrophe follows directly after the noun. If you move the apostrophe after the "s" (for example, if you write "dogs'" rather than "dog's"), you will change the meaning of the sentence (see the following section "The Possessive and Plural Nouns"). If you forget the apostrophe altogether, you will render the sentence meaningless.

The Possessive and Plural Nouns

Most plural nouns (for example: "the boys," "the dogs," "the bottles") can be made possessive by adding only an apostrophe. For example:

The *boys'* teacher was in the room.   *boys* (handwritten)

My mom forgot the *dogs'* food.   *'dogs* (handwritten)

We removed the *bottles'* labels.   *bottles* (handwritten)

The apostrophe directly follows plural nouns that end in "s" to make them possessive.

But for plural nouns that do not end in "s" (for example, "women"), you should treat the plural form as a singular noun (i.e., add an apostrophe followed by an "s"). For example:

woman   women's man men's (handwritten)

The *women's* locker room needs to be cleaned.

The Possessive and Multiple Nouns

Sometimes you'll want to indicate the possessive of more than one noun ("Nick and Nora," "Dan and Johann"). The placement of the apostrophe depends on whether the possessors share the possession. For example:

Nick and Nora's dog solves crimes.

Dan's and Johann's socks are dirty.

(handwritten at top: children's food / Fungus's / smells)

In the example of Nick and Nora, the dog belongs to both of them, so you treat "Nick and Nora" as a single unit, followed by a single apostrophe and "s." In the second example, both Dan and Johann have dirty socks, but they don't share the same dirty socks, so you treat Dan and Johann as separate units, giving each an apostrophe and "s."

The Possessive and Pronouns

Unlike nouns and proper nouns, the possessive case of pronouns does not use an apostrophe. The following chart gives you nominative pronouns (the ones you use as subjects) and the corresponding possessive pronouns:

(handwritten above table: subject)

Nominative Pronoun	Possessive Pronoun
I	my
you *(s.)*	your
she	her
he	his
we	our
you *(pl.)*	your
they	their
it	its
who	whose

(handwritten to right of table: Who = he/she / whom = him/her)

For example:

> The dog chewed on *its* tail.
>
> You should give him *your* wallet.

Don't confuse the "its" and the "your" above with "it's" and "you're." This mistake is frequently tested on the English Test.

Its/It's, Their/They're

The ACT will test you on your ability to distinguish between "its" and "it's." "Its" is the possessive form of "it." "It's" is the contraction of "it is." This can be tricky to remember, since you are normally trained to associate apostrophes with possession. But when you're dealing with "its" versus "it's," the apostrophe signals a contraction. The same is true for "their/they're/there," "your/you're," and "whose/who's." Make sure you are aware of these exceptions to the apostrophe rule of possession.

Try the following practice problem:

Your face is red.
9

9. **A.** NO CHANGE
    B. You're face
    C. Your nose
    D. OMIT the underlined portion.

You can eliminate **C** and **D** immediately: **C** changes the meaning of the sentence for no particular reason, and **D** leaves you without a complete sentence. The decision comes down to "Your" and "You're." If you don't know the correct answer, try replacing "You're" with "You are." The resulting sentence is "You are face is red"—an odd remark. The correct answer is **A**, "NO CHANGE." You can employ this replacement technique whenever you don't know the answer to a possessive-or-contraction question. Once you replace the contraction with the full phrase, your ear will tell you which choice is right.

Semicolons

You'll usually find several questions dealing with semicolons on the English Test. The main functions of a semicolon that you should know for the test are its ability to join related independent clauses and its use in a series.

The Semicolon and Two Independent Clauses

Semicolons are commonly used to separate two related but independent clauses. For example:

Julie ate five brownies; Eileen ate seven.

Josh needed to buy peas; he ran to the market.

In these cases, the semicolon functions as a "weak period." It suggests a short pause before moving on to a related thought, whereas a period suggests a full stop before moving on to a less-related thought. Generally, a period between these independent clauses would work just as well as a semicolon, so the ACT won't offer you a choice between period or semicolon on the English Test. But you may see the semicolon employed as a weak period in an answer choice; in that case, you should know that it is being used correctly.

Frequently, you will see two independent clauses joined by a semicolon and a transitional adverb (such as *consequently*, *however*, *furthermore*, *indeed*, *moreover*, *nevertheless*, *therefore*, and *thus*). For example:

Julie ate five brownies; *however*, Eileen ate seven.

Josh needed to buy peas; *thus* he ran to the market.

These sentences function similarly to those joined by a comma and a conjunction. Here, the semicolon replaces the comma, and the transitional adverb replaces the conjunction. Most transitional adverbs should be followed by a comma, but for short adverbs such as "thus," the comma should be omitted.

The Semicolon and the Series: When the Comma's Already Taken

The semicolon replaces the comma as the structural backbone of a series if the items already contain commas. For example:

> The tennis tournament featured the surprise comeback player, Koch, who dropped out last year due to injuries; the up-and-coming star Popp, who dominated the junior tour; and the current favorite, Farrington, who won five of the last six tournaments.

If you used commas rather than semicolons in the above sentence, anyone reading the sentence would feel pretty confused. The semicolons in this example function exactly as commas do in a series, but they allow you to avoid overpopulating the sentence with commas.

Colons

You'll probably be tested on your knowledge of colons a couple of times on the English Test. The ACT writers want to be sure that you know how colons introduce lists, explanations, and quotations.

The Colon and Expectation

Colons are used after complete sentences to introduce related information that usually comes in the form of a list, an explanation, or a quotation. When you see a colon, you should know to expect elaborating information. For example:

> The wedding had all the elements to make it a classic: *the elegant bride, the weeping mother, and the fainting bridesmaids.*

In this example, the colon is used to introduce a list of classic wedding elements. Without the list following the colon, the sentence can stand alone ("The wedding had all the elements to make it a classic"). By naming the classic elements of a wedding, the list serves mainly to explain and expand upon the independent sentence that precedes it.

Check out this example of another way to use colons:

> The wedding had all the elements to make it a classic: *the elegant bride beamed as her mother wept and as the bridesmaids fainted.*

Here, the clause following the colon also has an explanatory function. In this case, the colon joins two independent clauses, but the clause following the colon is used to explain and expand the first.

Colons can also be used to introduce quotations. For example:

> The mother's exclamation best summed up the wedding: *"If only the bridesmaids hadn't fainted!"*

Here, the colon is used to introduce the mother's exclamation. Make sure the quotation following the colon is related to the sentence.

Colon Problems

You should learn the following rules in order to avoid erroneous colon use on the English Test:

A Colon Should Always Be Preceded by an Independent Clause.

> *WRONG:*   The ingredients I need to make a cake: flour, butter, sugar, and icing.
>
> *RIGHT:*   I need several ingredients to make a cake: flour, butter, sugar, and icing.

In the "WRONG" example, a sentence fragment precedes the list of items. The sentence should be reworked to create an independent clause before the colon.

There Should Never Be More Than One Colon in a Sentence.

> *WRONG:*   He brought many items on the camping trip: a tent, a sleeping bag, a full cooking set, warm clothes, and several pairs of shoes: sneakers, boots, and sandals.
>
> *RIGHT:*   He brought many items on the camping trip: a tent, a sleeping bag, a full cooking set, warm clothes, sneakers, boots, and sandals.

If you see a sentence that contains more than one colon, the sentence needs to be rephrased. Lists within lists or explanations within explanations do not work in standard written English.

Other ACT Punctuation

The English Test rarely tests punctuation marks other than the ones listed above. But in the odd case that the test writers do throw in some other punctuation errors, you should know what to expect. The ACT officially states that it covers, in addition to the punctuation mentioned above, the following punctuation marks:

Parentheses and Dashes

Parentheses usually surround words or phrases that break a sentence's train of thought but provide explanatory information for it. For example:

> Their road trip *(which they made in a convertible)* lasted three weeks and spanned fourteen states.

Similarly, parenthetical sentences can be inserted between other sentences, adding additional information to them without diverting their flow. For example:

> Their road trip lasted three weeks and spanned fourteen states. *(The one they took two years ago lasted two weeks and covered ten states.)* When they got home, they were exhausted.

In this example, the parenthetical information about the previous road trip is interesting but not completely relevant to the other sentences. Note that when an entire sentence is enclosed within parentheses, the period should be inside them as well.

Dashes function similarly to parentheses. Dashes indicate either an abrupt break in thought or an insertion of additional, explanatory information.

> He walked so slowly—*with his lame leg he couldn't go much faster*—that even his neighbor's toddler eventually overtook him.
>
> I don't have the heart to refuse a friend's request for help—*do you?*

Periods, Question Marks, and Exclamation Points

These are the least common forms of punctuation tested by the ACT. The ACT writers probably realized that these sentence enders are easier to grasp than other forms of punctuation because they basically each have only one function:

> The sentence ends here.
>
> Does the sentence end here?
>
> Hooray, the sentence ends here!

The period in the first example indicates that the sentence has ended. In the second example, the question mark indicates that a question is being asked. The third example is an exclamatory statement marked by an exclamation point. Exclamation points should be used sparingly to indicate statements made with great emotion (for example, anger, excitement, or agitation).

Basic Grammar and Usage

As you've probably already gathered, the English Test will never *explicitly* ask you to name a grammatical error. But in order to identify and fix errors, you should know what they are. While you'll often be able to rely on your ear to detect errors, many of the questions will ask you to fix phrases that are fine for spoken English but not for formal written English.

In the following section, we'll cover these grammar issues, which appear on the English Test:

1. Subject-Verb Agreement
2. Pronoun-Antecedent Agreement
3. Pronoun Cases
4. Verb Tenses
5. Adverbs and Adjectives
6. Idioms
7. Comparative and Superlative Modifiers

Subject-Verb Agreement

Singular verbs must accompany singular subjects, and plural verbs must accompany plural subjects. For example:

SINGULAR:	The *man wears* four ties.
	His favorite *college is* in Nebraska.
	Matt, along with his friends, *goes* to Coney Island.
PLURAL:	The *men wear* four ties each.
	His favorite *colleges are* in Nebraska.
	Matt and his friends go to Coney Island.

In the first example with Matt, the subject is singular because the phrase "along with his friends" is isolated in commas. But in the second example with Matt, his friends join the action; the subject becomes "Matt and his friends," calling for the change to a plural verb.

Subject-verb agreement is a simple idea, but ACT writers will make it tricky. Often, they'll put the subject at one end of the sentence and the verb a mile away. Try the following example:

An audience of thousands of expectant

people who have come from afar to listen

to live music in an outdoor setting seem
17

terrifying to a nervous performer.

17. **A.** NO CHANGE
B. seems
C. have seemed
D. to seem

To solve this problem, cross out the junk in the middle that separates the subject, "an audience," from the verb "seem." Remember that the subject of a sentence can never be part of a phrase that begins with "of."

You're left with:

> An audience *seem* terrifying to a nervous performer.

Now you can see what the verb should be:

> An audience *seems* terrifying to a nervous performer.

So the correct answer is **B**. Double-check by eliminating **C** and **D** because they are grammatically incorrect (and because they don't make much sense in the sentence).

As long as you can isolate the subject and verb, handling subject-verb agreement is relatively simple. But certain cases of subject-verb agreement can be tricky. The ACT writers like to test you on several of these difficult types of subject-verb agreement.

Collective Nouns

Collective nouns (such as *committee, family, group, number,* and *team*) can be either singular or plural. The verb depends on whether the collective noun is being treated as a single unit or as divided individuals. For example:

> SINGULAR: The *number* of people living in Florida varies from year to year.
>
> PLURAL: A *number* of people living in Florida wish they had voted for Gore.
>
> SINGULAR: The *committee decides* on the annual program.
>
> PLURAL: The *committee have disagreed* on the annual program.

You can often determine whether a collective noun is singular or plural by examining the article (*the* or *a*) that precedes it. As in the first example, "*The* number" is generally singular, while "*A* number" is generally plural. This difference is demonstrated in the first example above. "*The* number" of people in Florida is a single entity—even though it comprises multiple individuals—so it takes a singular verb, "varies." "*A* number" of people, on the other hand, behave as multiple individuals—even though they wish for the same thing, they act independently of each other—so these people require a plural verb, "wish."

Looking to the article preceding a noun is a useful trick when deciding whether the noun is singular or plural, but it doesn't always work. In the second example, "*The* committee" can be both singular and plural. How the committee behaves (do they act together or apart?) decides whether the verb is singular or plural. If the committee does something as a unified whole ("*decides* on the annual program"), then the verb is singular. If the committee are divided in their actions ("*have disagreed* on the annual program"), then the verb is plural.

Indefinite Pronouns

Indefinite pronouns refer to persons or things that have not been specified. Matching indefinite pronouns with the correct verb form can be tricky because some indefinite pronouns that seem to be plural are in fact singular. Questions dealing with singular indefinite pronouns are popular with ACT writers, so you'd be wise to memorize a few of these pronouns now. The following indefinite pronouns are always singular, and they tend to appear on the English Test:

Another	Everybody	Nobody
Anybody	Everyone	No one
Anyone	Everything	Somebody
Anything	Each	Someone

each + another singular

All the indefinite pronouns in the list above should be followed by singular verbs. For example:

> *Anyone* over the age of 21 *is* eligible to vote in the United States.
>
> *Each has* its own patch of grass.

If you're used to thinking these pronouns take plural verbs, these sentences probably sound weird to you. Your best bet is to memorize the list above (it's not very long!) and to remember that those pronouns take singular verbs.

You should also be aware that not all indefinite pronouns are singular. Some (for example: *all*, *any*, *none*, and *some*) can be either singular or plural depending on the context of the sentence. Other indefinite pronouns (for example: *both*, *few*, *many*, and *several*) are always plural. The differences among these indefinite pronouns can be very confusing; determining what's right often requires an astute sense of proper English (or good memorization). If you're struggling to remember the different indefinite pronouns, take comfort in these two things:

1. The most commonly tested indefinite pronouns are the singular ones in the list we gave you.
2. You probably won't come across more than a couple of indefinite pronouns on the English Test you take.

Compound Subjects

Most compound subjects (subjects joined by *and*) should be plural:

Kerry and Vanessa live in Nantucket.

The blue bike and the red wagon need repairs.

The reasoning behind this rule is fairly simple: you have multiple subjects, so you need a plural verb. Thus "Kerry and Vanessa *live*" and the "bike and wagon *need*."

"There Is" or "There Are"?

Whether to use "there is" or "there are" depends on the singularity or plurality of the noun that the phrase is pointing out. If you have five grapes, you should say: "There *are* five grapes." If you have a cat, you should say: "There *is* a cat." The "is" and the "are" in these sentences are the main verbs, so they must agree with the noun.

"Or" and "Nor"

If you have singular subjects joined by an "or" or "nor," the sentence always takes a singular verb. For example:

Either Susannah or Caitlin is going to be in trouble.

If one of the subjects is plural and the other is singular, the verb agrees with the subject closer to it. For example:

Neither the van nor the buses were operating today.

Either the dogs or the cat is responsible for the mess.

Both of these examples contain a singular and a plural subject. The main verb of the sentence is determined by the subject nearest it: in the first example, "buses" is closer to the verb, so the verb is plural, and in the second example, "cat" is closer to the verb, so the verb is singular.

Mathematics, News, Dollars, Physics

These and other words look plural but are singular in usage:

Today's *news was* full of tragic stories.

Trust your gut instinct with these words. You'll probably know they're singular from everyday usage. "Dollars" is an exceptional case—it's singular when you're talking about an amount of money ("ninety dollars is a big chunk of change") but plural when you're discussing a particular group of bills ("the dollars in my pocket are green").

Pronoun-Antecedent Agreement

The ACT writers usually include several pronoun-antecedent agreement errors on the English Test. An antecedent is a word to which a later pronoun refers back. For example, in the sentence "Richard put on his shoes," "Richard" is the antecedent to which "his" refers. When the pronoun does not agree in gender or number with its antecedent, there's an agreement error. For example:

> *WRONG:*   Already late for the show, Mary couldn't find *their* keys.
>
> *RIGHT:*   Already late for the show, Mary couldn't find *her* keys.

Unless another sentence states that the keys belong to other people, the possessive pronoun should agree in gender and number with "Mary." As far as we can tell, Mary is a singular, feminine noun, so the pronoun should be singular and feminine too.

The example of Mary contained a fairly obvious example of incorrect agreement, but sometimes the agreement error isn't as obvious on the ACT. In everyday speech, we tend to say "someone lost *their* shoe" (wrong) rather than "someone lost *his* shoe" (correct) or "someone lost *her* shoe" (also correct) because we don't want to exclude either gender and because "someone lost *his* or *her* shoe" sounds cumbersome. The common solution? We attempt gender neutrality and brevity by using "their" instead of "his" or "her." In informal speech, such a slip is okay. But if you see it on the test, it's an error.

You will also run into agreement errors where the antecedent is unclear. In these cases, the pronoun is ambiguous. We use ambiguous pronouns all the time in everyday speech, but on the test (you guessed it) they're wrong. For example:

> *WRONG:*   Trot told Ted that *he* should get the mauve pants from the
> sale rack.

This sentence is wrong because we don't know to whom "he" refers. Should Ted get the pants, or should Trot? Or should neither, because mauve pants are never a good idea? You should restate the original sentence so all the pertinent information is relayed without confusion or multiple meanings, such as "Trot told Ted that Ted should get the pants…."

Pronoun Cases

The ACT writers will definitely include some questions on pronoun cases. Pronoun case refers to the role of the pronoun in a sentence. There are three cases: nominative, objective, and possessive. You don't need to know the names of these cases, but you do need to know the differences between them (and knowing the names doesn't hurt). Here, we'll briefly describe each case.

The Nominative Case

The nominative case should be used when a pronoun is the subject of a sentence—for example, "*I* went to the store" and "*They* walked to the park." You should also use a nominative pronoun after any form of *to be*:

WRONG:	It was *me* on the phone.
RIGHT:	It was *I* on the phone.

The right sentence may sound awkward to you, but it's the correct use of the nominative. The people who laid down the rules of grammar considered *to be* a grammatical equal sign, so when you have a sentence like "It was I on the phone," you should be able to do this: "It" = "I." If that equation holds true, "I" should be able to take the place of "It" in the sentence: "I was on the phone."

It = I .

Pronoun Comparisons

The nominative also follows comparative clauses that usually begin with "as" or "than." When a pronoun is involved in a comparison, it must match the case of the other pronoun involved. For example:

Add is at the end .

WRONG:	I'm fatter than *her*, so I'll probably win this sumo wrestling match.
RIGHT:	I'm fatter than *she*, so I'll probably win this sumo wrestling match.

In this sentence, "I" is being compared to "her." Obviously, these two pronouns are in different cases, so one of them must be wrong. Since only "her" is in question, it must be wrong, and therefore "she" is the correct answer.

Another way to approach comparisons is to realize that comparisons usually omit words. For example, it's grammatically correct to say, "Alexis is stronger than Bill," but that's an abbreviated version of what you're really saying. The long version is, "Alexis is stronger than Bill is." That last "is" is invisible in the abbreviated version, but you must remember that it's there. Now let's go back to the sumo sentence. As in our Alexis and Bill example, we don't see the word "is" in the comparison, but it's implied. If you see a comparison using a pronoun and you're not sure if the pronoun is correct, add the implied "is." In this case, adding "is" leaves us with "I'm fatter than her is." That sounds wrong, so we know that "she" is the correct pronoun in this case.

The Objective Case

As may be obvious from its name, the objective case should be used when the pronoun is the object of another part of speech, usually a preposition or a transitive verb (a verb that takes a direct object):

PREPOSITION:	She handed the presents *to them*.
	Olivia made a cake *for* Emily, Sarah, and *me*.
	Between whom did you sit?
TRANSITIVE VERB:	Harry *gave me* the tickets.
	Call *me!*
	Did you *take him* to the movies?

In the second preposition example, two names appear between "for" and "me." If this confuses you, eliminate "Emily, Sarah, and" to get "Olivia made a cake *for me*." Then you'll see that "me" is the correct pronoun case, not "I" (as in "Olivia made a cake for I"). This strategy of crossing out intervening words also works in spotting the correct case for an object of a transitive verb.

In informal, spoken English, you will not hear "whom" used frequently, but in written English (particularly written ACT English), you must remember the all important "m." As in the third preposition example, "between whom" is correct; "between who" is not. A good way to figure out if you should use "who" or "whom" in a sentence is to see whether the sentence would use "he" or "him" (or "they" or "them") if it were rearranged a little. If the sentence takes "he" or "they," you should use "who"; if it takes "him" or "them," you should use "whom."

[handwritten margin note: He, They] WHO / Him] / Them } whom]

If you rearrange "Between whom did you sit?" you get:

Did you sit between *them*?

Now you can see that you need to use "whom" in the original sentence.

The Possessive Case
You already know to use the possessive case when indicating possession of an object (see "The Possessive and Pronouns" under "Apostrophes"):

My car

Her dress

Its tail

Whose wheelbarrow

You should also use the possessive case before a gerund, a verb form that usually ends with "ing" and is used as a noun. For example:

When it comes to *my studying* for the ACT, "concentration" is my middle name.

Despite hours of practice, *her playing* is really terrible.

You can think of gerunds as turncoat verbs that are now nouns, so they need to be preceded by the same possessive pronouns that precede noun objects.

The following chart shows you all the pronoun cases we've just discussed:

Nominative Case	Objective Case	Possessive Case
I	me	my
you *(s.)*	you	your
she	her	her
he	him	his
we	us	our
you *(pl.)*	you	your
they	them	their
it	it	its
who	whom	whose

Now that you know something about pronoun cases, try the following sample problem:

Me and Jesse went to Cosmic Bowling
      4
Night at the Bowladrome.

4. F. NO CHANGE
    G. Jesse and me
    H. Jesse and I
    J. I and Jesse

Knowing when to use "I" and when to use "me" can be difficult, especially within compound nouns. If you're not sure which is correct, use the crossing-out trick: cross out "and Jesse" and see what you have left.

Me went to Cosmic Bowling Night at the Bowladrome.

Unless you're doing your Ralph Wiggum imitation, that sentence sounds (and is) wrong. The correct sentence?

Jesse and I went to Cosmic Bowling Night at the Bowladrome.

So the answer to the problem is **H. J**, which also contains the correct pronoun "I," is wrong because the conventional rules of grammar require that you show a little deference in forming sentences involving yourself. "I" should always come after the other people involved in the activity.

Verb Tenses

Most verb tense errors on the English Test will be pretty easy to spot, since we don't often make tense errors in everyday speech. When you read a tense error on the test, it will most likely sound wrong to you. Your ear is your most reliable way of spotting tense errors.

Different Verb Tenses in One Sentence

Nowhere is it written that you must use the same tense throughout a sentence. For example, you can say, "I used to eat chocolate bars exclusively, but after going through a conversion experience last year, I have broadened my range and now eat gummy candy too." That sentence has tense switches galore, but they are logical: the sentence uses past tense when it talks about the past, and present tense when it talks about the present, and the progression from past to present makes sense. Another acceptable example:

> They *are* the best team in baseball, and I think they *will* triumph over what *could have been* devastating injuries.

But you can't throw in different tenses willy-nilly. They have to make sense. You can't say:

> Next year, I *was* on an ocean voyage.

"Next year" refers to the future, and "was" refers to the past. The sentence doesn't make any sense unless you're doing some time travel. Your most powerful weapon against tense switch questions is logic. We could prattle on for paragraph after paragraph about present tense, simple past, general present, and present perfect, but remembering the millions of different tense forms, and when to use which, is both difficult and unnecessary. For the English Test, if you don't hear an error the first time you read a sentence, and you don't see a pronoun problem, check out the tenses and figure out whether they're OK.

Tricky Verbs You're Likely to See on the ACT

By tricky verbs, we mean those verbs that never sound quite right in any tense—like "to lie," or "to swim." When do you lay and when do you lie? When do you swim and when have you swum? Unfortunately, there's no easy memory trick to help you remember when to use which verb form. The only solution is to learn and remember.

You LIE down for a nap.

You LAY something down on the table.

You LAY down yesterday.

You SWIM across the English Channel.

You SWAM across the Atlantic Ocean.

You HAD SWUM across the bathtub as a child. *Remote past.*

"To lie" and "to swim" aren't the only two difficult verbs. Below, you'll find a table of difficult verbs in their infinitive, simple past, and past participle forms. You don't have to memorize all of these forms; you'll probably only see one tricky-verb question. Still, it is well worth your time to read the list below carefully, and especially to make sure you understand those verbs that you've found confusing before.

Infinitive	Simple Past	Past Participle	Infinitive	Simple Past	Past Participle
Arise	Arose	Arisen	Lead	Led	Led
Become	Became	Become	Lie (to recline)	Lay	Lain
Begin	Began	Begun	Lie (tell fibs)	Lied	Lied
Blow	Blew	Blown	Put	Put	Put
Break	Broke	Broken	Ride	Rode	Ridden
Choose	Chose	Chosen	Ring	Rang	Rung
Come	Came	Come	Rise	Rose	Risen
Dive	Dived/dove	Dived	Run	Ran	Run
Do	Did	Done	See	Saw	Seen
Draw	Drew	Drawn	Set	Set	Set
Drink	Drank	Drunk	Shake	Shook	Shaken
Drive	Drove	Driven	Shine	Shone	Shone
Drown	Drowned	Drowned	Shrink	Shrank	Shrunk
Dwell	Dwelt/dwelled	Dwelt/dwelled	Shut	Shut	Shut
Eat	Ate	Eaten	Sing	Sang	Sung
Fall	Fell	Fallen	Sink	Sank	Sunk
Fight	Fought	Fought	Sit	Sat	Sat
Flee	Fled	Fled	Speak	Spoke	Spoken
Fling	Flung	Flung	Spring	Sprang	Sprung
Fly	Flew	Flown	Sting	Stung	Stung

Infinitive	Simple Past	Past Participle	Infinitive	Simple Past	Past Participle
Forget	Forgot	Forgotten	Strive	Strove/strived	Striven/strived
Freeze	Froze	Frozen	Swear	Swore	Sworn
Get	Got	Gotten	Swim	Swam	Swum
Give	Gave	Given	Swing	Swung	Swung
Go	Went	Gone	Take	Took	Taken
Hang (a thing)	Hung	Hung	Throw	Threw	Thrown
Hang (a person)	Hanged	Hanged	Wake	Woke	Woke/woken
Know	Knew	Known	Wear	Wore	Worn
Lay	Laid	Laid	Write	Wrote	Written

The ACT writers are going to get a little sneaky and use the tenses we *do* get wrong when we talk. One notoriously annoying trick is the difference between "lie" and "lay" and all their variations. Here are the rules:

> *LIE:*   to recline or to disguise the truth
>
> *RIGHT:*   We *lie* down on the hammocks when we want to relax.
>
>   I *lie* to my mother about eating the cookies.
>
> *LAY:*   to place
>
> *RIGHT:*   Just *lay* down that air hockey table over there.
>
>   I *lay* the book on the table.

The tricky part is that the past tense of "lie" is "lay."

> She *lay* down yesterday, and today she'll *lie* down again.

The past tense of "lay" is "laid."

> She *laid* down the law with an iron fist.

The Conditional

Another thorny tense issue arises with something called the conditional. The conditional is the verb form we use to describe something uncertain, something that's conditional upon something else. You can memorize the conditional formula; it goes "If . . . were . . . would." Look at this sentence:

If were would.

> *WRONG:*   If I were running for president, my slogan *will be* "I'll Fight for Your Right to Party."

The use of "will be" in this sentence is wrong because you're not certain you're going to run for president (as suggested by "If I were"); consequently, the word "will" is too strong. "Will" implies you're definitely going to campaign for president. You should use "would" instead—the conditional form of "will"—to indicate that running is still only a possibility.

would is a possibility; will certainty

> *RIGHT:*   If I were running for president, my slogan *would be* "I'll Fight for Your Right to Party."

Notice also that the correct form is "If I *were*," not "If I *was*." You'll often hear people use "was" incorrectly in "If . . ." phrases like this, but now you'll know better. Sentences beginning with "If . . ." call for the subjunctive form of the verb. In English, the subjunctive is often the same as the regular past tense verb, but in certain cases, notably *to be*, the forms are irregular:

> *If I* were, *you* were, *s/he* were, *we* were, *they* were, *who* were, *it* were

Adverbs and Adjectives

The ACT writers will test you once or twice on your ability to use adjectives and adverbs correctly in sentences. To describe a noun, you use an adjective. To describe a verb, adjective, or adverb, you use an adverb. Look at the following example:

> *WRONG:*   My mom made a *well* dinner.
>
> *RIGHT:*   My mom made a *good* dinner.

Since "dinner" is a noun, the descriptive word modifying it should be an adjective.

Now look at this example:

WRONG:	My mom made dinner *good*.
RIGHT:	My mom made dinner *well*.

Here, the word modified is "made," a verb, so the descriptive word modifying it should be an adverb. Don't let the placement of the adverb fool you: just because it's next to the noun "dinner" doesn't mean that "dinner" is the word modified. Often, though, you *will* find the modifier next to the modified word:

WRONG:	I didn't do *good* in the game last night.
RIGHT:	I didn't do *well* in the game last night.

In the example above, how the athlete did (a verb) is being described, so you need an adverb ("well") rather than an adjective ("good").

Adverb/adjective errors are pretty common in everyday speech, so don't rely entirely on your ear. For example:

WRONG:	She shut him up *quick*.
RIGHT:	She shut him up *quickly*.
WRONG:	I got an A *easy*.
RIGHT:	I got an A *easily*.

The wrong examples above may sound familiar to you from everyday speech, but they are incorrect in written English.

Idioms

You *should* trust your ear when you're being tested on idioms. Idioms are expressions and phrasings that are peculiar to a certain language—in the ACT's case, the English language. They include odd expressions like "through the grapevine" and "rain check" as well as simple ones like "bring up" (meaning "raise"). Idiom questions on the English Test will often ask you to identify the correct prepositions used in certain expressions. This task is difficult because there are no laws governing idioms. You have to be able to read a sentence and think, "That sounds plain old wrong." Fortunately, you probably won't encounter more than a few idiom errors on the English Test you take. Take a look at this idiom error:

WRONG:	We spent days *wading into* the thousands of pages of reports.

"Wading into" sounds wrong. Instead, we say:

RIGHT:	We spent days *wading through* the thousands of pages of reports.

Why do we use some prepositions instead of others? That's just the way it is.

The following is a list of proper idiomatic usage:

He can't *abide by* the no-spitting rule.

She *accused me of* stealing.

I *agreed to* eat the broccoli.

I *apologized for* losing the hamsters in the heating vent.

She *applied for* a credit card.

She pretends to *approve of* my boyfriend.

She *argued with* the bouncer.

I *arrived at* work at noon.

You *believe in* ghosts.

I can't be *blamed for* your neuroses.

Do you *care about* me?

He's *in charge of* grocery shopping.

Nothing *compares to* you.

What is there to *complain about*?

He can always *count on* money from his mommy.

Ice cream *consists of* milk, fat, and sugar.

I *depend on* no one.

That's where cats *differ from* dogs.

It's terrible to *discriminate against* parakeets.

I have a plan to *escape from* this prison.

There's no *excuse for* your behavior.

You can't *hide from* your past.

It was all he'd *hoped for.*

I must *insist upon* it.

It's impossible to *object to* her arguments.

I refuse to *participate in* this discussion.

Pray for me.

Protect me from evil.

Provide me with plenty of Skittles.

She stayed home to *recover from* the flu.

I *rely on* myself.

She *stared at* his chest.

He *subscribes to* several trashy magazines.

I *succeeded in* fooling him.

Wait for me!

Work with me, people!

Comparative and Superlative Modifiers

Comparative modifiers compare one thing to another, while superlative modifiers tell you how one thing compares to everything else. For example:

COMPARATIVE: My boyfriend is *hotter* than yours.

✓   That purple-and-orange spotted dog is *weirder* than the blue cat.

Dan paints *better* than the other students.

SUPERLATIVE: My boyfriend is the *hottest* boy in the world.

✓   That purple-and-orange spotted dog is the *weirdest* pet on the block.

Of all the students, Dan paints *best*.

You will probably see only one or two comparative and superlative modifier questions on the English Test, and they will likely ask you to distinguish between the two types of modifiers. Remember that comparative modifiers are used in relative statements; in other words, they compare one thing to another. Just because my boyfriend is *hotter* than yours, it doesn't mean that my boyfriend is hotter than Sue's. However, if I used the superlative and told you that my boyfriend is the *hottest* boy in the world, then there's no way that Sue's boyfriend is hotter than mine, unless, as is probably the case, I'm exaggerating.

Comparative statements always require a comparison with something else. Simply saying "my boyfriend is hotter" may get your meaning across in a heated dispute with your friends, but in proper English you need to finish that sentence with a "than" phrase: "my boyfriend is hotter *than Jude Law*" or "my boyfriend is hotter *than your dog*."

Sentence Structure

Sentence structure is the big deal when it comes to Usage/Mechanics problems. Of the 40 Usage/Mechanics questions, almost half of them (18 to be exact) will test you on your knowledge of sentence structure, the topics of which include:

1.   Connecting and Transitional Words
2.   Subordinate or Dependent Clauses
3.   Sentence Fragments
4.   Comma Splices
5.   Run-on Sentences
6.   Misplaced Modifiers
7.   Parallelism

Connecting and Transitional Words

We've already mentioned coordinating conjunctions (*and*, *but*, *for*, etc.) and transitional adverbs (*however*, *nevertheless*, *moreover*, etc.) in "Punctuation." Here you'll learn more about these and other transitional words.

Coordinating Conjunctions

Coordinating conjunctions (*and, but, or, nor, for, yet*) connect words, phrases, and independent clauses of equal importance in a sentence.

independent clauses of equal importance'

> WORDS: You can hand the bottle to Seamus *or* Bea.
>
>   Liz *and* Amanda got down on the dance floor.
>
> PHRASES: To get there, you must drive over a bridge *and* through a farm.
>
>   We walked by the park *but* not by the river.
>
> CLAUSES: Tim can go to the store, *or* Jen can go instead.
>
>   It's only ten o'clock, *yet* I feel really sleepy.

When joining two words or phrases, you should not use a comma, but (as demonstrated in "Commas") if you have a list of more than two words or phrases, commas should separate them and precede the conjunction. A comma also needs to precede the coordinating conjunction when it joins two independent clauses, as in the sentence "Tim can go to the store, or Jen can go instead," above.

Transitional Adverbs

Like coordinating conjunctions, these adverbs (*however, also, consequently, nevertheless, thus, moreover, furthermore,* etc.) can join independent clauses. When they do, they should be preceded by a semicolon (see "Semicolons") and followed, most of the time, by a comma. Short adverbs, such as "thus," do not need a comma. Here are some examples of transitional adverbs in action:

> Joe always raves about soccer; *however*, he always refuses to watch a match.
>
> If you can't go to the prom with me, let me know as soon as possible; *otherwise*, I'll resent you and your inability to communicate for the rest of my life.

You need to remember that transitional adverbs must be accompanied by semicolons. If you see a transitional adverb on its own or preceded by a comma on the English Test, you should immediately know there's an error.

Subordinating Conjunctions

When you have two independent clauses, but you feel that one is more important than the other, you can use a subordinating conjunction to connect them. In other words, you use a subordinating conjunction (*because, when, since, after, until, although, before,* etc.) to make one clause dependent on the other. By subordinating one clause, you show the reader the relationship between the two clauses. For example, take the following two sentences:

AA
BB

> I ate a rotten egg.
>
> I became violently ill.

It seems likely that eating the rotten egg caused the violent illness. To make that relationship grammatically clear, you can rephrase the sentences as:

> *Because* I ate a rotten egg, I became violently ill.

Let's try another example:

> I found out my dog was really a rat.
>
> I called the exterminator.

Put them through the subordinating conjunction transformation machine:

> *After* I found out my dog was really a rat, I called the exterminator.
>
> I called the exterminator *after* I found out my dog was really a rat.

In these examples, "I found out my dog was really a rat" becomes subordinate to "I called the exterminator." You can base your decision on which clause to subordinate by determining the relationship between the clauses. In the example above, the discovery about the "dog" leads to the call; in other words, the discovery is the cause and calling the exterminator the result. Subordinating the cause to the result often makes the most sense when forming these sentences. For further discussion of this topic, move on to the next section.

Subordinate or Dependent Clauses

When you're tested on subordinate conjunctions, you'll need to select the most appropriate conjunction and place it correctly within the sentence. When you're tested on subordinate and dependent clauses, you'll need to decide how to form the whole sentence correctly. As touched upon above, not all clauses deserve the same emphasis in a sentence. Equality is a good thing, but in the writing world you've got to give preference to some clauses over others.

You can run into problems if you're too liberal with your coordinating conjunctions and transitional adverbs (the adverbs that link independent clauses). These adverbs assume that the clauses being connected deserve equal weight in a sentence. Take a look at this sentence:

Everyone regards Ginger as the most promising student in the class, and she gets the highest grades; also, she is the president of the student council.

This sentence doesn't read very well. Subordinating some of the clauses will improve the flow of the sentence:

Everyone regards Ginger as the most promising student in the class because she gets the highest grades and is the president of the student council.

This new sentence explains why Ginger is "the most promising student" by subordinating the clauses that cite her high grades and student council presidency.

Sentence Fragments

Sentence fragments are incomplete sentences that tend to look like this on the English Test:

We didn't go outside. *Even though the rain had stopped.*

Tommy could not pay for his lunch. *Having spent his last dollars on sunglasses.*

Always a bit shy. She found herself unable to talk to the other kids.

The sentence fragments above are not sentences on their own. They can be attached to the independent clauses next to them to form complete sentences:

We didn't go outside*, even though the rain had stopped.*

Having spent his last dollars on sunglasses, Tommy could not pay for his lunch.

Always a bit shy, she found herself unable to talk to the other kids.

The answer choices on English Test questions will often make clear whether you should incorporate a fragment into a neighboring sentence. For example:

We didn't go <u>outside</u>. Even though the rain

17
had stopped.

17. **A.** NO CHANGE
    B. outside;
    C. outside; even
    D. outside, even

Notice how **B**, **C**, and **D** all give you the option of combining two sentences into one. That should give you a good clue as to what's required. The variation between the last three choices occurs in punctuation. If you agree that **A** is incorrect, you can rely on your punctuation skills to decipher the correct answer. The answer, by the way, is **D** because **B** and **C**, with their use of the semicolon, continue to isolate the sentence fragment from the sentence.

Other sentence fragment questions on the English Test will ask you to turn a fragment into its own full sentence rather than simply to incorporate it into a different sentence. Again, you'll be able to tell from the answer choices what the ACT writers want:

We didn't go outside. <u>While</u> the rain continued
                                              18
 	
to fall.
	18. **F.** NO CHANGE
	        G. Although the
	        H. The
	        J. Since the

F, **G**, and **J** don't solve the sentence fragment problem. By choosing those, you still end up with a subordinate clause posing as a sentence (**G** and **J** simply replace one subordinating conjunction with another). But by getting rid of the subordinating conjunction altogether, you form a real sentence: "The rain continued to fall." The correct answer is **H**.

Most sentence fragments on the English Test will be subordinate or dependent clauses trying to be complete sentences. By studying your subordinate and dependent clauses and learning what they look like, you'll be able to catch them committing sentence fragment crime.

Comma Splices

The ACT writers may test your ability to weed out illegal comma splices. A comma splice occurs when two independent clauses are joined together by a comma with no intervening conjunction. For example:

put a period

Bowen walked to the *park, Leah* followed behind.

The comma between "park" and "Leah" forms a comma splice. Although the sentence may sound correct because the comma demands a short pause between the two related clauses, the structure is wrong in written English. Instead, two sentences are necessary:

Bowen walked to the *park. Leah* followed behind.

Or, if you explicitly want to show the relationship between the clauses, you can write:

Bowen walked to the *park, while* Leah followed behind.

OR

Bowen walked to the *park, and* Leah followed behind.

while : subordinate
and : equal

Inserting "while" subordinates the "Leah" clause to the "Bowen" clause. In the second sentence, the "and" joins the two clauses on equal footing.

Think about the comma splice in construction terms: the comma (a wimpy nail) is too weak a punctuation mark to join together two independent clauses (two big heavies). In order to join them, you have to add a conjunction (super glue) to the comma or use a period (a bolt) instead.

Run-on Sentences

You can think of run-on sentences as comma splices minus the commas. For example:

> Joan runs every day she is preparing for a marathon.
>
> John likes to walk his dog through the park Kevin doesn't.

To fix run-on sentences, you need to identify where they should be split. The first example should be broken into two parts: "Joan runs every day" and "she is preparing for a marathon." These are two independent clauses that can stand on their own as sentences:

> Joan runs every day. She is preparing for a marathon.

Alternatively, you may choose to show the relationship between these sentences by subordinating one to the other:

> Joan runs every day *because* she is preparing for a marathon.

The second example, when split, becomes: "John likes to walk his dog through the park" and "Kevin doesn't." The following sentences are correct alternatives to the original run-on:

> John likes to walk his dog through the park. Kevin doesn't.
>
> John likes to walk his dog through the park, *but* Kevin doesn't.
>
> John likes to walk his dog through the park; *however,* Kevin doesn't.

These are just a few ways you can join the two clauses. We could go on and on, showing different relationships between the two clauses (but we won't).

Misplaced Modifiers

Does the following sentence sound odd to you?

> Having eaten six corn dogs, nausea overwhelmed Jane.

Nausea didn't eat six corn dogs. Gluttonous Jane did. However, the sentence above says that nausea was the one "having eaten six corn dogs." This is a case of a misplaced modifier. When you have a modifier like "having eaten six corn dogs," it must come either directly before or directly after the word that it is modifying.

> *Having eaten six corn dogs,* Jane was overwhelmed by nausea.
>
> Jane, *having eaten six corn dogs,* was overwhelmed by nausea.

These two sentences make it clear that Jane was the one wolfing down the corn dogs.

Modifiers are not necessarily phrases like the one above. They can be adverbial phrases, adverbial clauses, or single-word adverb modifiers. You've already seen how adverbial-phrase modifiers work in the example above. The simple rule for phrase modifiers is to *make sure phrase modifiers are next to the word(s) they modify*. The same rule applies to clause modifiers. Misplaced clause modifiers look like this:

> Bill packed his favorite clothes in his suitcase, *which he planned to wear on vacation.*

Now do you really think this guy is planning to wear his suitcase on vacation? Well, that's what the sentence says. It'll be a pretty heavy outfit too, since the suitcase is packed with clothes. If Bill decides to wear his clothes instead of his suitcase, you should say:

> Bill packed his favorite clothes, *which he planned to wear on vacation,* in his suitcase.

Of course, he'll be a slightly more conventional dresser, but the clothes will probably fit better than the suitcase.

The placement of single-word adverbs is slightly trickier than that of clause and phrase modifiers. You need to make sure that adverb modifiers (such as *just, almost, barely, even,* and *nearly*) are modifying the word you intend them to modify. If they aren't, the sentence will probably still make sense, but it will have a different meaning than you intended.

Take the sentence "Jay walked a half hour to the grocery store." Now add to that sentence the adverbial modifier "only." The placement of "only" within the sentence will alter the meaning of the sentence:

Only Jay walked a half hour to the grocery store.

The sentence above means that no one but Jay made the walk.

Jay *only walked* a half hour to the grocery store.

Here, "only" modifies the verb "walked," and the sentence means that Jay did nothing but walk—he didn't run, and he didn't swim—to the store.

Jay walked *only a half hour* to the grocery store.

Hey, the walk to the grocery store isn't too bad. According to the sentence above, it took Jay only a half hour to get there.

Jay walked a half hour to *only the grocery store*.

Now we find out that Jay's single destination was the grocery store (and we were about to accuse him of having ulterior motives for taking that walk).

Parallelism

When you see a list underlined on the English Test, look for a parallelism error. Parallelism errors occur when items in a list are mismatched. For example, if you have a list of verbs, then all items in the list must be verbs of the same tense. For example:

WRONG: In the pool area, there is no *spitting*, no *running*, and *don't throw* your cigarette butts in the water.

The first two forbidden activities end in "ing" (they're called gerunds, though that doesn't really matter), and because of that, the third activity must also end in "ing." For example:

> *RIGHT:*   In the pool area, there is no *spitting*, no *running*, and no *throwing* your cigarette butts in the water.

By simply converting the final verb to gerund form, you have parallel structure. Parallelism is also important when you have expressions linked by the verb *to be*. Because you should think of *to be* as an equal sign, the words on either side of the sign must be parallel. For example:

> *WRONG:*   *To grow* tired of London is *growing* tired of life.
>
> *RIGHT:*   *To grow* tired of London is *to grow* tired of life.
>
> *WRONG:*   *Growing* tired of London is *to grow* tired of life.
>
> *RIGHT:*   *Growing* tired of London is *growing* tired of life.

The examples above are not parallel when the verb forms are different on either side of "is." You can make them parallel by simply changing the form of one verb to the form of the other.

If you have a list of nouns, you must also maintain parallel construction. For example:

> The personal ad said that she likes "*books*, good *food*, and *to take* long walks on the beach."

She apparently *doesn't* like parallelism. "Books" and "food" are nouns, but "to take" is a verb infinitive. If she's hoping to get a call from the grammarian of her dreams, she should rewrite her ad to look like this:

> The personal ad said that she likes "*books*, good *food*, and long *walks* on the beach."

Now that's one grammatically correct lady.

RHETORICAL SKILLS

The ACT writers break Rhetorical Skills questions into three categories:

1. Writing Strategy
2. Organization
3. Style

Some people may find these questions more challenging than the Usage/Mechanics questions because there are no rules that strictly determine the Rhetorical Skills answers. Others may find them easier for that very reason—there's little to memorize. In any case, to answer Rhetorical Skills questions correctly you must develop an intuitive sense for good English writing. We'll show you how.

Read the Whole Passage

Yes, we already gave you this advice in the "Strategies" section earlier in the book. But we think it's such good advice that we'll give it again: You should read (or at least skim) the whole passage. You may want to underline key phrases or transitions that help you decode the passage and that help you understand how its parts fit together. This strategy is particularly important for answering Rhetorical Skills questions. Quite a few Rhetorical Skills questions demand that you have a good understanding of the passage's content, tone, and purpose. You won't have that understanding if you haven't read (or at least skimmed) the entire passage.

Writing Strategy Questions

Writing strategy involves improving the effectiveness of a passage through careful revision and editing. Frequently, strategy questions will ask you to choose the most appropriate topic or transitional sentence for a paragraph. Almost as frequently, you will have to choose the best option for strengthening an argument by adding information or evidence. In other questions, you may also have to choose which sections of an argument can be deleted. You will also have to identify the purpose of a passage—its audience or its message—in other strategy questions.

The following strategy topics are covered in this section:

1. Transitions and Topic Sentences
2. Additional Detail and Evidence
3. Big Picture Purpose

Transitions and Topic Sentences

These questions ask you to figure out the best way to open or conclude paragraphs within a passage. Here's an example of a strategy question:

[2]

Victorian novelists were often concerned with issues of character, plot, and the Victorian social world. Dickens's novels, for example, were several-hundred-page-long works documenting the elaborate interweaving of his characters.

[3]

47 Their "modernist" novels tended to focus on the characters' inner lives, which they depicted through a stylistic technique called "stream of consciousness." Several of the best-known modernist novels were written in this stream-of-consciousness style.

47. The writer wishes to begin paragraph 3 with a sentence that strengthens the focus of the paragraph, while providing a transition from paragraph 2. Which of the following would be the best choice?

A. In the early twentieth century, novelists began to reject the Victorian emphasis on social context and look for a new focus for the novel.
B. Victorian novels ended with the Victorian era.
C. In the early twentieth century, novelists further developed this emphasis on characters' inner lives.
D. World War I significantly affected British culture in the twentieth century.

Question 47 asks you to choose a sentence that will simultaneously serve as a topic sentence ("a sentence that strengthens the focus of the paragraph") for paragraph 3 and as a transition sentence between the two paragraphs ("while providing a transition from paragraph 2"). In order to answer this question correctly, you need to understand what the two paragraphs are saying. We suggest that you reread paragraph 3 first. By developing a good sense of what that paragraph says, you can eliminate answer choices that clearly do not work as topic sentences. After you've eliminated any choices, make sure that you understand paragraph 2. From the remaining choices, you can identify the best transition sentence.

Done that? We hope that you immediately eliminated **B** and **D** from your list of possible topic sentences. **B** talks exclusively about the Victorian novel, making it an inappropriate topic sentence for a paragraph on modernist novels. **D** doesn't talk specifically about novels at all. Its focus is World War I, which is not mentioned elsewhere in the paragraph. So now you've narrowed the selection down to **A** and **C**. These sentences have similar constructions, but they say radically different things: **A** claims that twentieth-century novelists rejected Victorian ideas, while **C** claims that they embraced and developed

Victorian ideas. In order to figure out which one of these claims is true, you need to have read paragraph 2 in addition to paragraph 3. Paragraph 2 tells you that Victorian novelists were primarily concerned with the social world. In paragraph 3, you discover that modernist novelists were primarily concerned with characters' thoughts and inner lives. Thus paragraph 3 describes a *change* in novel writing that occurred between the Victorian era and the early twentieth century. The correct answer to the question is **A**.

The example above is fairly typical of transition and topic sentence questions you will encounter on the English Test. Sometimes you'll be asked to select only a topic sentence or only a transition sentence from the answer choices. Those questions are usually less complex than the example above because you have to perform one fewer step. You may also be asked to choose a concluding sentence for a paragraph. These questions are similar to transition questions because a good concluding sentence tends to be one that easily and sensibly makes the transition to the next paragraph.

Additional Detail and Evidence

These questions ask you to flesh out a paragraph by selecting the answer choice that provides the best additional detail or evidence. For example:

[3]

47 Their "modernist" novels tended to focus on the characters' inner lives, which they depicted through a stylistic technique called "stream of consciousness." Several of the best-known modernist novels were written in this stream-of-consciousness style. 48

48. The writer wishes to add information here that will further support the point made in the preceding sentence. Which of the following sentences will do that best?

   F. Today, this style is not as popular as it once was.
   G. However, there are many famous early twentieth-century works not written in this style.
   H. Joyce's Ulysses, for example, was written in this style, and it is widely considered one of the most important books of the century.
   J. Ford's The Good Soldier, although less read today, is a great example of this style.

This question asks for additional information to support the point of the preceding sentence ("Several of the best-known modernist novels were written in this stream-of-consciousness style"). To answer this question correctly, you need to understand the point being made, so read the sentence carefully. You should be able to eliminate **F** and **G** immediately. **F** talks about the popularity of this style among contemporary authors—an issue that the preceding sentence does not address. You can eliminate **G** almost immediately because it starts with "however," which indicates that it is going to make a statement that attempts to contradict, not support, the previous point. Now you've successfully limited the answer choices to **H** and **J**. Both would provide the paragraph with an example of a stream-of-consciousness work. The key to deciding which of these sentences is correct lies in the preceding sentence, which talks about the "best-known modernist novels." On the one hand, **J** tells you that *The Good Soldier* is "less read today" and also, presumably, less well known. On the other hand, **H** tells you that *Ulysses* is "widely considered one of the most important books of the century." This statement suggests that the novel is famous, so **H** is the best answer to the question.

Big Picture Purpose

On each English Test, you'll probably encounter a few Big Picture Purpose (BPP) questions. These questions always come at the end of a passage. We call them Big Picture Purpose questions because they ask you to look at the big picture and identify a passage's main point, intended purpose, or intended audience.

These questions in many ways resemble some of the questions on the Reading Test. BPP questions do, after all, test your comprehension of the passage—and comprehension is also what the Reading Test assesses. Because these questions test your overall comprehension, they are difficult to prepare for outside the context of a whole passage. Therefore, we suggest you prepare for these questions by studying our Reading Test chapter.

Before you start flipping through the book, we'll give you an idea of how these questions look on the English Test. They will often be phrased like this:

> Suppose the writer has been assigned to write an essay explaining the development of the British novel from 1799 to 1945. Would this essay successfully fulfill the assignment?

The answer choices to these questions come in two parts: the first part will respond either "No" or "Yes" to the question, and the second part will give an explanation for this answer. For example:

A. No, because the essay restricts its focus to the American novel from 1850 to 1945.
B. No, because the essay omits mention of famous poets.
C. Yes, because the essay focuses on the novel's birth in the eighteenth century.
D. Yes, because the essay describes changes in novel writing from the end of the French Revolution to the end of World War II.

Without reading the entire passage, you're probably unable to answer a definite "No" or "Yes" to this question, but you can eliminate an incorrect answer or two because of irrelevant or nonsensical explanations. In this example, you can immediately cross off **B** because the explanation calls for a discussion of famous poets in the essay. Famous poets, however, do not necessarily belong in an essay on the novel's development. You can also cross off **C**. It claims that the passage *successfully* fulfills the essay requirements because it discusses the novel's birth in the eighteenth century. However, the assignment calls for a discussion of the novel starting in 1799 (the end of the eighteenth century), so **C** cannot be correct. By reading and understanding the passage, you'll be able to choose from the two remaining answers. If the passage indeed focuses on the American novel, **A** is correct, and the essay does not succeed; if the essay describes the novel from the end of the French Revolution (1799) to the end of the World War II (1945), **D** is correct, and the essay does succeed.

Organization

Organization questions deal with the logical structuring of the passage on the level of the sentence, the paragraph, and the passage as a whole. These questions ask you to organize sections to maximize their coherence, order, and unity by asking three types of questions:

1. Sentence Reorganization
2. Paragraph Reorganization
3. Passage Reorganization

Sentence Reorganization

Sentence reorganization questions often involve the placement of a modifier within a sentence. Your ability to reorder a sentence correctly will depend on how well you have absorbed your grammar lessons from the previous section—specifically the "Misplaced Modifiers" section. For example:

> Austen wrote about a society of manners, in which
>
> love triumphs over a rigid social hierarchy
>
> <u>despite confinement to her drawing room</u>.
>   43

43. **A.** NO CHANGE
    B. (place after *love*)
    C. (place after *Austen*)
    D. (place after *society*)

You probably guessed that the underlined phrase does not modify "hierarchy," "love," or "society." The pronoun "her" in the underlined phrase should tip you off that "Austen" is being modified. If you read "Misplaced Modifiers" in the previous chapter, you should already know the cardinal rule of placing the modifier next to the modified word. So the correct answer is **C** because the underlined part modifies "Austen."

Approximately half of the organization questions on the English Test will ask you to reorder sentences. All of these sentence reorganization problems will look similar to the one above. Study up on your modifier placement in order to get them right.

Paragraph Reorganization

A couple of questions will ask you to reorder sentences within a paragraph. They will look much like this:

[1] In April, I'm usually in a bad mood because of my debilitating pollen allergies. [2] In November, despite the graying trees and the short days, I'm elated because I can celebrate both Thanksgiving and my birthday. [3] My mood changes with the months. [4] In the summer months I feel happy from days spent in the sun. ☐ 61

61. Which of the following provides the most logical ordering of the sentences in the preceding paragraph?
A. 1, 4, 3, 2
B. 3, 4, 2, 1
C. 3, 1, 4, 2
D. 2, 1, 4, 3

The best way to approach these questions is to decide which sentence should come first, and then to eliminate incompatible answer choices. Ask yourself: which sentence logically comes first in this sequence? Sentence 3 makes a good topic sentence because it provides a general argument that can be followed and supported by examples. By deciding that Sentence 3 should come first, you can immediately eliminate **A** and **D** because they do not begin with Sentence 3. Now you can move on to arranging the rest of the paragraph. Each of the remaining sentences talks about a different time of year: April, summer, and November. The three sentences should fall in that chronological order (April, summer, November), as this is the most logical arrangement in this example. Therefore, the correct answer is **C**.

If you are totally lost on a paragraph reorganization question, you can often look to the answer choices for clues. You can look at the first sentences given to you by the answer choices and see whether any of them sound like topic sentences. If you can identify a topic sentence, you're well on your way to getting the correct answer.

Passage Reorganization

These appear at the end of passages. They will ask you either to insert a sentence where it best belongs in the passage or to move a paragraph to a different location in the passage. Questions that ask you to insert a sentence will generally look like this:

72. The writer wishes to include
the following sentence in the
essay: "That summer, I spent so
much time on the beach that I
could smell only a combination of
sand and seaweed when I finally
returned to school." That sentence
will fit most smoothly and
logically into paragraph:
   F. 2, before the first sentence.
   G. 3, after the last sentence.
   H. 4, before the first sentence.
   J. 5, after the last sentence.

This question is basically a strategy question disguised as an organization question. It asks you to identify the sentence provided as an appropriate topic or concluding sentence for paragraphs 2, 3, 4, or 5. When the answer choice calls for the sentence to be placed "before the first sentence," then it would become the topic sentence of the paragraph. When the answer choice calls for the sentence to be placed "after the last sentence," then it would become the concluding sentence.

Questions that ask you to relocate a paragraph will generally look like this:

74. For the sake of the unity and
coherence of this essay, paragraph
4 should be placed:
   F. where it is now.
   G. after paragraph 1.
   H. after paragraph 2.
   J. after paragraph 5.

To answer this question, look at (and perhaps underline) the topic sentences of each paragraph. These topic sentences, removed from the passage, should follow a logical chain of thought. For example, look at these topic sentences:

Topic Sentence 1:	Seasonal variations affect many aspects of my life.
Topic Sentence 2:	This April, the sight of leaves and the sounds of returning birds cheered me so much that I hugged a tree.
Topic Sentence 3:	The return of the warm weather also meant that I got some much-needed exercise after being stuck indoors all winter.
Topic Sentence 4:	My mood changes with the months.
Topic Sentence 5:	The weather's effect on my mood and my fitness always reminds me of the undeniable connection between people and nature.

Even without reading the whole passage, you can take an educated stab at the correct answer. Consider the logical organization of an essay: introduction, supporting paragraphs, and conclusion. According to this structure, Topic Sentence 1 should present the passage's argument, and it should be followed by three paragraphs supporting the argument and a final paragraph presenting a conclusion.

Now take a look at Topic Sentence 4. It makes a general argument about the weather's effect on the author's mood. Ask yourself where the paragraph best fits into the passage: is it a supporting paragraph or a conclusion? It's unlikely that paragraph 4 is a conclusion because it narrows the focus of the essay to talk about the author's mood, while other paragraphs in the essay discuss the author's physical condition. If it's a supporting paragraph, then where does it belong? Eliminating **J** (which would make it the conclusion) leaves you with three options for a supporting paragraph.

Your next step should be to take a look at the remaining topic sentences. Topic Sentence 2 also discusses the weather's effect on the author's mood, but it deals specifically with April weather. Topic Sentence 3 discusses the weather's effects on the author's physical health. If you choose **F** and keep paragraph 4 where it is, the passage will be ordered like this: introduction, weather/mood, weather/health, weather/mood, conclusion. This order doesn't make much sense because it inexplicably divides the weather/mood discussions. **G** and **H** place the weather/mood paragraphs side by side. **G** puts paragraph 4 (general weather/mood) before paragraph 2 (April weather/mood), while **H** puts 2 before **4**. When writing an essay, moving from the general to the specific makes more sense than moving in the opposite direction because you want to support your claims with specific evidence. So by using good writing strategy, you will arrive at the correct answer: **G**.

Style

Style questions generally concern effective word choice. They often ask you to choose the most appropriate word for a sentence in terms of its tone and clarity. Other times, they'll ask you to eliminate redundant words or phrases. In the next section, we discuss the following style topics:

1. Redundancy
2. Appropriate Word Choice and Identifying Tone

Redundancy

The ACT writers will test you on your ability to spot redundant statements. Redundant statements say the same thing twice, and you should always avoid redundancy on the English Test (in life too, if possible). For example:

WRONG:	The diner closes at 3 A.M. in the morning.
RIGHT:	The diner closes at 3 A.M.

"In the morning" is redundant because it is implied in "A.M." Here's another example of a redundant statement:

> *WRONG:* In my opinion, I think we should go get some food.

"I think" and "In my opinion" mean the same thing, so you can eliminate one of the phrases from the sentence:

> *RIGHT:* In my opinion, we should go get some food.
>
> *ALSO RIGHT:* I think we should go get some food.

Either one of those phrases gets the point across; using both merely makes the sentence cumbersome.

Redundancy questions almost always give you the option to "OMIT the underlined portion." If you spot a phrase or word that means the same thing as the underlined portion, then you should always choose to "OMIT." (For more on "OMIT," refer to "Don't Hesitate to Choose 'OMIT'" on page 21.)

Appropriate Word Choice and Identifying Tone

Identifying the appropriate word choice can be as simple as figuring out whether a sentence should use the word *their*, *there*, or *they're*. But word choice can also be more complicated, involving many words working together to create a tone. For example, the sentence "Lloyd George rocks!" probably does not belong in an essay on World War I. It doesn't fit because it's written in a casual, slangy tone, and history essays are generally neither casual nor slangy. The sentence might belong, however, in a passage on your awesome new friend, Lloyd George.

The content of a passage will generally give you a clue about the appropriate tone. Essays on history and culture will probably be written in a fairly formal style—a style that omits youthful slang, casual contractions, and familiar personal pronouns (such as "I" and "you"). A personal essay on your experiences driving a bulldozer, on your great-grandmother, or on your new skateboard calls for a relatively informal style of writing. These personal essays can exhibit varying degrees of informality. An essay by a young writer may be more colloquial and relaxed than an essay by a mature writer recalling past experiences.

Tone is one of the most important elements in correctly answering word choice questions. You will encounter quite a few questions that look like this:

During the Great War, the British Public believed that Lloyd George <u>rocks!</u> He was widely admired for his ability to unify the government and thus to unify Britain.

7. A. NO CHANGE
    B. rocked!
    C. was an effective political leader.
    D. had the ability to unify the government and thus to unify Britain.

Because we already told you that informality does not belong in a history essay, you can immediately eliminate **A** and **B**, even though **B** correctly changes the verb tense. If you read the section above, you should also be able to eliminate **D** because it is redundant—it repeats the information given in the next sentence. That leaves the correct answer, **C**.

PRACTICE FOR THE ACT ENGLISH TEST

ENGLISH TEST

45 Minutes—75 Questions

DIRECTIONS: There are five passages on this test. You should read each passage once before answering the questions on it. In order to answer correctly, you may need to read several sentences beyond the question.

There are two question formats within the passages. In one format, you will find words and phrases that have been underlined and assigned numbers. These numbers will correspond with sets of alternative words/phrases, given in the right-hand column of the test booklet. From the sets of alternatives, choose the answer choice that works best in context, keeping in mind whether it employs standard written English, whether it gets across the idea of the section, and whether it suits the tone and style of the passage. You will usually be offered the option "NO CHANGE," which you should choose if you think the version found in the passage is best.

In the second format, you will see boxed numbers referring to sections of the passage or to the passage as a whole. In the right-hand column, you will be asked questions about or given alternatives for the sections marked by the boxes. Choose the answer choice that best answers the question or completes the section. After choosing your answer choice, fill in the corresponding bubble on the answer sheet.

PRACTICE SET 1

PASSAGE I

Tiger Woods: The Essence of Focus

[1]

People inside and outside of the golf world

have marveled at Tiger Woods' success for years.
1

1. **A.** NO CHANGE
   B. marvel
   C. are marveling
   D. do marvel

At age 21 he became the youngest player ever to
²

win the Masters championship, and he won it with

the lowest score ever. Despite this, between 2000
³

and 2001, he won all four of golf's major

championships consecutively, an unprecedented

and unrepeated feat who many rank as one
⁴

of the greatest accomplishments in sports history.

Intrinsic to Woods' success has been his

extraordinary focus, commitment, and

determination to reach his goals.

[2]

Commentators have noted Woods' appealing
⁵

ability to handle the pressure of competition

during a tournament. One example is during a

six-tournament stretch in Woods' 2006 season.

Woods had three dramatic victories all in the final

hole, and two were in the playoffs. Woods credits

his ability to handle the stress to his powers of

concentration. In an interview with Ed Bradley,

he explained "your concentration is so high,
⁶

so keen, because all this pressure's on you.

Your senses are more heightened, everything
⁷

seems to flow better. It's a great feeling." One of

Woods' favorite activities when he is not on the
⁸

golf course is spear fishing.

2. F. NO CHANGE
   G. At age 21 he became the
       youngest player,
   H. At age 21, he became the
       youngest player
   J. At age, 21, he became the
       youngest player

3. A. NO CHANGE
   B. Finally,
   C. For example,
   D. Later,

4. F. NO CHANGE
   G. that many
   H. which many
   J. many

5. Which of the choices would be
   most appropriate here?

   A. NO CHANGE
   B. intimidating
   C. aggravating
   D. disarming

6. F. NO CHANGE
   G. he explained, "your
   H. he, explained, "your
   J. he explained your

7. A. NO CHANGE
   B. heightened;
   C. heightened and
   D. heightened

8. F. NO CHANGE
   G. Woods first took an interest
       in golf when he was only six
       months old.
   H. Woods' greatest childhood
       ambition was to beat his
       father in golf.
   J. OMIT the underlined
       portion.

[3]

Woods credits much of his success to his late father, Earl Woods, <u>who helped coach, nurtured, and was managing</u> his son's career from the
9
beginning. The senior Woods, a former Green Beret who served in Vietnam, <u>instilled during competition in his son the ability to maintain a keen sense of focus.</u> After an emotional victory at the British
10
Open in July 2006 following his father's recent death, Woods said he had played the tournament in a way that his father would have appreciated, by "thinking his way around the course." [11]

Woods' mental conditioning <u>allowed</u> him to keep his focus and strategize about the course ahead, rather than <u>dwelling</u> on his last mistake or on
12
a competitor's advances.

[4]

[13] Changing his golf swing twice in an effort to become more consistent—and consequently falling out of the number-one ranking—brought criticism from many analysts. "You can always become better," he said in speaking with Ed Bradley, and the changes have paid off. Answering his critics in 2005, Woods won his fourth Masters tournament

9. A. NO CHANGE
   B. who coached him, nurtured him, and was managing
   C. who coached, nurtured, and managed
   D. who helped coach, was nurturing, and who managed

10. F. NO CHANGE
    G. instilled in his son the ability to maintain a keen sense of focus during competition.
    H. during competition instilled in his son the ability to maintain a keen sense of focus.
    J. instilled in his son during competition the ability to maintain a keen sense of focus.

11. The writer is thinking of revising the preceding sentence to read:
    Woods won the British Open in July 2006 following his father's death.
    If this revision were made, the sentence would primarily lose:
    A. unnecessary information that does not relate to the topic.
    B. information that should be included elsewhere in the essay.
    C. descriptive details that enhance the narrative.
    D. confusing details that serve only to distract the reader.

12. F. NO CHANGE
    G. to dwell
    H. be dwelling
    J. dwell

13. Given that all the answers are true, which of the following sentences, if added here, would most effectively introduce the new subject of paragraph 4?
    A. Woods has also been willing to take risks in pursuit of excellence.
    B. Playing golf has not always been Woods' primary goal in life.
    C. Breaking golf records is of little importance to Woods.
    D. For Woods, improving his golf swing takes time and patience.

and <u>again regained the number-one ranking.</u>
14

We can take inspiration from the elements of

Woods' phenomenal success that are available to

each <u>of us</u>: commitment, focus, and determination.
15

14. **F.** NO CHANGE
    G. again, regained the number-one ranking.
    H. regained the number-one ranking.
    J. regained again the number-one ranking.

15. **A.** NO CHANGE
    B. of us;
    C. of us,
    D. of us

PRACTICE SET 1: ANSWERS & EXPLANATIONS

1. **A** Verb Tense
   The sentence informs the reader that people have been amazed by Tiger Woods *for years*. The phrase *for years* indicates that the action of the sentence has continued to occur over time, so there is no change.

2. **H** Commas
   A comma is placed after an introductory phrase, which in this sentence is the phrase *At age 21*. The comma signals that the main part of the sentence is about to begin. **H** is the correct answer.

3. **D** Connecting and Transitional Words
   A transitional word indicating the passage of time is needed in this sentence to show what Tiger Woods accomplished at the age of 21 and in the following years. While both *finally*, **B**, and *later*, **D**, are transition words that indicate time, *finally* makes it seem as if Tiger Woods took a really long time to win championships, which was not the case. Therefore, **D** is correct.

4. **G** Pronoun-Antecedent Agreement
   In this sentence, the pronoun *who* does not agree with its antecedent, *feat*, because *who* refers to a person. The pronoun *that*, **G**, should be used instead.

5. **D** Word Choice
   Woods handles pressure so well that he wins many tournaments in the final hole, as indicated in the second sentence of the paragraph. Woods' competitors are unable to beat him because his concentration during tough situations reduces their ability to win, which is *disarming*, **D**.

6. **G** Commas
   When a quotation is introduced with an expression such as *he said* or *he explained*, a comma is needed. Quotation marks are placed after the comma and before the quoted statement begins, so **G** is correct.

7. **B** Run-on Sentences
   A run-on sentence consists of two complete sentences that need to be firmly separated by a period, a semicolon, or a comma followed by a conjunction, such

as *and*. A comma alone does not sufficiently separate the two thoughts, so the sentences need a semicolon, **B**.

8.   **J**   Paragraph Reorganization
The focus of the paragraph is Woods' ability to handle pressure, as noted in the first sentence. All of the paragraph's details should relate to Woods' amazing ability to concentrate. Otherwise, the topic of the paragraph will be lost. The choices given in **F**, **G**, and **H** do not have a connection to Woods' concentration.

9.   **C**   Parallelism
Two or more items in a sentence should be parallel and expressed with similar words, or else the sentence does not flow well. All three words used to describe what Earl Woods did for his son should be past tense, so the sentence will be more balanced. In **C**, *coached*, *nurtured*, and *managed* are all past tense. Therefore, **C** is correct.

10.   **G**   Misplaced Modifiers
The original sentence makes it sound as if Earl Woods is teaching his son in the middle of a golf tournament. The phrase *during competition* describes when Woods is able to focus, so it should be next to the word *focus* for a clearer meaning. **G** is correct.

11.   **C**   Additional Detail and Evidence
The topic of this paragraph is the close relationship between Tiger Woods and his father. Earl Woods taught his son how to stay focused during tournaments, and the extra details in the original sentence support this idea. Therefore, **C** is correct.

12.   **J**   Parallelism
Sentences should be as concise and well-structured as possible. *Keep*, *strategize*, and *dwell* are the three words that should match and be parallel for a balanced sentence. **J** adheres to this rule and keeps all three words parallel.

13.   **A**   Transitions and Topic Sentences
The purpose of a paragraph's topic sentence is to state the main point of the paragraph. Paragraph 4 describes how Woods has been willing to make changes in his game in order to improve it, even if that meant not being successful for a time, so **A** is correct.

14.   **H**   Redundancy
The sentence states that Woods *regained* his number-one position, which means he earned it again. So, the word *again* is unnecessary in the sentence, and **H** is correct.

15.   **A**   Colons
A colon is used to call attention to the words that follow it, as long as a complete sentence exists to the left of the colon. In this case, there is a complete sentence before the colon, so this sentence reflects an accurate way to use the punctuation.

PRACTICE SET 2

PASSAGE II

Ireland: A Celebration of Old and New

[1]

[1] I discovered the union of ancient and modern throughout my travels, as well as a notable reverence for heritage. [2] Many rich experiences awaited me on my first visit to Ireland, the land of my ancestry. [3] The opportunity to learn more about my family's background proved a rewarding experience. ☐1

[2]

Todays Dublin is a fascinating blend of old
2

and new. Irish Castles appear on the same block as
3

historic churches and stone buildings. ☐4

1. Which of the following sequences of sentences makes paragraph 1 most logical?
   A. NO CHANGE
   B. 1, 3, 2
   C. 3, 1, 2
   D. 2, 1, 3

2. F. NO CHANGE
   G. Today
   H. Today's
   J. Todays'

3. Given that all are true, which of the choices would provide the best example of the "union" described in paragraph 1?
   A. NO CHANGE
   B. Automated teller machines
   C. Century-old pubs
   D. Cobblestone streets

4. The writer wishes to include another example illustrating the coexistence of ancient and modern Ireland. Which of the following true sentences, if inserted in paragraph 2, would best fulfill that goal?
   F. Traditional Irish music can be heard all over the country, from rural festivals to country pubs.
   G. Ireland is a culturally rich country that is youthful as well, since more than half of the population is under 30.
   H. Ireland's spectacular coastline offers visitors pristine beaches, towering cliffs, and clear water.
   J. All street signs are printed in both Irish and English, hearkening to the Celtic heritage.

Driving in Dublin, a harrowing experience, as
my taxicab driver maneuvered through narrow
winding streets clearly not designed for automobiles.
My discovery of ancient treasure continued at the
library at Trinity College, which houses the Book
of Kells, an ornately illuminated manuscript of the
four Christian gospels in Latin that dates back to
medieval times.

[3]

Traveling west by train across Ireland from
Dublin to Galway, the Irish landscape, restful to the
eye, unfolded in a wonderland of green. As pastoral
images of the countryside streamed by I marveled
that the barns fences, and train depots had likely
been there for generations. Arriving in Galway,
County Mayo, I stopped into a pub that displayed an

interesting sign that I saw, "Irish Spoken, English
Understood." I had traveled into western Ireland,
where Irish-speaking citizens keep the heritage
of that Celtic language and culture alive. Despite,
this on a day trip by ferry to the Aran Islands off
the coast of Galway—famous for their ancient forts,
woolen sweaters, and windy weather—the clerk who
sold me a sweater seemed to speak only Irish.

[4]

My experience of western Ireland was
especially poignant as my great grandmother
immigrated from County Mayo in the late 19th
century and married my Italian grandfather five
years later. Seeing the extremely rocky land in the

5. A. NO CHANGE
   B. Driving in Dublin such a harrowing experience,
   C. Driving in Dublin was a harrowing experience,
   D. The drive in Dublin, a harrowing experience,

6. F. NO CHANGE
   G. a manuscript ornately illuminated
   H. a manuscript, which was ornately illuminated
   J. an illuminated manuscript, which was ornate

7. A. NO CHANGE
   B. by; I marveled that the barns, fences, and train depots
   C. by I marveled, that the barns, fences, and train depots
   D. by, I marveled that the barns, fences, and train depots

8. F. NO CHANGE
   G. which I read,
   H. that I saw on the building,
   J. OMIT the underlined portion.

9. A. NO CHANGE
   B. Indeed,
   C. Nevertheless,
   D. However,

10. F. NO CHANGE
    G. whom
    H. which
    J. whose

11. A. NO CHANGE
    B. century, marrying my Italian grandfather five years later.
    C. century. She married my Italian grandfather five years later.
    D. century.

western coastal area, I <u>could easily imagine</u> the
                              12

potato famine that caused so much desperation. The

experience of walking in the land of my ancestors

<u>were</u> powerful. From east to west on this emerald
 13

isle, my journey offered a <u>different</u> experience of
                             14

Irish culture and <u>their</u> own heritage.
                    15

12. F. NO CHANGE
     G. could of easily imagined
     H. easily imagine
     J. will easily imagine

13. A. NO CHANGE
     B. are
     C. have been
     D. was

14. F. NO CHANGE
     G. plain
     H. rich
     J. genuine

15. A. NO CHANGE
     B. its
     C. my
     D. our

PRACTICE SET 2: ANSWERS & EXPLANATIONS

1. **D** Paragraph Reorganization
    Paragraphs are typically organized from a broad statement to a narrower one.
    In this opening paragraph, the sentence beginning with *Many rich experiences* is
    a general introduction to the essay, so it should be first, **D**.

2. **H** Apostrophes
    The word *today* is showing ownership of Dublin to emphasize that the writer is
    describing the modern city, not yesterday's Dublin. **H** is the best answer.

3. **B** Analysis
    The writer is trying to illustrate the *union* of old and new in Ireland by
    providing examples in the essay. Old churches and buildings contrast with the
    modern convenience of automated teller machines, so **B** is correct.

4. **J** Additional Detail and Evidence
    The focus of the essay is how Ireland maintains old traditions while embracing
    modern life. Traditional music, the population of Ireland, and the Irish
    coastline do not support the idea of contrasts seen in Ireland. **J** must be the
    answer.

5. **C** Sentence Fragments
    The underlined section is missing a verb, which has caused a sentence fragment.
    With the addition of the verb *was*, **C**, the sentence now makes sense.

6. **F** Adverbs and Adjectives
    Adverbs and adjectives usually come before the words they modify. *Ornately
    illuminated*, **F**, describes the manuscript, so the way it is written is correct.

7. **D** Commas

This sentence begins with an introductory phrase, so a comma should be placed after *by* to show that the main part of the sentence is beginning. Additional commas are needed to separate the items in the series, so **D** fits.

8. **J** Redundancy

The writer indicates that a sign was displayed in a pub, and including *that I saw* is redundant. It is understood that the writer saw and read the sign, so the underlined portion should be deleted.

9. **B** Connecting and Transitional Words

The writer is trying to provide more examples that depict old and new Ireland living side by side. *Despite this*, *nevertheless*, and *however* would be used if the writer were trying to provide an example that did not support her main point. **B**, *indeed*, fits.

10. **F** Pronoun-Antecedent Agreement

The sentence is written correctly because the pronoun *who* is used in reference to people, such as *the clerk*. The pronoun *which*, **H**, is used when referring to things; *whose*, **J**, shows possession; and *whom*, **J**, is an objective pronoun.

11. **D** Sentence Reorganization

The underlined information is unimportant because it does not relate to the topic. While the information about the writer's grandfather may be interesting, it should be removed from the sentence because it distracts from the focus of the essay.

12. **F** Verb Tenses

The writer's trip to Ireland occurred in the past, and she is reflecting on her experience. The original verb phrase *could easily imagine* indicates how she felt when she was in Ireland during the past.

13. **D** Subject-Verb Agreement

The subject of the sentence is *experience*, and the verb should be *was*, **D**, for proper agreement. Although *ancestors* precedes the verb, it is part of a phrase and is not the subject of the sentence. The correct answer is **D**.

14. **H** Word Choice

Words should be as specific and concrete as possible to make writing clear. The adjective *rich*, **H**, accurately describes the writer's journey, which was full of the sights and sounds of Ireland.

15. **C** Possessives

The writer has discussed her family's Irish background in the final paragraph, using the pronoun *my*, **C**, many times. The *heritage* belongs to the writer, not to Ireland or anyone else.

PRACTICE SET 3

PASSAGE III

J. K. Rowling: Magic

[1]

It seems that the life story of British writer

J. K. Rowling the author, of the much-beloved,
₁

widely acclaimed Harry Potter fantasy

séries, has its own elements of magic. Joanne

Rowling had written "almost continuously,"

1. **A.** NO CHANGE
   B. J. K. Rowling, the author of the much-beloved, widely acclaimed
   C. J. K. Rowling, the author of the much-beloved widely acclaimed
   D. J. K. Rowling the author of the much-beloved, widely acclaimed

she says, since age six but had not published
₂

any writing, when perhaps the most magical

moment of her life happened. While riding on

a crowded train from Manchester to London

in 1990, the idea for Harry Potter occurred to

her. The ensuing story of a young boy which
₃

did not know he was a wizard has enthralled

millions of readers. ☐4

2. **F.** NO CHANGE
   G. have not published
   H. is not publishing
   J. was not published

3. **A.** NO CHANGE
   B. whom
   C. who
   D. and he

4. The writer is considering revising "has enthralled millions of readers" to read "has been read by many people." If this revision were made, the sentence would primarily lose:
   F. important details about the Harry Potter novels.
   G. specific information about Rowling's writing abilities.
   H. characteristics of individuals who read Rowling's books.
   J. the extensive emotional impact of Rowling's series.

[2]

Rowling and her young daughter were,

when she wrote, living on state benefits, the
₅

first Harry Potter novel, *Harry Potter and the*

Philosopher's Stone. Rowling who completed

5. **A.** NO CHANGE
   B. as she wrote, were living on state benefits,
   C. were living on state benefits, which was when she wrote
   D. were living on state benefits when she wrote

the manuscript on an old manual typewriter.
6

The first twelve publishers rejected the

6. F. NO CHANGE
   G. Rowling completed the manuscript
   H. Rowling, after completing the manuscript
   J. Rowling's completed manuscript

manuscript, finally a small British publisher
7

named Bloomsbury accepted it, after the

eight-year-old daughter of the company's

chairman read the first chapter and

demanded the second. A year later, Scholastic,

Inc., won the publishing rights to the novel

in the United States and paid Rowling

more than $100,000, a sum which shocked
8

Rowling reportedly. The book also won several

prestigious awards prior to being published in

the United States in October 1998.

7. A. NO CHANGE
   B. manuscript, but
   C. manuscript but
   D. manuscript; but

8. F. NO CHANGE
   G. reportedly shocked Rowling.
   H. which shocked reportedly Rowling.
   J. which reportedly shocked Rowling.

[3]

9 The last three volumes in the Harry

Potter series (books four through six) have all

9. Given that all are true, which of the following sentences, if added here, would best introduce the new subject of paragraph 3?
   A. The heroine in a fairy tale is often quite wealthy, and Rowling is no exception.
   B. Included in Rowling's storybook lifestyle are the author's husband and family.
   C. The Harry Potter novels stimulate children's minds and encourage them to read.
   D. The Harry Potter movies have found almost as much success as the novels.

been the fastest-selling books in history. Prior
10

to the release of book six, *Forbes* had

10. F. NO CHANGE
    G. faster-selling
    H. fast-selling
    J. most fast selling

estimated Rowlings fortune at £576 million,
11

equivalent to slightly more than $1 billion

in the United States. The reading world now

awaits with great anticipation the release

11. A. NO CHANGE
    B. Rowlings'
    C. Rowling's
    D. Rowling

of the seventh book in the Harry Potter

series, which is slated to be the series' final

publication. <u>The film version of *Harry Potter*</u>
<u>*and the Philosopher's Stone* earned more than</u>
<u>$960 million.</u>
[12]

[4]

<u>You wonder</u> if Rowling sometimes questions
[13]
whether she will wake up from the fantastic

magic spell she fell into when she first met

Harry in her imagination. The adventures of

a <u>scrawny black-haired, bespectacled</u> boy who
[14]
attended a school for wizardry have taken

J.K. Rowling on quite a magic carpet ride. [15]

12. **F.** NO CHANGE
    G. Some of Rowling's income supports research into multiple sclerosis, the condition from which her mother died.
    H. Rowling and her family reside in a large estate in Scotland.
    J. OMIT the underlined portion.

13. **A.** NO CHANGE
    B. I wonder
    C. One wonders
    D. Oneself wonders

14. **F.** NO CHANGE
    G. scrawny, black-haired, bespectacled
    H. scrawny, black-haired bespectacled
    J. scrawny black-haired bespectacled

15. What function does paragraph 4 serve in relation to the rest of the essay?
    A. It refers back to the opening sentence of the essay, suggesting that Rowling's life has been as magical as her book series.
    B. It states that Rowling's good fortune will soon end because of the cyclical nature of good fortune.
    C. It summarizes the essay's main point that hard work and determination can lead to success.
    D. It indicates that Rowling's monetary wealth is secondary only to the wealth of her imagination.

PRACTICE SET 3: ANSWERS & EXPLANATIONS

1. **B** Commas
    Two commas are needed in the underlined section to make the sentence flow well. One comma should be placed after *Rowling* to set off the phrase that begins with *the author* and ends with *series*. A second comma is needed between *beloved* and *widely* to separate the two adjectives. So, the sentence now reads: *It seems that the life story of British writer J. K. Rowling, the author of the much-beloved, widely acclaimed Harry Potter fantasy series, has its own elements of magic.* **B** is correct.

2. **F** Verb Tenses

The underlined section is correct as written because *had not published* is past tense, and the writer is discussing Rowling's failure to publish for many years. In addition, *had not published* matches *had written* in the first part of the sentence, making the verbs parallel.

3. **C** Pronoun-Antecedent Agreement

Usually, the pronouns *who* and *whom* refer to people, while the pronouns *that* and *which* are most often applied to animals and things. *A young boy* is part of the sentence's subject, so *who*, **C**, instead of *whom*, **B**, would be the correct pronoun to choose.

4. **J** Analysis

The phrase *has enthralled millions of readers* indicates that the Harry Potter books have charmed and enchanted an extensive number of people. The emotional impact, **J**, and appeal of the series would be lost with the revision.

5. **D** Sentence Reorganization

When phrases and words are positioned incorrectly, sentences can become difficult to understand. The sentence should be revised by moving *when she wrote* after *state benefits,* **D**.

6. **G** Sentence Fragments

The underlined section is missing a verb, thus creating a sentence fragment. By adding the verb *completed*, **G** turns the fragment into a complete sentence.

7. **B** Comma Splices

The original sentence contains a comma splice because it joins two independent clauses with only a comma. To connect the two independent clauses, the comma after *manuscript* should be followed by a conjunction, such as *but*, as in **B**.

8. **J** Adverbs and Adjectives

For clarity, adverbs should be placed next to the words they describe. In this sentence, the adverb *reportedly* describes how Ms. Rowling was *shocked*, so the two words should be next to each other instead of separated, as in **J**.

9. **A** Transitions and Topic Sentences

The focus of paragraph 3 is the amount of money Rowling has earned from the Harry Potter novels. The topic sentence should unify the paragraph and prepare the reader for the upcoming information, which **A** does.

10. **F** Comparative and Superlative Modifiers

The phrase *in history* tells the reader that no other novels have sold as many copies as the Harry Potter books. Since more than two books are being compared, the superlative form of *fast*, which is *fastest*, should be used.

11. **C** Apostrophes

The *fortune* belongs to Rowling, so possession needs to be indicated. An apostrophe should be added before the *s*, as it is in **C**.

12. **J** Paragraph Reorganization

While it is tempting to include interesting information, a writer needs to make sure the information fits with the topic of a paragraph. The topic of paragraph 3 is the amount of money Rowling has made from her books, not her movies, so the underlined sentence should be omitted.

13. **C** Pronoun Cases

The essay is not written in first-person, *I*, or second person, *you*. Replacing *you* with *one*, **C**, makes the essay more consistent.

14. **G** Commas

Commas should separate a series of descriptive words. By including commas after *scrawny* and *black-haired*, the writer is indicating that Harry is *scrawny* and *black-haired* and *bespectacled*, so **G** is correct.

15. **A** Big Picture Purpose

Conclusions should bring the reader back to the focus and intent of the essay. Throughout the essay, the writer refers to Rowling's magical life, and the concluding paragraph completes that circle for the reader. Therefore, **A** is correct.

PRACTICE SET 4

PASSAGE IV

A Sensory Paradise

[1]

Give chores their due; they're advocates
                    1
put up a valiant fight. They just could not

overcome the yearning for adventure and the

delight that laid ahead.
            2

[2]

After meeting a friend for Sunday

breakfast, and I returned to my car and
        3
pondered my activities for the remainder

of the summer day. Immediately, my list

of projects beckoned me, berated me.

1. **A.** NO CHANGE
    B. there due; their advocates
    C. their due; its advocates
    D. their due; their advocates

2. **F.** NO CHANGE
    G. lay
    H. lie
    J. laying

3. **A.** NO CHANGE
    B. breakfast, so I
    C. breakfast and I
    D. breakfast, I

Insistent voices reminded me of housework, responsibilities, and attentions needed. But the lobbyists for my conscience were losing: I could not be convinced to drive home. Starved

4. F. NO CHANGE
G. losing, I
H. losing and I
J. losing so I

for adventure, I drove on rebelliously not
knowing my destination.

[3]

"Sensory paradise" was my journal notation, as I described my perceptions of the many sights of the hypnotic rushing waterfalls and the minty fragrance oozing from the peppermint geranium. Meditating in this quiet, I am transporting a world away from the bustling, concrete city that lay just outside the gates.

5. A. NO CHANGE
B. I rebelliously drove on,
C. rebelliously, I drove on,
D. I drove on, which was rebellious,

6. F. NO CHANGE
G. of what I saw
H. and the many thoughts I had
J. OMIT the underlined portion.

7. A. NO CHANGE
B. will transport
C. was transported
D. have been transporting

[4]

What appeared was a grand idea—a spontaneous expedition to the botanic gardens—and what was the next occurrence was pure delight. The August afternoon was unusual: perfect "Monet painting" daylight, overcast but still iridescent, with comfortable air that seemed to ensconce me. Wandering the Romantic Gardens, I encountered First Love Dianthus and knelt to feel the luxurious down of Lamb's Ear. I chuckled to myself when, in disbelief, I overheard Italian being spoken as I contemplated an exquisite arrangement of water platters and one lotus flower. Some people were also exploring this sensory paradise; I wondered how they would

8. F. NO CHANGE
G. what was happening
H. what happened
J. whatever happened next

9. A. NO CHANGE
B. unusual; perfect
C. unusual, and perfect
D. unusual. Perfect

10. F. NO CHANGE
G. Italian travelers
H. visitors
J. OMIT the underlined portion.

describe the unusual and magnificent water

platters.

[5]

Furthermore, as if my time for reflection
11
had ended by design, the gathering clouds

finally turned to rain, so I completed the

entry in my notebook and headed toward my

car. Arriving home, I discovered I had a new

perspective and renewed energy to tackle my

project list! no longer dreading my chores, I
12
accomplished 90 percent of them in very short

order. The real magic of the day was the gift

of relaxation and rejuvenation and enjoying
13
the magnificent gardens had been the perfect

idea after all.

11. A. NO CHANGE
    B. Then,
    C. Moreover,
    D. Although,

12. F. NO CHANGE
    G. list, no
    H. list! No
    J. list no

13. A. NO CHANGE
    B. rejuvenation, enjoying
    C. rejuvenation; enjoying
    D. rejuvenation, by enjoying

Questions 14 and 15 refer
to the essay as a whole.

14. For the sake of unity and
    coherence of the essay, paragraph
    3 should be placed:
    F. where it is now.
    G. after paragraph 1.
    H. after paragraph 4.
    J. after paragraph 5.

15. Suppose the writer had been
    assigned to write a brief
    essay illustrating a personal
    experience with nature. Would
    this essay successfully fulfill the
    assignment?
    A. Yes, because the essay
       describes the author's day
       spent in a botanical garden.
    B. Yes, because the essay depicts
       the satisfaction felt by the
       author for the work she
       completed in her garden.
    C. No, because the essay was not
       autobiographical.
    D. No, because the essay
       focuses on avoiding work
       and not necessarily on
       enjoying nature.

PRACTICE SET 4: ANSWERS & EXPLANATIONS

1. **D** Possessives
    The word *their* indicates ownership. *They're* means "they are," while *there* indicates location. Neither of which would be appropriate in the underlined section of the sentence.

2. **G** Verb Tenses
    The verb *lie* and its past tense form *lay* refer to something resting or reclining, while the verb *lay* and its past tense form *laid* refer to putting something down. The sentence should be reworded to say *the delight that lay ahead* because it is the past tense form of *lie*, so **G** is correct.

3. **D** Connecting and Transitional Words
    After meeting a friend for Sunday breakfast is an introductory clause, which needs a comma to show that the main part of the sentence is about to begin. A connecting word such as *and*, in **C**, or *so*, in **B**, is not necessary here. **D** is correct.

4. **F** Semicolons
    Semicolons can be used to join two related sentences. Using only a comma to separate the sentences would cause a run-on sentence, as would using a conjunction without a comma.

5. **B** Adverbs and Adjectives
    The word *rebelliously* describes how the author *drove*, so it should be placed before the word it modifies, as in **B**. The other options are awkward and confusing.

6. **J** Redundancy
    The reader can figure out that the author saw *many sights* during her garden visit. The underlined phrase should be deleted because it is redundant.

7. **C** Verb Tenses
    The author is reflecting about an event that happened in the past, so a past tense verb should be used, **C**. As it is written in **A**, *am transporting* makes it seem as if the garden visit is happening right now, instead of in the past.

8. **H** Parallelism
    Sentences should be parallel, so they will flow well. *What was the next occurrence* should be rewritten as *what happened*, **H**, to make it parallel with *what appeared*.

9. **A** Colons
    Colons call attention to the words that follow them, as long as a complete sentence exists to the left of the colon. *The August afternoon was unusual* is a complete sentence, so a colon appropriately introduces the list that follows. The list also elaborates on the sentence to the left of the colon.

10. **G** Vague Words
As it is written, *some people* does not provide the reader with much information. Changing *people* to *Italian travelers* further explains the previous sentence in which the author mentioned overhearing Italian voices, so **G** is correct.

11. **B** Connecting and Transitional Words
The transitional word *furthermore* is used to introduce additional arguments or points, so it is not necessary in this sentence. The author is merely telling the reader what happened next during her adventure, so *furthermore* should be replaced with *then*, **B**.

12. **H** Periods, Question Marks, and Exclamation Points
Although exclamation marks should not be overused, the exclamation mark is appropriate in this sentence because the author is expressing a feeling of excessive joy. Exclamation marks end sentences, so the word *no*, **H**, should be capitalized.

13. **C** Semicolons
As it is written, the sentence is a run-on because it lacks either a semicolon or a comma followed by a conjunction. A semicolon is appropriate in this sentence because the second part of the sentence further explains the first part. This makes **C** correct.

14. **H** Passage Reorganization
As the passage is currently organized, paragraph 3 is confusing because it describes the author's sensory experience, but the reader does not find out the author's location until paragraph 4. By placing paragraph 3 after paragraph 4 in **H**, the reader discovers that the author is in a garden, which makes the essay more logical.

15. **A** Big Picture Purpose
This essay describes the author's experience at a botanical garden. She describes in detail the different sights, sounds, and smells of her garden visit, which fulfills the assignment. Therefore, **A** is correct.

PASSAGE V

What's Your Major? Give It Time

[1]

It seems that high school seniors have barely submitted their college applications when people begin asking them, "What do you plan to major in?" Choosing a major for college studies is an important decision. The choice is also one that does not need to be rushed or "cast of stone" early in a student's college career. It may be best to think of that decision as [2]

[2]

The process of choosing a college major begins in high school, as students discover specific interests and aptitudes in the course

of their studies. They meet with academic counselors to discern those aptitudes and interests and then narrow their list of college

1. **A.** NO CHANGE
   B. "cast in stone"
   C. "cast under stone"
   D. "cast from stone"

2. The writer wishes to introduce the main topic of the essay by indicating how choosing a career path involves determining one's true interests. Which of the following phrases would best do so, in keeping with the way the topic is developed throughout the essay?
   F. a time-consuming process.
   G. an arduous undertaking.
   H. a discernment process.
   J. a necessary experience.

3. **A.** NO CHANGE
   B. Juniors and seniors, in meeting to discern, with academic counselors
   C. In meetings with juniors and seniors, academic counselors discern
   D. Juniors and seniors, who along with discerning counselors, meet

choices, based on individual interests. ☐4

4. With the intention of adding more information, the writer is considering inserting at this point the following true statement:

> Some students determine what college to attend based on the rankings of a university's football and basketball teams.

Should the writer insert the new sentence here? Why, or why not?

F. Yes, because the sentence gives the reader some serious information about how some students select a college, as a contrast to the trivial information given earlier.

G. Yes, because the sentence provides information that supports the idea that choosing a college requires discernment.

H. No, because the sentence provides information that undermines the writer's argument that a college major should be chosen quickly.

J. No, because the sentence provides incidental details that are not of sufficient relevance for inclusion.

[3]

☐5 The college experience is designed as a continuation of the self-discovery process, a process intended to guide the individual to a satisfying career. While students often enter college with a certain direction in mind, it is not uncommon for that direction to <u>change;</u>

<u>and sometimes</u> to a very different area.
6

[4]

Susan's experience is a good example.

<u>She excelled in math and logic, as well as her</u>
7
<u>interests and abilities which included writing,</u>
<u>music, and literature.</u> Her father

5. Which of the following sentences would most effectively guide the reader from paragraph 2 into paragraph 3?

A. Academic counselors help students make important decisions.

B. Those areas are just a starting point, however.

C. Many college freshmen are unprepared for university life.

D. College counselors encourage freshmen to choose their major.

6. **F.** NO CHANGE

G. change and sometimes

H. change—and sometimes

J. change! Sometimes

7. **A.** NO CHANGE

B. Her interests and abilities included writing, music, and literature and also math and logic.

C. Her interests and abilities included writing, music, literature, but she was also good in math and logic.

D. While her interests and abilities included writing, music, and literature, she also excelled in math and logic.

had worked in the computer field for years,
                                        8

she entered college strongly considering a

computer science major, and she enrolled

in a programming class her freshman year.

In the course of the class, however, Susan
                              9

discovered that while she could appreciate the

logic and challenge involved in programming,

she did not have a passion for it. Ultimately,

she discovered that the passion she had for

literature and the humanities, as well as her
                      10

verbal and cognitive abilities, would

eventually best be applied in English and
                  11

philosophy studies.

[5]

One can see from the example that, in

addition to aptitude and inclinations, several

other factors, including family and cultural

expectations, often contributes to
                          12

your choice of study. She is glad she briefly
 13

investigated the option of computer science
                              14

(even for a short time), and she still uses her

analytical skills in her teaching and writing

career. Ultimately, Susan is grateful for

8.
  F. NO CHANGE
  G. for years. She
  H. for years and she
  J. for years she

9.
  A. NO CHANGE
  B. class; however, Susan
  C. class however; Susan
  D. class however, Susan

10.
  F. NO CHANGE
  G. the passion she had for literature and the humanities, and the way she excelled in verbal and cognitive activities,
  H. her interests were in literature and the humanities, and she also excelled in areas requiring verbal and cognitive abilities,
  J. her passion for literature and the humanities, as well as her verbal and cognitive abilities,

11.
  A. NO CHANGE
  B. finally would best be applied
  C. would best be applied
  D. would best be applied at last

12.
  F. NO CHANGE
  G. contributed
  H. have contributed
  J. contribute

13.
  A. NO CHANGE
  B. one's
  C. ones'
  D. their

14.
  F. NO CHANGE
  G. of computer science, even for a short time,
  H. for a short time, of computer science,
  J. of computer science,

the experience and process that helped her

discern her true passion. ⬚15

15. Suppose the writer had been assigned to write a short essay on a specific problem faced by college first-years at large public universities. Would this essay successfully fulfill the assignment?
   A. Yes, because the essay defines an issue for students at large universities.
   B. Yes, because the essay describes something that happened to one person, Susan.
   C. No, because the essay primarily describes the process students go through to determine their field of study.
   D. No, because the essay focuses only on the problems faced by high school seniors.

PRACTICE SET 5: ANSWERS & EXPLANATIONS

1. **B** Idioms
Cast in stone, **B**, is a saying that means something is fixed and cannot be changed. The writer is pointing out that college majors can be altered.

2. **H** Big Picture Purpose
The writer discusses how the college experience helps students learn what truly interests them. The example of Susan illustrates the idea that students often enter college assuming they want to pursue one career, but after taking classes, they discern that their interests may lie elsewhere. Therefore, **H** is correct.

3. **A** Sentence Reorganization
The underlined section conveys its meaning clearly and is grammatically correct. The other answer choices offer different ways to reword the sentence, but none improve the original.

4. **J** Additional Detail and Evidence
Paragraph 2 is about high school students taking the time to determine their interests and skills before selecting a college. The statement about sports determining college selections does not relate to the paragraph's topic, so **J** is correct.

5. **B** Transitions and Topic Sentences
Paragraph 2 discusses the first steps of choosing a major, while paragraph 3 elaborates further on the same idea. The topic sentence of paragraph 3 should make a connection between the self-discovery process that occurs in both high school and college. **B** is the best answer.

6. **H** Periods, Question Marks, and Exclamation Points
A dash, in **H**, is needed in this sentence to emphasize the idea that college students sometimes go through big changes. The dash adds more emphasis than a comma, but the statement is not emotional enough to deserve an exclamation point.

7. **D** Subordinate or Dependent Clauses
The purpose of the underlined sentence is to contrast Susan's diverse interests. While Susan's skills could be listed out in a series, emphasizing the differences in her abilities makes the sentence flow better with the entire paragraph. **D** is correct.

8. **G** Comma Splices
The comma in the underlined section causes the sentence to form a comma splice, in which two independent clauses are joined with only a comma. One way to correct the sentence is to place a period after *years* in order to stop the first sentence and begin the next, so **G** is correct.

9. **A** Connecting and Transitional Words
In the original, the word *however* is correctly separated from the rest of the sentence with two commas. *However* is a transitional word, and it needs a comma on both sides to indicate that it is interrupting the sentence.

10. **J** Parallelism
For the clearest sentence, two or more items in a sentence should be parallel and expressed with words of similar form. In the underlined section, the parallel words should be *her passion* and *her verbal and cognitive abilities*, as in **J**.

11. **C** Redundancy
The sentence first states that Susan *ultimately* determined what major was best for her. Words such as *eventually*, *finally*, and *at last* would be redundant here, so **C** is correct.

12. **J** Subject-Verb Agreement
The phrase *including family and cultural expectations* separates the subject and verb of the sentence. The subject (*factors*) and the verb must agree, so the correct expression would be *factors contribute*, **J**.

13. **B** Pronoun-Antecedent Agreement
Pronouns in a sentence need to match, and the underlined section should agree with *one*, which is used at the beginning of the sentence. The section should be rewritten as *one's* choice of study, with an apostrophe before the *s* to indicate ownership. So, **B** is correct.

14. **J** Redundancy
The sentence states that Susan is glad she *briefly* investigated computer science. The phrase *for a short time* is redundant here, so the correct answer is **J**.

15. **C** Big Picture Purpose
The focus of the essay is the self-discovery process that students must go through when determining their college major. No reference is made to a school's size. Therefore, **C** is correct.

PRACTICE SET 6

PASSAGE VI

Counting Crows

[1]

Formed in 1991 in San Francisco, the

rock band <u>Counting Crows for inspiration</u>
₁
<u>turned to English literature</u>

1. **A.** NO CHANGE
    B. Counting Crows turned to English literature for inspiration
    C. for inspiration the Counting Crows turned to English literature
    D. to English literature the Counting Crows turned for inspiration

<u>by naming</u> their group. The moniker Counting
₂
Crows derives from an old English rhyme

whose theme implies that life is as pointless

as counting crows, "One for sorrow, two for

mirth, three for a wedding, four for a birth . . ."

2. **F.** NO CHANGE
    G. and naming
    H. having named
    J. when naming

<u>While the verse suggests</u> the futility of
₃

3. **A.** NO CHANGE
    B. While, the verse suggests
    C. While the verse suggests,
    D. While, the verse suggests,

counting crows, oddly enough, 4

[2]

The perception that crows count dates

to the 18th century, when a black bird built a
                                              5

nest on an estate, much to the exasperation

of the squire. Whenever the squire entered

the tower, the crow would disappear until his

human adversary departed and it was safe

to return to his roost. To exterminate the

nest with an unwavering desire, the owner
                                    6

dispatched two employees into the tower—one

would leave, suggesting a vacant tower, while

the other would lie in wait but the ruse failed
                                7

to hoodwink the ingenious crow. Each day the

squire increased the number of individuals,

until finally the crow was outwitted. Five

people entered the tower, one remained to
                            8

eradicate the unwanted houseguest and
                                    9

eliminate it.

[3]

Behavioral scientists studying animal

4. The writer wishes to introduce
the main topic of the essay by
indicating what people believe
about the intelligence of crows.
Which of the following would best
do so, in keeping with the way the
topic is developed throughout the
essay?
   F. some behavioral scientists
   do not believe that crows can
   count.
   G. crows are a nuisance to
   people, as shown in numerous
   behavioral studies.
   H. many people have contended
   that crows possess surprising
   mathematical ability.
   J. some historians report that
   more than 200 years ago,
   homeowners began devising
   ways to get rid of crows.

5. Given that all the choices are
true, which of the following gives
the most descriptive details about
nest building to the reader at this
point in the essay?
   A. NO CHANGE
   B. an uninvited crow
   constructed a nest in an
   estate's watchtower,
   C. a crow built a nest in a tower,
   D. an annoying bird made a
   home in a building,

6. F. NO CHANGE
   G. With an unwavering desire to
   exterminate the nest,
   H. His unwavering desire to
   exterminate the nest,
   J. In order to exterminate the
   nest he needed an unwavering
   desire,

7. A. NO CHANGE
   B. wait; however,
   C. wait, however
   D. wait however,

8. F. NO CHANGE
   G. tower and one
   H. tower, and one
   J. tower and the one

9. A. NO CHANGE
   B. eradicate and eliminate the
   unwanted houseguest.
   C. eradicate the unwanted
   houseguest.
   D. eliminate the unwanted
   houseguest and eradicate it
   forever.

The ACT
English &
Reading
Workbook

intelligence conducted an experiment to [10]

During testing, a number of covered cups

were filled with varying amounts of meat

pieces, ranging in number from zero to three,

and were made available to the crows trained
                                          11

to be able to remove the lids, the crows
   12

consumed as many pieces from each container

as desired. Beside the cups was a plate

containing meat pieces totaling more than

the sum found in the individual containers.

The objective for the avian subjects was to

eat an equal number of pieces from the plate

as the total consumed from the cups, with

punishment a deterrent for overindulging.

The assignment was accomplished when the

crows distinguished amounts up to seven but

no higher. Observers have witnessed crows

drop walnuts into busy intersections so that
                    13

passing cars will crack them open. Whether

the birds were actually counting or merely

recognizing patterns fuels some debate,

although no one questions the inadequate
                                       14

intelligence of crows.

[4]

While the author of the old English

poem suggests counting crows is a seemingly

pointless activity. It seems crows, on the other
              15

hand, view counting people a worthwhile

endeavor—as long as no more than seven are

involved, anyway.

10. Which choice best leads the reader into the subject matter of paragraph 3?
F. substantiate the stories regarding counting crows.
G. determine whether crows can be trained to open containers.
H. disprove the hypothesis that crows can count as high as ten.
J. reenact the story of the crow in the watchtower.

11. A. NO CHANGE
B. crows, trained
C. crows who were trained
D. crows. Trained

12. F. NO CHANGE
G. be motivated to remove
H. be removing
J. remove

13. A. NO CHANGE
B. Crows have the largest brain of any animal relative to their body size.
C. Because crows are so clever, many people consider them pests.
D. OMIT the underlined portion.

14. F. NO CHANGE
G. uncanny
H. miraculous
J. marginal

15. A. NO CHANGE
B. activity, it
C. activity; it
D. activity, and it

PRACTICE SET 6: ANSWERS & EXPLANATIONS

1. **B** Sentence Reorganization
   As it is written, the phrase *for inspiration* is awkwardly placed after *Counting Crows*. By moving *for inspiration* after *English literature*, as in **B**, the reader can then understand the meaning of the sentence.

2. **J** Idioms
   The first sentence conveys that the Counting Crows were inspired by English literature during the process of naming their group. This meaning is clarified by the phrase *when naming*, **J**. The other answer options make the meaning of the sentence unclear.

3. **A** Connecting and Transitional Words
   As written, the underlined section is part of the introductory phrase *while the verse suggests the futility of counting crows*. A comma is not needed until the end of the whole clause.

4. **H** Big Picture Purpose
   The main point of the essay is that crows can count, a belief held by many people for hundreds of years. The other choices do not support the writer's argument, so **H** is correct.

5. **B** Word Choice
   Specific details create a vivid picture for readers. Descriptive words, such as *uninvited crow* and *watchtower*, **B**, are more precise than *bird* and *building*, **D**.

6. **G** Sentence Reorganization
   The underlined section describes the owner's attitude—the owner had *an unwavering desire to exterminate the nest. Unwavering desire* needs to come before *exterminate* because it explains the owner's feelings about exterminating the nest. Only **G** solves this problem.

7. **B** Connecting and Transitional Words
   However connects two independent clauses, which could both stand alone as sentences. When *however* joins two independent clauses, a semicolon should be placed on the left of *however* and a comma on the right. So, the sentence now reads: *To exterminate the nest with an unwavering desire, the owner dispatched two employees into the tower—one would leave, suggesting a vacant tower, while the other would lie in wait; however, the ruse failed to hoodwink the ingenious crow.* Therefore, **B** is correct.

8. **H** Comma Splices
   Two sentences have been joined together incorrectly here with only a comma. One way to correct the comma splice is to place a conjunction after the comma, so **H** is correct.

9. **C**   Redundancy
The sentence states that the people entering the tower planned to eradicate and eliminate the crow. *Eradicate* and *eliminate* have the same meaning, so the words are redundant. Therefore, **C** must be the right answer.

10. **F**   Transitions and Topic Sentences
Paragraph 3 details the study that attempted to confirm stories about counting crows; however, no reenactment occurred during the experiment. Although crows open containers, that task is not the focus of the paragraph. While the experiment indicated that crows can count to seven, the scientists were not attempting to disprove a hypothesis that crows can count to ten. **F** is correct because it explains the topic of the paragraph.

11. **D**   Run-on Sentences
The original creates a run-on sentence by joining two complete sentences with no punctuation. One complete sentence ends with *available to the crows*, and the next sentence begins with *trained*. **D** provides one way to repair the run-on sentence by inserting a period between *crows* and *trained*.

12. **J**   Verb Tenses
In the past, the crows were taught how to remove the lids. Extra words such as *be motivated* and *be able* do not improve the clarity of the sentence, so **J** is correct.

13. **D**   Paragraph Reorganization
The subject of paragraph 3 is a specific study that tested the ability of crows to count. While the other statements support the idea that crows are intelligent, none of them should be included in the paragraph because they do not relate to the experiment. Therefore, **D** is correct.

14. **G**   Word Choice
Because no miracles occurred during the experiment, a crow's intelligence is not *miraculous*, **H**. *Marginal* and *inadequate* would suggest crows are not intelligent, but the experiment revealed that crows have an unexpected, or *uncanny*, intelligence. So, **G** must be correct.

15. **B**   Sentence Fragments
The first part of the sentence, *while the author of the old English poem suggests counting crows is a seemingly pointless activity*, introduces the main part of the sentence that begins with *it seems*. A period after *activity* creates a sentence fragment, so the period should be replaced with a comma, **B**.

OVERVIEW OF THE ACT READING TEST

Time is certainly of the essence on the ACT Reading Test. It gives you 35 minutes to read four rather lengthy passages and answer 40 passage questions. You'll have little time to do a lot of work. Becoming familiar with the format and content of this subject test before you actually have to take it will help you use your time efficiently and effectively. After reviewing this section, be sure to practice with our Reading practice sets.

THE INSTRUCTIONS

There's no reason to waste a single minute (or even a fraction of one) glancing at the instructions during the test. Do yourself a favor and learn them before test day. You should know the drill by now: read, repeat, remember.

> **DIRECTIONS:** On this test, you will have 35 minutes to read four passages and answer 40 questions (ten questions on each passage). Each set of ten questions appears directly after the relevant passage. You should select the answer choice that best answers the question. There is no time limit for work on the individual passages, so you can move freely between the passages and refer to each as often as you'd like.

Got that? These directions are pretty straightforward. If you do feel any confusion, rest assured it will be gone by the time you finish this chapter and are familiar with the layout of the test. Let's move on.

FORMAT OF THE READING TEST

The Reading Test has two main components: the passages and the questions.

The Passages

Each of the four passages is approximately 750 words long and presented in two columns. They'll basically look like the following (except they'll be longer and have words other than "blah"):

This is a sample passage.

Blah blah blah blah blah blah blah blah blah blah blah blah blah blah blah blah blah blah blah blah blah blah blah blah blah blah blah blah blah blah blah blah blah blah blah blah blah blah blah blah blah blah blah blah blah blah blah blah blah blah blah blah blah blah blah blah blah blah blah blah blah blah blah blah blah blah blah blah blah blah

5 blah blah blah blah blah blah blah blah blah blah blah blah blah blah blah blah blah blah blah blah blah blah blah blah blah blah blah blah blah blah.

Blah blah blah blah blah blah blah blah blah blah blah blah blah blah blah blah blah blah blah blah blah blah blah blah blah blah blah blah blah blah blah blah blah blah blah blah blah blah blah blah blah blah blah blah blah blah blah blah blah blah

10 blah blah blahblah blah blah blah blah blah blah blah blah blah blah blah blah blah blah blah blah blah blah blah blah blah blah blah blah blah blah blah blah blah blah blah blah blah blah blah blah blah blah blah blah.

Blah blah blah blah blah blah blah blah blah blah blah blah blah blah blah blah blah blah blah blah blah blah blah blah blah blah blah blah blah blah

15 blah blah blah blah blah blah blah blah blah blah blah blah blah blah blah blah blah blah blah blah blah blah blah blah blah blah blah blah blah blah blah blah blah blah blah blah blah blah blah blah blah blah blah blah blah blah blah blah blah blah blah blah blah blah blah blah blah blah blah blah blah blah blah.

The numbers along the left side of the column are line numbers (the "5" means that you're reading the fifth line of the passage, the "15" means you're reading the fifteenth line, etc.). Line numbers appear on every fifth line of the passage. They are useful primarily to refer to specific line-numbered sections addressed by select questions.

The Questions

Each passage is directly followed by 10 questions of varying difficulty, making a total of 40 questions on the Reading Test. The ACT includes a number of different types of questions in each batch of 10. We'll provide in-depth examples of each type below.

CONTENT OF THE READING TEST

There are two different types of content we refer to when we say "the content of the Reading Test."

The first type of content refers to the subject matter of the passages. The second type refers to the sorts of questions asked about the passages.

The Reading Passages

The Reading Test consists of four passages: Prose Fiction, Social Science, Humanities, and Natural Science—always appearing in that order. Prose Fiction is the only fiction passage on the test; the other three are nonfiction. All four passages are given equal weight in scoring.

Later in this workbook, we will present you with two practice sets for each of the four content areas. For now, just read the brief descriptions of each passage type.

Prose Fiction

Prose Fiction passages are usually excerpts from novels or short stories. You should approach this passage as you would an assignment for your high school English class, not as you would a book you read in your spare time. When you read fiction for pleasure, you may be tempted to read simply for the story. Yet while the plot is an important element of most fiction, and one on which the questions will test you, it is certainly not the only element.

In addition to the plot of the passage, pay attention to character development. Since plot and character are usually essential to a story, your ability to identify and comprehend them is probably pretty strong already. You should also pay attention to tone, style, and mood when reading the passage. Ask yourself questions like: "Who is the narrator?"; "Does the narrator exhibit any sympathies or biases?"; "What are the relationships between the characters?" These questions will help you keep on top of the passage as you read.

Social Science

The Social Science passage can cover a variety of subjects ranging from anthropology to economics to politics. All of the subjects that appear in the Social Science passage essentially deal with the ways societies and civilization work, and most of them have a political context.

When reading the passage, you should pay attention to the key names, dates, and concepts mentioned, and you want to underline this information as you read over the passage. Because the subject of this passage is often historical, you should also pay attention to cause-effect relationships and the chronology of events.

Social Science writing is often research-based and, as a result, relatively formal in tone. Despite the relative objectivity implied by words like *research* and *science*, the authors of Social Science passages often express strong and controversial views on their subjects. You should try to decipher the author's standpoint—if he or she has one—from the general argument of the passage and individual statements.

Humanities

Humanities passages cover cultural matters, particularly art and literature. These passages tend to be written analytically or journalistically. On rare occasions, you might encounter a Humanities passage that is an excerpt from a personal essay.

In some respects, the Humanities passage closely resembles the Social Science passage. They both deal with either historical or contemporary figures and events, so they are both full of specific information that you should underline as you read the passage. The difference between the two types of passages lies in their emphasis. Whereas the Social Science passage usually provides a political context for figures and events, the Humanities passage focuses on their artistic or literary significance.

As in the Social Science passage, the writer of the Humanities passage will often have a slant or bias, and your reading of the passage should be sensitive to that.

Natural Science

Natural Science passages discuss, unsurprisingly, scientific topics. These passages present scientific arguments or experiments and explain the reasoning behind them and their significance.

These passages are usually heavy on facts and scientific theories. Underline these theories so you can refer back to them later. You should keep an eye out for cause-effect relationships and comparisons when reading Natural Science passages.

Question Types

The 40 questions found on the Reading Test can be broken down into several types according to what each tests. Most broadly, the questions can be categorized by the way in which they force you to interact with the passage. One type will ask you to deal with the passage in a very straightforward way and to identify details, facts, and specific information that is clearly stated in the passage. The second type will ask you to take a further step and to use the information in the passage to figure out larger issues, such as the main idea, relationships, and point of view.

More specifically, the different types of questions test your ability to:

- Identify specific details and facts
- Determine the meaning of words through context
- Draw inferences from given evidence
- Understand character and character motivation
- Identify the main idea of a section or the whole passage
- Identify the author's point of view or tone
- Identify cause-effect relationships
- Make comparisons and analogies

Some of the question types apply primarily—and sometimes solely—to certain passages. For instance, understanding character questions appear only in the Prose Fiction passage, since it's the only passage that will have characters. On the other hand, you won't find a main idea question on the Prose Fiction passage, since works of fiction generally don't present arguments.

This list of question types is designed to give you a general impression of the questions asked on the Reading Test. Next, we will cover the strategies you need to know to ace the Reading Test.

STRATEGIES FOR THE READING TEST

Doing well on the Reading Test is not a matter of having tricks up your sleeve. When you come to a question that asks about a passage's main point, you can't rely on some handy main-point trick to figure out the answer. Either you know it, or you don't; either you understood the passage, or you didn't.

That said, you can use a general strategy to improve your performance on the test. We like to think of this general strategy as a macro approach to the entire Reading Test, rather than micro tips to get you from question to question. The crux of the strategy is your ability to read well—that is, with speed and without sacrificing comprehension.

Read!

Before we go on to discuss specific strategies for the Reading Test, we want to give you this piece of advice: Reading during the months and weeks before the ACT is the best preparation for the Reading Test. The Reading Test assesses one main thing: your reading comprehension skills. Every time you read, regardless of *what* you read, you exercise your reading comprehension skills. And the more you read, the better you'll become at quickly and thoroughly comprehending what's written. So it makes sense that the best practice for the Reading Test is reading.

While reading this SparkNotes workbook will have you well on your way toward ACT success, we encourage you to improve your score and your mind by reading other things in your spare time. Newspapers, novels, and homework assignments provide good reading material. You may particularly want to focus on reading science articles in a newspaper or scientific magazine, as many students have less familiarity with this type of material. The more challenging the material, the more exercise your brain will get, so don't just read comic books and cereal boxes.

Take the Practice Sets

Practice sets are a useful tool for spotting your weaknesses. Take a Reading practice set before you begin studying and then another after you've done some preparation. We've also categorized the Reading practice sets by passage type so you can focus on specific passage types. When you score your practice sets, you'll be able to see how you did on each type of question, so you can pinpoint your weak and strong areas for focused study.

Know Your Strengths and Weaknesses

Knowing your strong and weak points is important for developing a simple but effective Reading Test strategy. On the actual test, play to your strong points and play down your weak ones. For example, after all your studying, if you're still incapable of correctly answering cause-effect questions, don't waste valuable time struggling with them on the actual test. Instead, guess on those questions or save them for a second pass through the test. Play the percentages: Concentrate on questions you're more likely to get right to achieve your optimum score.

Optimize Your Time

As you know by now, the Reading Test demands a little extra something from you: In addition to answering its questions, you must digest approximately 3,000 words worth of information. In order to be effective on this test, you must achieve an optimum balance between the time you spend reading the passages and the time you spend answering the questions. For instance, if you sweat over the first passage, painstakingly making sure you know its every little detail, you'll probably run out of time before you get to the last passage. On the flip side, if you breeze through the passages, registering a word here and there, you'll probably have a hard time answering the questions. The lesson here is that you need to find the perfect balance.

There's no formula for this perfect balance; in fact, what's "perfect" varies from person to person. Below, we'll give you some general strategies for rationing your time on the Reading Test. We think these strategies work well for most people, but ultimately it's up to you to decide what works best. Our strategies can help you, but you should complement them by taking timed practice Reading Tests. By practicing frequently, you can determine your ideal reading speed—the speed that allows you to get through the passages quickly while understanding what's being said.

Scan Quickly for Details

Because the Reading Test quizzes you on your understanding of general themes and specific information in each passage, your instinct is probably to read the entire passage carefully, making sure you don't miss anything that can be covered in the questions. If you had unlimited time, this method of reading would probably make sense, but you don't have unlimited time; in fact, you have extremely limited time.

As you read, pay active attention to what's going on, but don't get bogged down trying to assimilate *every* detail. By the end of your first reading, you should understand the themes of the passage and the argument, if there is one. We definitely don't mean that you should ignore the meat of paragraphs and focus only on their first sentences; if you do that, you won't understand the passage.

Reading for a general understanding means you don't have to memorize all the specific facts of the passage. The author uses specific facts to support an argument, but as you read, you should be more concerned with their cumulative effect (i.e., the larger argument) than with the specific facts themselves. When you get to a point in a passage where the author lists a bunch of facts to support an idea, make a quick note of the list in the margin for future reference and keep going.

The only time you should slow down and go back is if you lose the flow of the passage—if you realize you don't know what's happening, what's being argued, or what in the world that entire last paragraph was about.

Remember: There are only ten questions accompanying each passage. These ten questions cannot cover the entire content of a passage, so reading for every detail is a waste of time. When reading an ACT passage, read carefully to understand general elements: the topic, theme, and argument. Read the passage with an awareness of the general questions you might be asked. What is the author's goal in writing the passage? What is the tone; what are the themes and major points of the passage? When you finish a passage, you should be able to answer these questions and also have a sense of the passage's layout. Reading on the ACT is like taking a tour of a room—you have to know the layout of the room, but you don't have to know the location of every knicknack.

When you see details that seem important, don't fuss painstakingly over those details. Instead, lightly note them in your mind and perhaps make a quick mark in the margin. This way, you'll reduce wasted time and gain a good enough comprehension of the passage to answer questions that cover general aspects of the passage correctly. You'll also have a good enough sense of the passage's layout so that when the passage asks about specific information, you'll be able to go back quickly to the passage, check the information, and choose the correct answer.

Scribble and Underline

Once upon a time, you learned that a pristine ACT test booklet is a wasted opportunity. Here, on the Reading Test, you have a chance to take advantage of your test book by scribbling and underlining away in it. Any marking you do will help you when it's time to answer the questions.

You're probably wondering how you'll know what to underline without having read the questions. Indeed, that does seem like the tricky part. But the point of underlining is not to pinpoint specific answers to questions; in fact, if you could underline answers, you'd be wasting time underlining them when you could be filling in a bubble on the answer sheet.

The point of underlining, then, is not to highlight correct answers, but to assist you when you refer back to the passage for those answers. You can use your underlines and notes as a map through the passage, so you don't waste time covering passage territory for a second time. As long as scribbling and underlining don't take up a significant amount of time (you should not be drawing straight lines or printing neatly), any marginal notes and underlines will help and guide you when you answer the questions.

Underlining the topic sentence of each paragraph (it's not always the first sentence) will help you keep on top of the argument's direction. These underlines will serve as handy reference tools when you need to refer back to the passage. Because you're reading for the general point of a passage and its component paragraphs, you do not need to know every single illustrative example. When you encounter a sentence or a section that looks like it will enumerate examples to support a point, you can quickly glance at the section, then scribble "eg" or "ex" or some other mark in the margin to let you know that this is an example. If a question asks you for specific evidence that demonstrates a certain point, you can refer back to the relevant passage by glancing at your notes and then moving down to the section marked "eg" or "ex." You can also use numbers to mark items in an extended list. Underlining key phrases that help relate parts of the passage, such as "subsequently," "on the other hand," and "in contrast," will also help you map your way through the passage.

Answer the Questions

After you finish the passage, go to the questions. Since you read the passage with the big picture in mind, you should be able to answer the general questions dealing with main points, point of view, or tone. When you get to a question on a specific detail, don't immediately look at the answer choices to avoid being influenced by "trick" answers. Instead, articulate to yourself exactly what the question is asking. Then quickly go back to the passage and come up with your own answer to the question. Finally, choose the answer that best matches yours.

If you get to a question that is very hard and threatens to take a lot of time, place a mark next to it, skip it, move on to the next question, and come back if you have time. You should *not*, however, move on to the next passage while leaving a blank question behind you. Answer all questions dealing with a passage while the passage is still fresh in your mind.

Why "Passage First, Questions After" Is a Good Strategy

Some test prep books advise you to look at the questions first to find key words and then to read the passage with an eye to answering the questions. While this strategy seems good on paper, it's really quite difficult in practice, especially in high-pressure situations like taking the ACT. Imagine trying to remember what 10 questions ask while reading an unfamiliar passage, simultaneously trying to get the gist of it, and looking for possible answers to the questions. That's like trying to chew gum while patting your head, rubbing your stomach, and singing "The Star Spangled Banner." In addition, because some of the questions ask for specific details, you'll feel pressured to pay close attention to the passage line by line, which takes too much time. Ultimately, the "questions first, passage after" strategy can be extremely confusing as well as extremely difficult to execute.

"Passage first, questions after" is really just common sense. Using this method, you can avoid the confusion caused by other strategies. Again, think about the passage as a room and the answers to the questions as objects within the room. If you follow the other test books' strategy of "questions first," you'll be left groping helplessly for the objects in a completely dark room. If you follow our strategy (in other words, if you use common sense), you'll have turned on the lights first, making the objects much easier to find.

Take our Reading Test practice sets and exercise your wrists by making marginal notes and underlines. Soon you should be able to develop a scribbling system that works for you. Ready? On to the Reading review!

REVIEW FOR THE ACT READING TEST

In the following chapter, you'll get an in-depth review of the passages tested on the Reading Test. We'll review four sample passages covering each topic area. You should read these sample passages to gain familiarity with the types of passages on the test.

Our four sample passages are accompanied by descriptions of the question types you're likely to encounter, along with examples of these questions and methods for answering the sample questions. Our goal in offering you these descriptions and examples is to increase your familiarity with the types of questions on the test. These descriptions are usually not heavy on suggested strategy. As we've mentioned before, there aren't many strategies you can use to answer individual questions on the Reading Test. The best thing you can do to prepare is to know what the test will ask you.

We've divided this section into two parts: Prose Fiction first and the other three tests (Social Science, Humanities, and Natural Science) second. We've made this division because the Prose Fiction passage differs the most from the others in terms of how you read it and what you're reading it for.

PROSE FICTION

As we've stated before, you should not read the ACT Prose Fiction passage as you would a novel that you casually pick up on a Saturday afternoon. Treat the Prose Fiction passage as you would an English homework assignment. In addition to understanding the story behind the passage, you should also strive to understand the passage's use of style and tone.

Sample Passage

The following sample is adapted from James Joyce's short story "Grace" from the book, Dubliners.

    She was an active, practical woman of middle age. Not long before she had celebrated her silver wedding anniversary and renewed her intimacy with her husband by waltzing with him to Mr. Power's accompaniment. In her days of courtship, Mr. Kernan had seemed to her a not ungallant figure: and she still
5   hurried to the chapel door whenever a wedding was reported and, seeing the bridal pair, recalled with vivid pleasure how she had passed out of the Star of the Sea Church in Sandymount, leaning on the arm of a jovial well-fed man, who was dressed smartly in a frock-coat and lavender trousers and carried a silk hat gracefully balanced upon his other arm. After three weeks she had found a wife's
10   life irksome and, later on, when she was beginning to find it unbearable, she had become a mother. The part of mother presented to her no insuperable difficulties and for twenty-five years she had kept house shrewdly for her husband. Her two eldest sons were launched. One was in a draper's shop in Glasgow and the other

was clerk to a tea merchant in Belfast. They were good sons, wrote regularly and
15   sometimes sent home money. The other children were still at school.

Mr. Kernan sent a letter to his office next day and remained in bed. She made
beef tea for him and scolded him roundly. She accepted his frequent intemperance as part of the climate, healed him dutifully whenever he was sick, and
always tried to make him eat a breakfast. There were worse husbands. He had
20   never been violent since the boys had grown up, and she knew that he would
walk to the end of Thomas Street and back again to book even a small order.

Two nights after, his friends came to see him. She brought them up to his
bedroom, the air of which was impregnated with a personal odor, and gave them
chairs at the fire. Mr. Kernan's tongue, the occasional stinging pain of which had
25   made him somewhat irritable during the day, became more polite. He sat propped
up in the bed by pillows and the little color in his puffy cheeks made them
resemble warm cinders. He apologized to his guests for the disorder of the room,
but at the same time looked at them a little proudly, with a veteran's pride.

He was quite unconscious that he was the victim of a plot that his friends, Mr.
30   Cunningham, Mr. M'Coy and Mr. Power had disclosed to Mrs. Kernan in the
parlor. The idea had been Mr. Power's, but its development was entrusted to Mr.
Cunningham. Mr. Kernan came of Protestant stock and, though he had been
converted to the Catholic faith at the time of his marriage, he had not been in the
pale of the Church for twenty years. He was fond, moreover, of giving side-thrusts
35   at Catholicism.

Mr. Cunningham was the very man for such a case. He was an elder col-
league of Mr. Power. His own domestic life was not very happy. People had great
sympathy with him, for it was known that he had married an unpresentable
woman who was an incurable drunkard. He had set up house for her six times;
40   and each time she had pawned the furniture on him.

Everyone had respect for poor Martin Cunningham. He was a thoroughly
sensible man, influential and intelligent. His blade of human knowledge, natural astuteness particularized by long association with cases in the police courts,
had been tempered by brief immersions in the waters of general philosophy. He
45   was well informed. His friends bowed to his opinions and considered that his
face was like Shakespeare's.

When the plot had been disclosed to her, Mrs. Kernan had said:
"I leave it all in your hands, Mr. Cunningham."

After a quarter of a century of married life, she had very few illusions left.
50   Religion for her was a habit, and she suspected that a man of her husband's age
would not change greatly before death. She was tempted to see a curious appro-
priateness in his accident and, but that she did not wish to seem bloody-minded,
would have told the gentlemen that Mr. Kernan's tongue would not suffer by
being shortened. However, Mr. Cunningham was a capable man; and religion

55 was religion. The scheme might do good and, at least, it could do no harm. Her beliefs were not extravagant. She believed steadily in the Sacred Heart as the most generally useful of all Catholic devotions and approved of the sacraments. Her faith was bounded by her kitchen, but, if she was put to it, she could believe also in the banshee and in the Holy Ghost.

Questions

Below, we'll give you a rundown of the questions you're most likely to find on the Prose Fiction passage and how to answer them. All of the examples below pertain to the above passage.

1.   Identify Specific Details and Facts. Specific detail questions are perhaps the most straightforward questions you'll encounter anywhere on the test. As the name suggests, these questions ask you to find specific details within the passage. They are very common on the Prose Fiction passage and throughout the rest of the test. You'll probably see three or four specific detail questions accompanying the Prose Fiction passage.

Here's an example of a relatively easy specific detail question:

According to his friends, Mr. Cunningham resembles:

A.   Mr. Kernan.
B.   a policeman.
C.   Shakespeare.
D.   Mr. Power.

If you know the answer to this question, you're all set. If you don't, you probably remember there was a section near the end of the passage that discussed Mr. Cunningham and his background. To answer this question, you should first look in that section because the answer is probably there. Have you looked yet? Well, the answer *is* there, on lines 45–46 ("his face was like Shakespeare's"). The correct answer is **C**.

That question was fairly simple, partly because it had a one-word answer, but specific detail questions can be more confusing when the answers are longer. Try another question about Mr. Cunningham:

According to the passage, people feel sorry for Mr. Cunningham because:

A.   he is sensible, influential, and intelligent.
B.   he was the victim of a plot by his friends.
C.   he has a long association with police courts.
D.   he is married to a drunkard.

While this question is not too difficult, it is slightly more confusing than the previous one simply because the answers are longer. If you've read the passage reasonably carefully and you've quickly double-checked the answer in the passage, you can correctly identify **D** as the answer. **A** and **C** are actually given as reasons why Mr. Cunningham is *respected* by his acquaintances, and **B** applies not to Mr. Cunningham but to Mr. Kernan.

While specific detail questions are generally straightforward, they can try to trick you by leading you to give an answer that seems correct if you read one sentence but that is revealed as incorrect by another. For example:

> How many children do the Kernans have?
>
> **A.** None
> **B.** One
> **C.** Two
> **D.** More than two

If you remembered that the Kernans' children were mentioned in the first paragraph, you'd look there, and perhaps your eye would fall on the sentence, "Her two eldest sons were launched." A quick glance at this sentence may miss the word "eldest," which indicates that there are younger children, so you may decide that there are only two children in the Kernan family and that the answer is **C**. But the word "eldest" and the last sentence of the paragraph, "The other children were still at school," indicate that there are other children in the family and that the correct answer is **D**.

2. Draw Inferences.

Inference questions ask for implied information. They want you to take a piece of information given in the passage and use it to figure out something else. Because the answers are not given explicitly within the passage, these questions are often significantly more difficult than specific detail questions. But they are just as common, so you need to get a handle on them.

You can usually spot an inference question from a mile away. Inference questions frequently use verbs such as *suggest*, *infer*, *imply*, and *indicate*.

As with specific detail questions, some inference questions are easier than others. Sometimes, the ACT writers will feel extra nice and refer you to a specific portion of the passage. For example:

> The second paragraph (lines 16–21) suggests that the Kernans' marriage is characterized primarily by:
>
> **A.** Mr. Kernan's violent behavior toward his wife.
> **B.** Mrs. Kernan's patience with her husband.
> **C.** Mr. Kernan's fondness for his wife's beef tea.
> **D.** Mr. Kernan's willingness to go to the store for his wife.

In some ways, this inference question resembles a specific detail question. Elements of all the answer choices are mentioned in the paragraph. Your job is to figure out which answer choice *best* answers the question. Perhaps **A** characterized the marriage at one point in time, but the narrator notes that Mr. Kernan "had never been violent since the boys had grown up," so **A** is wrong. Nowhere in the paragraph does it mention that Mr. Kernan likes the beef tea his wife makes for him, so you can rule out **C**. **D** seems to be a true statement, since the last sentence of the paragraph states, "she knew that he would walk to the end of Thomas Street and back again to book even a small order." But does this willingness adequately *characterize* their marriage? Not really. The specificity of the act makes it an unlikely candidate to be a characteristic. If **D** had said, "Mr. Kernan's courtesy to his wife" or "Mr. Kernan's consideration for his wife," the choice would have a little more promise as a characteristic (but then its validity would come into question). That leaves us with **B**. Although we eliminated the other answer choices, it doesn't hurt to make sure that **B** fits the bill. The key sentence in the paragraph that suggests **B** is the correct answer is the third one (lines 17–19): "She accepted his frequent intemperance as part of the climate, healed him dutifully whenever he was sick, and always tried to make him eat a breakfast." Words such as *accepted* and *dutifully* don't suggest that Mrs. Kernan takes care of her husband because she thinks it's fun; rather, these words suggest a patient resignation to her life and duties. So you can safely choose **B** as the correct answer.

Less direct inference questions will ask you to draw out character or plot details from the information given in the passage. These inference questions can be more difficult to answer than the one given above. Here's an example of a character inference question:

It can be reasonably inferred from this passage that Mrs. Kernan's attitude toward religion is:

A. fervently pious.
B. practical but faithful.
C. skeptical.
D. nonexistent.

If you read effectively, you'll remember that the last paragraph contains a description of Mrs. Kernan's brand of religious faith. There are several key phrases in this passage that should help you choose the correct answer: "Religion for her was a habit"; "Her beliefs were not extravagant"; "She believed steadily in the Sacred Heart as the most generally useful of all Catholic devotions"; "Her faith was bounded by her kitchen, but, if she was put to it, she could believe also in the banshee and in the Holy Ghost." We can't provide you with a strategy for interpreting this information. You must be able to comprehend the writing in order to get this question right. No matter what your understanding is, you'll probably realize that **D** is wrong because the existence of the phrases indicates that Mrs. Kernan has some kind of attitude toward religion. If you understand what's being said in the phrases above, you can eliminate **A** (because "Her beliefs were not extravagant") and **C** (because "she could also believe in the banshee and in the Holy Ghost"). So the correct answer is **B**, "practical but faithful," which is exactly what those phrases imply.

Now try this plot inference question:

One can reasonably infer from this passage that the goal of the friends' plan, mentioned in line 29, is to:

A. make Mr. Kernan a good, practicing Catholic.
B. cure Mr. Kernan of his alcohol abuse.
C. turn Mr. Kernan into a better husband.
D. go to Thomas Street for Mrs. Kernan while her husband recovers.

The nice thing about inference questions is that they do the inferring for you. If you have no idea what the friends are plotting for Mr. Kernan, don't worry: The ACT writers have given you the right answer already—along with three wrong answers. The best way to approach this question, and any like it, is to read the sentences around the provided section (line 29, in this case). For this question, the information following line 29 will help you decide on the correct answer. The rest of the paragraph is devoted primarily to Mr. Kernan's religious background and his attitude toward Catholicism, and it should give you a good clue that the answer is probably **A**. If you've gotten to this point but feel uncomfortable committing yourself to the answer, consider the other answer choices and how well they work. **B** suggests that the friends want Mr. Kernan to stop drinking; however, there is no mention of his drinking habit after lines 17–18 (in fact, there is only one reference to it in this passage), so it is most likely not the answer. **C** suggests the vague goal of turning Mr. Kernan into a better husband. While this may be a consequence of the desired change in his behavior, it doesn't seem to be the right answer because there is no mention of it in the passage; in fact, Mrs. Kernan seems reasonably content with their relationship. **D**, which offers Thomas Street as an answer, tries to lure you off track by mentioning an unrelated but specific piece of information from the passage. So **A** is the best answer to this question. Remember that, although **B** and **C** may be true desires of Mr. Kernan's friends, they are not the *best* answer to the question. **A** is the best answer because religion is specifically discussed in relation to the plot.

3. Understand Character. Character generalization questions appear only with the Prose Fiction passage. They ask you to reduce a lot of information about a character into a simple, digestible statement. For instance, if you have a character who hates children, kicks dogs, takes candy from babies, and steals his neighbors' mail, you could make the generalization that he is mean-spirited and cruel.

Let's take a look at a character generalization problem dealing with the sample passage:

Mrs. Kernan would most likely agree with which of the following characterizations of her husband:

A. He is foolish and excessive.
B. He is sensible and intelligent.
C. He is irreverent but generally considerate.
D. He is proud of his accomplishments.

As you can see, this question is similar to the inference questions discussed above in that it asks you to draw a conclusion from the information provided by the passage. You should note that the question doesn't ask you how *you* would characterize Mr. Kernan or how the narrator or any other character would, but how *Mrs. Kernan* would characterize him. Because this question is specific in its point of view, it helps you pinpoint the sections you must examine—the ones that give Mrs. Kernan's opinion of her husband. If you do that, you can figure out that nothing suggests **A** is true. **B** is also incorrect according to the passage; the words *sensible* and *intelligent* are actually used to describe Mr. Cunningham. **D** is not correct, although Mr. Kernan appears proud of his injury (line 28). **C** is the correct answer. You can arrive at this answer through process of elimination, but you can also get to it through understanding the passage. The last paragraph reveals that Mrs. Kernan apparently thinks her husband's "tongue would not suffer by being shortened." Earlier in the passage, the narrator also describes Mr. Kernan's verbal lack of respect for Catholicism, so *irreverence* seems to describe him accurately in Mrs. Kernan's eyes. The second part of the answer, his consideration, is implied in the second paragraph, which describes Mr. Kernan's willingness to run errands for his wife.

When answering inference and character generalization questions, you should remember that right answers are not necessarily perfect answers; they must simply be the best answer out of the four provided. For that reason, when answering these questions, you should read through all the answer choices and ask yourself which one best answers the question.

4. Point of View. Point-of-view questions accompanying the Prose Fiction passage will generally ask you to describe the narrator's point of view. Questions that deal with other characters' points of view usually fall under the heading of inference or character generalization. Point-of-view questions are fairly rare on the Prose Fiction passage, but you may encounter one of them on the test.

These questions tend to be pretty obvious when they're asked because they usually look like this:

> The narrator's point of view is that of:
>
> **A.** a detached observer.
> **B.** Mr. Kernan.
> **C.** a biased observer.
> **D.** the Kernans' child.

Again, answering this question is a matter of understanding the material, not of tricks and strategies. You can eliminate **B** and **D** immediately if you recognize that the passage is not written in the first person. Then ask yourself whether the narrator expresses any biases (does he obviously prefer one character to another, for instance?). In this passage, the narrator is fairly bias-free, so the best answer to this question is **A**, a detached observer.

5. Cause-Effect. These questions ask you to identify either the cause or the effect of a situation. These questions are fairly rare on the Prose Fiction passage, but you should still be prepared to answer one. You will generally recognize these questions from cue words in the question, such as *resulted in* and *led to* for effect questions, and *caused by* and *because* for cause questions.

On the Prose Fiction passage, cause-effect questions will generally ask you to identify how one character's actions affected another's. For example:

> According to the passage, the visit paid by Mr. Kernan's friends resulted in:
>
> **A.** his unpleasant behavior toward them.
> **B.** a completely healed tongue.
> **C.** his boasting of weathering two days of sickness.
> **D.** his politeness.

As in the example above, cause-effect questions will not make you draw inferences (only inference questions will). Cause-effect questions are interested in the facts of the passage. Both the cause (the visit paid by Mr. Kernan's friends) and the effect (one of the answer choices) should be clearly stated in the passage. You should not choose an answer choice that requires you to make an inference. After you eliminate **A** and **B**, which are contrary to facts stated in the third paragraph of the passage, you must choose between **C** and **D**. You should eliminate **C**, though, because it is an inference and involves guessing on your part rather than referring specifically to the text. Although the last line of the third paragraph states that Mr. Kernan appears to feel "a veteran's pride," it is never explicitly stated within the passage that this feeling arises from the visit by his friends. Because you are looking for the *best* answer choice—not the *perfect* answer choice—**D** is correct. The passage explicitly states that the visit causes Mr. Kernan to become "more polite" after having been cantankerous.

SOCIAL SCIENCE

In many ways, you can think of the Social Science passage as the standard nonfiction passage on the Reading Test because it can cover all of the question types and because it represents a middle ground between the Humanities and Natural Science passages. In this section, you'll read a sample Social Science passage and learn about all the possible question types associated with Social Science:

1. Specific Detail
2. Inference
3. Main Idea and Argument
4. Cause-Effect
5. Point of View
6. Comparison
7. Vocabulary

These questions types are also found on the Humanities and Natural Science passages, so the descriptions we give of them here also apply to those passages.

Sample Passage

The following passage is adapted from an essay on Malcolm X.

During 1963 the nation became aware of a civil rights leader making a dramatic impact on the black community. Malcolm X, the charismatic, ferociously
eloquent preacher and organizer for the Nation of Islam, had been preaching his
message to (usually poor) black communities since the early 1950s. Malcolm X

5   was a "black Muslim," a member of a small but crucial religious organization that
proved instrumental in giving birth to the modern Black Power Movement. The
Nation of Islam, led by Elijah Muhammed, believed that whites had systemati-
cally and immorally denied blacks their rights and that blacks therefore had no
reason to act peacefully or lovingly towards whites. Instead of supporting the phi-

10 losophy of nonviolence embraced by Martin Luther King, Jr., the Nation of Islam
believed that whites should repay blacks for slavery and allow them to set up
their own nation within America. Until that day arrived, the Nation encouraged
blacks to defend themselves against white supremacy "by any means necessary."

The membership and influence of the Nation of Islam grew tremendously

15 during the late 1950s and early 1960s, in large part due to the dedication and
speaking skills of Malcolm X. Like King, Malcolm X mobilized the people, leading them in rallies, protest marches, and demonstrations. Though he was widely
known among the black underclass and in civil rights circles, it was not until
his famous "Chickens Coming Home to Roost" speech on December 1, 1963, that

20 he truly blasted his way into the consciousness of most Americans. X gave the
speech in reference to the November 22 assassination of President John F. Ken-
nedy, and described the killing as "chickens coming home to roost." The media,
which had negatively portrayed the Nation of Islam in general and Malcolm X
in particular, jumped on the speech immediately, claiming it as an example of

25 Malcolm X's divisive hatred and blatant disrespect for the U.S. government. In
the face of public reaction, officials within the Nation silenced X for 90 days. The
speech not only brought Malcolm X to the forefront of the civil rights struggle
but also highlighted and helped solidify a strand of civil rights activism that
found inadequate the nonviolent policies the movement had so far used.

30 Malcolm X is a highly controversial figure in black history. Many see him
as a spouter of hatred and divisiveness. Certainly it is true that a fair portion
of X's rhetoric—his references to "white devils" and "Uncle Tomming Negro
leaders"—was angry and inflammatory, and did little to promote the cause of
integration. However, X represented an element of black consciousness that

35 white people refused to face: the incredible rage that most black people felt
after suffering so many years of oppression.

For all of his fame, it is interesting to note that his mobilization and participation in the civil rights movement was actually fairly slim. He respected some
civil rights leaders (King, for example), though for much of his life he believed

40 that the idea of integration was merely playing into the hands of the white
man. For the most part, Malcolm X's role in the civil rights movement was
merely to preach, to pass on the crucial message of black rage to white America,

and to become a role model for those who began the Black Power Movement a
few years later. He is vitally important not because of what he actually did, but
45   because of what he said and how he said it.

Malcolm X's own biography reveals that he was more nuanced and interesting than the simple role of black rage that he was sometimes assigned by both
whites who held him up as an example of rage gone wild, and blacks who saw
him as a warrior willing to express that which most blacks could not. After
50   years of service, X eventually broke with the Nation of Islam. Then, after a
life-changing visit to Mecca in 1964, he broke with his own previous thought
and began preaching a message of cross-cultural unity, and founded the Organization for Afro-American Unity. With his fire-and-brimstone oratory, broad
base of black community support, and knack for attracting media attention,
55   X's new path might have forged major interracial inroads. But before he could
follow this new path of more general inclusion, X was assassinated on February 21, 1965, shot as he was giving a speech in New York. The perpetrators
have never been found, though many presume the Nation of Islam to have been
responsible. X's autobiography, *The Autobiography of Malcolm X*, is an abiding
60   document of both his own personal journey and of his time.

The Questions

Below, we'll give you a rundown of the questions you'll likely encounter on the Social Science passage. All of the questions below pertain to the above passage on Malcolm X.

1. Specific Detail. These questions on the nonfiction passages are as straightforward as
they are on the fiction passage. They ask you to identify a specific detail or piece of evidence from the passage. For example:

> According to the passage, some critics of Malcolm X censured him for being:
>
> **A.**   an "Uncle Tomming Negro leader."
> **B.**   an example of rage gone wild.
> **C.**   a warrior for African Americans.
> **D.**   a civil rights leader.

If you read the section dealing with specific detail for Prose Fiction, you probably have a
pretty good idea of how to answer this question. Getting the right answer is really a matter of
careful reading, but you can use the question to help you eliminate answers that are clearly
wrong. For instance, because the question asks you for criticisms of Malcolm X, it is probably
a safe bet to eliminate **C** and **D**, which give positive interpretations of his career. Choosing
the right answer from **A** and **B** is really a matter of understanding the material. If you read
the passage carefully, you probably remember that Malcolm X used **A** as a criticism for black
leaders whom he considered panderers to white supremacists. In the last paragraph of the
passage, the writer notes that some white people "held him up as an example of rage gone
wild"—a pretty clear criticism of Malcolm X; thus **B** is the correct answer to the question.

2. Inference. You may remember that inference questions ask for implied information. The answers to inference questions won't be stated explicitly in the nonfiction passages; instead, you must ferret out the answer from the evidence provided by the passage. For example:

> One can reasonably infer from the passage that the Nation of Islam is widely thought responsible for Malcolm X's assassination because:
>
> **A.** X broke with the group politically and philosophically.
> **B.** X gave a controversial speech after Kennedy's assassination.
> **C.** X visited Mecca in 1964.
> **D.** X began to write an autobiography.

You should look to the last paragraph, where Malcolm X's assassination is described. Ask yourself what this paragraph focuses on. The paragraph mentions that Malcolm X broke with the Nation of Islam, **A**, and that he visited Mecca, **C**. You can safely eliminate **B** because his controversial "Chickens Coming Home to Roost" speech occurred well before his break with the Nation of Islam; moreover, the author explicitly states the Nation of Islam's response to the speech in line 26. Now you must choose between the remaining three answer choices: **A**, **C**, and **D**. If you can't figure out the correct answer, consider which answer choices make sense and which one best answers the question. **C**, which points to Malcolm X's trip to Mecca, would probably not make sense as an answer choice, as this pilgrimage is a central element of the Islamic faith. Like **C**, **D** also does not seem to offer the proper detail. The passage offers no connection at all between Malcolm X's autobiography and his assassination. **A**, meanwhile, fits the bill: Malcolm X not only split from the Nation of Islam, but also began to preach a message opposed to the group's—a message of unity and nonviolence rather than of separate nations and cultures. **A** is the correct answer to the question because it best describes why the Nation of Islam would assassinate Malcolm X.

3. Main Idea and Argument. On the nonfiction passages, you'll encounter quite a few main idea questions. Some of the questions will deal with the passage as a whole, while others will deal with sections of the passage. In both cases, these questions will ask you to identify the main ideas or arguments presented within the passage.

Here's an example of a main idea question:

> The main point made in the third paragraph (lines 30–36) is that:
>
> **A.** the "Chickens Coming Home to Roost" speech propelled Malcolm X to the forefront of the civil rights debate.
> **B.** Malcolm X's rhetoric promoted hatred and divisiveness.
> **C.** Malcolm X was an important role model for the future leaders of the Black Power Movement.
> **D.** although his message was controversial, Malcolm X successfully gave a voice to black people who had been oppressed for generations.

This question refers you to a specific paragraph and asks you for that paragraph's main point. For questions that direct you to a specific section, you should glance back at that section to ensure that you don't confuse it with another. If you don't glance back, you may mistake the paragraph for the one before or the one after and choose the wrong answer, such as **A** (which deals with the second paragraph) or **C** (which deals with the fourth). Also make sure that you understand the point of the whole paragraph. If you read just the first couple sentences, you may think the correct answer to this question is **B**. But the rest of the paragraph goes on to talk about Malcolm X's impact despite that controversial side of him, and ultimately the point of the paragraph is **D**. **D** is the best answer because it incorporates both aspects of the paragraph: The first part of it, which discusses his controversial method, and the second part, which talks about why he was an important civil rights figure.

Many main point questions will cover the entire passage. These questions will generally be posed in one of the following three ways:

- The main idea of the passage is that:
- One of the main ideas of the passage is that:
- Which of the following best states the main point of the passage?

Here's where having read the passage carefully (but quickly) will work to your advantage. You should be able to answer general questions like these without referring back to the passage *if* you did a good job of reading the first time. Reading with an eye to answering specific questions may be an effective strategy for most questions, but you will inevitably encounter general questions like these on the Reading Test. If you choose the strategy of reading for answers, you will have to reread the passage in order to answer these questions. Ultimately, you'll waste more time than you'll save.

Another kind of main idea question asks you to identify the main *purpose* of the passage—in other words, to determine why the author wrote it. For example:

The author's purpose in writing this passage seems to be:

A. to portray Malcolm X as the man responsible for the civil rights movement.

B. to reveal an overlooked event in Malcolm X's life.

C. to give a relatively balanced account of the positive and negative sides of Malcolm X's career.

D. to expose the Nation of Islam's role in the assassination of Malcolm X.

You should be able to answer this question without referring back to the passage because it deals with the general theme and argument of the entire passage. When you come to a question like this, ask yourself what the author has accomplished with the passage. If you form your answer before looking at the answer choices, you're less likely to be swayed by a wrong but convincing answer choice. The author of this passage describes both negative and positive aspects of Malcolm X's career. For example, the author mentions X's early rage and unwillingness to integrate, but balances that with X's crucial representation of African Americans. **C** seems the best answer to the question, but you can always double-check by eliminating the other answer choices. **A** is wrong because the author states in lines 37–38 that X's "participation in the civil rights movement was actually fairly slim." **B** is also wrong; the author never mentions an overlooked event in X's life. **D** is wrong even though the author suggests the Nation of Islam's culpability in X's death; this suggestion is not the focus of the entire passage, and it is only briefly mentioned in the last paragraph. So you can safely select **C** as the best answer.

4. Cause-Effect. As with their Prose Fiction counterparts, cause-effect questions on the nonfiction passages will ask you to identify either the cause or the effect of a particular situation. You are more likely to see these questions on Social Science and Natural Science passages than on Humanities passages because the "science" passages often describe sequences of events.

Cue words in the question will let you know whether you must identify the cause or the effect of the relationship. Words such as *because* warn you that the question seeks the cause of an event, while words such as *resulted in*, *led to*, and *caused* let you know you'll need to identify the effect of a situation.

Here's an example of a nonfiction cause-effect question:

According to the passage, Malcolm X came to the forefront of the American civil rights struggle because:

A. of his "Chickens Coming Home to Roost" speech, which generated a media frenzy.
B. he was silenced by the Nation of Islam for 90 days.
C. he rejected King's nonviolent message.
D. he founded the Organization for Afro-American Unity.

As with almost all questions on the ACT Reading Test, answering this question correctly requires a careful reading of the passage. From the cue word *because*, you know that the question asks you for the *cause* half of the relationship. If you're unable to answer this question without referring back to the passage, you should at least have an idea of where to look. The second paragraph deals with Malcolm X's increasing fame. There are a couple of sentences within this paragraph that clearly indicate **A** as the correct answer to this question: "[I]t was not until his famous 'Chickens Coming Home to Roost' speech on December 1, 1963, that he truly blasted his way into the consciousness of most Americans," and "[t]he speech . . . brought Malcolm X to the forefront of the civil rights struggle."

5. Point of View. Point-of-view questions on the nonfiction passages differ somewhat from those on the Prose Fiction passage. As opposed to the fiction point-of-view questions, which ask you to identify the point of view of the narrator (a fictional invention), the nonfiction point-of-view questions ask you to identify how the writer (a real person) views his or her subject. As you read a passage, consider whether the writer's argument seems to support or attack the passage's subject, and pay attention to the language the writer uses. The writer's tone (is it angry? is it sympathetic?) will be a good indication of his or her feelings about the subject.

Here's an example of a point-of-view question:

The relatively objective tone of this particular Social Science passage makes this point-of-view question difficult—more difficult, at least, than answering a point-of-view question for a passage written by an obviously biased author. Still, you should be able to pinpoint the author's tone even here, especially with assistance from the answer choices. In this passage, the author pretty clearly does not feel negatively about Malcolm X, although she may disagree with some of his tactics, so you can eliminate **A** and **C**, which indicate negative sentiments. Now you are left with a positive feeling, **D**, and a mixed one, **B**. Which one more accurately describes the author's feelings for Malcolm X? While the author is fairly objective in her writing, her attitude cannot be described as mixed or ambivalent. Although she does mix praise for Malcolm X with some condemnation, her overall tone is one of respect, so the best answer is **D**.

As you can see in the example above, the answer choices for a point-of-view question can seem similar to one another, but there are always crucial differences. For example, words like *anger* and *disapproval* both express negative sentiments. If "anger" and "disapproval" were the two most promising answer choices for a question, you would have to know more than whether the writer approves or disapproves of the subject. You would have to identify the degree of passion in the writer's negativity. If the writer cares deeply about the subject, then "anger" may be the correct answer. If the writer is intellectually opposed to the subject, then "disapproval" may be correct.

6. Comparison. As the name implies, comparison questions ask you to make comparisons, usually between different viewpoints or data. Comparisons can be tricky questions to handle because you need to assimilate information on both sides of the comparison and then see how the sides compare. You'll see these types of questions more frequently on the Social Science and Natural Science passages than on the Humanities passage because the science passages usually contain a lot of factual information. You probably won't encounter more than a couple of these questions on the entire test.

The question will contain cue words or phrases that indicate it's a comparison question. *Compares* and *analogy* are two words that frequently appear in comparison questions.

Here's an example of a comparison question:

Two key points in the passage can help you answer this question: lines 9–12 and lines 27–29. If you refer to those sections, you'll be able to select **A** as the best answer to the question. You can also go through the list and eliminate incorrect answers. **B** is incorrect because the author explicitly states that X's role in the civil rights movement was limited. **C** is incorrect because the author never connects King to the Nation of Islam (to which King did not belong). **D** doesn't work because the author never discusses King's influence on future leaders.

7. **Vocabulary.** Vocabulary questions ask you to decipher the meaning of a word given its context. Usually, these words will have multiple meanings, so you must decide the function of the word in the specific context.

You will immediately recognize these questions from their formulaic phrasing. They provide you with a line number along with an italicized word or short phrase in quotation marks, and then they ask you to provide the meaning of the word in context. For example:

As it is used in line 33, the word *inflammatory* most nearly means:

A. revolutionary.
B. flammable.
C. violent.
D. agitating.

To answer this particular vocabulary question (a rather difficult one), you must also know what the answer choices mean. This is where having a good vocabulary will help you on the ACT. In line 33, the author discusses how X's language was "angry and inflammatory." In the surrounding lines, you get a sense that X's speech was designed to provoke anger and disorder. Thus the correct answer to this question is **D** because "agitating" provides that sense of provocation. If you cannot figure out the answer directly, you should try to eliminate the other choices. **A**, "revolutionary," is related to "inflammatory," but it is incorrect. You can think of it as a subset of inflammatory: Revolutionary speech tends to be inflammatory, but inflammatory speech is not always revolutionary. "Revolutionary" contains a political connotation that "inflammatory" and "agitating" lack, so it is not as good an answer as **D**. **B**, "flammable," applies to physical objects and means that something is capable of being lit on fire. While you may be tempted to choose this answer because both the tested word and the answer choice contain the root "flam," there is a crucial difference between their definitions. **C**, "violent," is incorrect because it lacks the element of provocation present in "inflammatory."

HUMANITIES

The Humanities passage will generally deal with a topic of cultural interest. You can think of it as a "softer" version of the Social Science passage, which tends to have more of an analytical and political angle. Still, the general approach to answering Social Science questions should apply to Humanities questions.

Sample Passage

The following passage is adapted from the chapter "How I Came to Play Rip Van Winkle" in The Autobiography of Joseph Jefferson *(©1890, 1891 by the Century Company, New York).*

The hope of entering the race for dramatic fame as an individual and single attraction never came into my head until, in 1858, I acted Asa Trenchard in *Our American Cousin*; but as the curtain descended the first night on that remarkably successful play, visions of large type, foreign countries, and increased
5 remuneration floated before me, and I resolved to be a star if I could. A resolution to this effect is easily made; its accomplishment is quite another matter.

Art has always been my sweetheart, and I have loved her for herself alone. I had fancied that our affection was mutual, so that when I failed as a star, which I certainly did, I thought she had jilted me. Not so. I wronged her. She only
10 reminded me that I had taken too great a liberty, and that if I expected to win her I must press my suit with more patience. Checked, but undaunted in the resolve, my mind dwelt upon my vision, and I still indulged in day-dreams of the future.

During these delightful reveries it came up before me that in acting Asa-
15 Trenchard I had, for the first time in my life on the stage, spoken a pathetic speech; and though I did not look at the audience during the time I was acting—for that is dreadful—I felt that they both laughed and cried. I had before this often made my audience smile, but never until now had I moved them to tears. This novel accomplishment was delightful to me, and in casting about
20 for a new character my mind was ever dwelling on reproducing an effect where humor would be so closely allied to pathos that smiles and tears should mingle with each other. Where could I get one? There had been many written, and as I looked back into the dramatic history of the past a long line of lovely ghosts loomed up before me, passing as in a procession: Job Thornberry, Bob Tyke,
25 Frank Ostland, Zekiel Homespun, and a host of departed heroes "with martial stalk went by my watch." Charming fellows all, but not for me, I felt I could not do them justice. Besides, they were too human. I was looking for a myth—something intangible and impossible. But he would not come. Time went on, and still with no result.

30 During the summer of 1859 I arranged to board with my family at a queer old Dutch farmhouse in Paradise Valley, at the foot of Pocono Mountain, in Pennsylvania. A ridge of hills covered with tall hemlocks surrounds the vale, and numerous trout-streams wind through the meadows and tumble over the rocks. Stray farms are scattered through the valley, and the few old Dutchmen
35 and their families who till the soil were born upon it; there and only there they have ever lived. The valley harmonized with me and our resources. The scene was wild, the air was fresh, and the board was cheap. What could the light heart and purse of a poor actor ask for more than this?

40   On one of those long rainy days that always render the country so dull I had
climbed to the loft of the barn, and lying upon the hay was reading that delightful book *The Life and Letters of Washington Irving.* I had gotten well into the
volume, and was much interested in it, when to my surprise I came upon a passage which said that he had seen me at Laura Keene's theater as Goldfinch in
Holcroft's comedy of *The Road to Ruin,* and that I reminded him of my father "in
45   look, gesture, size, and make." Till then I was not aware that he had ever seen
me. I was comparatively obscure, and to find myself remembered and written
of by such a man gave me a thrill of pleasure I can never forget. I put down the
book, and lay there thinking how proud I was, and ought to be, at the revelation
of this compliment. What an incentive to a youngster like me to go on.

50   And so I thought to myself, "Washington Irving, the author of *The Sketch-
Book,* in which is the quaint story of Rip Van Winkle." Rip Van Winkle! There
was to me magic in the sound of the name as I repeated it. Why, was not this
the very character I wanted? An American story by an American author was
surely just the theme suited to an American actor.

The Questions

As we stated above, your approach to questions on the Humanities passage should be
essentially the same as your approach to Social Science questions. For that reason, in
this section we'll skip most of the commentary on the question types and go straight to
the examples.

    To start with, we'll give you a rundown of the types of questions that appear most
frequently on the Humanities passage, in decreasing order:

---

1.   Specific Detail
2.   Inference
3.   Vocabulary
4.   Main Idea
5.   Comparison

---

1.   Specific Detail. Specific detail questions on the Humanities passage are exactly the
same as on the rest of the test. Because you should already have a good grasp of how to
answer these questions, we'll just give you some examples of questions that could accompany the passage above.

According to the passage, Washington Irving saw the author perform:

A. Asa Trenchard in *Our American Cousin*.
B. Goldfinch in *The Road to Ruin*.
C. Rip Van Winkle in *The Sketch-Book*.
D. Job Thornberry in *John Bull, or the Englishman's Fireside*.

The author considers the following to be attractions of Paradise Valley EXCEPT:

F. the fresh air.
G. the untamed scenery.
H. the long rainy days.
J. the inexpensive board.

As you already know, the best way to answer these questions is to read the passage carefully enough the first time around that you either know the answer or can quickly find the answer in the passage. If you made marginal notes and underlines during your preliminary reading, you will be able to refer easily to the relevant sections of the passage for these questions.

The correct answers to these questions are **B** and **H**, respectively.

2. Inference. By now, you should have a good idea of how to answer inference questions. An inference question on this sample Humanities passage could look like this:

It can be reasonably inferred from the passage that the character of Rip Van Winkle is:

A. charming.
B. very human.
C. like Washington Irving's father.
D. mythical.

This inference question is slightly complicated because Rip Van Winkle is mentioned in the last paragraph of the passage, but you need to refer to the third paragraph in order to answer the question. In the third paragraph, the author describes the types of characters he is unable to play and the type of character that he would like to play. The inference you must make to answer this question is that Rip Van Winkle represents an ideal character for the author and therefore must fit the description in paragraph 3: "a myth." The correct answer to this question is **D**.

3. **Vocabulary.** The Humanities passage often contains a number of vocabulary questions, so be on the lookout. Vocabulary questions on the passage above could look like this:

As it is used in line 15, the word *pathetic* most nearly means:

A. moving.
B. pitiful.
C. contemptible.
D. weak.

As it is used in line 30, the word *board* most nearly means:

F. a rectangular piece of wood.
G. a group of people with managerial powers.
H. to walk onto a ship or aircraft.
J. to lodge and eat at an inn or residence.

These vocabulary questions deal with words that have multiple meanings. They ask you to decide which meaning best suits the context. When you see vocabulary questions like these, go to the indicated line number without even looking at the answers. Read the relevant sentence, ignoring the tested word and coming up with a different word to fill its place. This new word will be a synonym for the tested word. If you can't come up with a word by looking at the individual sentence, read the sentences around it as well. Once you have your synonym, go back to the question and compare your synonym to the answers. When you've found a match, you have your answer. If you're at a loss for words when using this strategy, you can substitute the answer choices (as long as you know what they mean) into the sentence to see whether they make sense.

If you employ the strategy above, you should see that **A** and **J**, respectively, make the most sense in the sentences and thus are correct.

4. **Main Idea.** Main idea questions tend to accompany Humanities passages that are more analytical or journalistic in tone than the sample passage above. With anecdotal passages like this, it's unlikely that you'll be asked to identify the main point of the passage or of a paragraph—the anecdote itself is usually the point. If you do face a main idea question, use the same strategy that we covered under the question strategy section for the Social Science passage.

5. **Comparison.** Though some Humanities passages may be accompanied by more than one comparison question, this particular passage is not very fact-heavy, so it likely would not have any comparison questions. If a comparison question did appear with this sample passage, it might look like this:

In the second paragraph of the passage, the author compares art to:

A. a profession.
B. a sweetheart.
C. a star.
D. a daydream.

The comparison in this paragraph is actually a metaphor, in which the author doesn't explicitly say that art is *like* something, but says that it *is* something that it clearly isn't. You don't need to know this literary term or any other to answer this question. The first sentence of the paragraph ("Art has always been my sweetheart") should make the answer to this comparison question pretty clear. The correct answer is **B**.

NATURAL SCIENCE

On the continuum of Reading Test passages, the Prose Fiction passage would be on one extreme, the Social Science and Humanities passages in the middle, and the Natural Science passage at the other extreme end. The Natural Science passage is heavy on scientific facts, argument, cause-effect logic, and details.

Sample Passage

The following passage is adapted from an essay on Lamarckian evolutionary theory.

For many centuries, scientists and scholars did not question the origin of life on Earth. They accepted the authority of the Book of Genesis, which describes God as the creator of all life. This belief, known as creationism, was supported by observations made by scientists about the everyday world. For instance, organisms seemed
5　well adapted to their environments and ways of life, as if created specifically to fill their roles; moreover, most organisms did not seem to change in any observable manner over time. About two centuries ago, scientists began accumulating evidence that cast doubt on the theory of creationism. As scientists began to explore remote parts of the natural world, they discovered seemingly bizarre forms of life.
10　They also discovered the fossils of animals that no longer existed. These discoveries led scientists to develop new theories about the creation of species.

Count George-Louis Leclerc de Buffon was an early pioneer of these new theories, proposing that the species he and his contemporaries saw had changed over time from their original forms. Jean Baptiste Lamarck was
15　another early pioneer. Lamarck proposed ideas involving the mechanisms of use and disuse and inheritance of acquired traits to explain how species might change over time. These theories, though in many ways incorrect and incomplete, paved the way for Charles Darwin, the father of the theory of evolution.

Although he built on the work of his mentor Leclerc, Lamarck often receives
20　credit for taking the first step toward modern evolutionary theory because he proposed a mechanism explaining how the gradual change of species could occur. Lamarck elaborated on the concept of "change over time," saying that life originated in simple forms and became more complex. In his 1809 publication of *Philosophie Zoologique*, he describes the two part mechanism by which change
25　was gradually introduced into species and passed down through generations. His theory is referred to as the theory of transformation or, simply, Lamarckism.

The classic example used to explain the concept of use and disuse is the elongated neck of the giraffe. According to Lamarck's theory, a giraffe could,

over a lifetime of straining to reach food on high branches, develop an elongated
30   neck. Although he referred to "a natural tendency toward perfection," Lamarck
could never offer an explanation of how this development could occur, thus
injuring his theory. Lamarck also used the toes of water birds as an example in
support of his theory. He hypothesized that water birds developed elongated,
webbed toes after years of straining their toes to swim through water.

35   These two examples attempted to demonstrate how use could change an
animal's trait. Lamarck also believed that disuse could cause a trait to become
reduced in an animal. The wings of penguins, he believed, are smaller than
those of other birds because penguins do not fly.

        The second part of Lamarck's theory involved the inheritance of acquired
40   traits. Lamarck believed that traits changed or acquired over an individual
animal's lifetime could be passed down to its offspring. Giraffes that had acquired
long necks would have offspring with long necks rather than the short necks their
parents were born with. This type of inheritance, sometimes called Lamarckian
inheritance, has since been disproved by the discovery of hereditary genetics.

45   An extension of Lamarck's ideas of inheritance that has stood the test of time,
however, is the idea that evolutionary change takes place gradually and constantly.
Lamarck studied ancient seashells and noticed that the older they were, the
simpler they appeared. From this, he concluded that species started out simple and
consistently moved toward complexity or, as he said, "closer to perfection."

The Questions

Since Natural Science passages contain so many facts, many of the questions on this passage will test whether you know these facts. These questions will come in many guises besides the standard specific detail format. For example, some questions will ask you to build on information in the passage by making you identify cause-effect relationships or comparisons. Here's a breakdown of the question types commonly asked on the Natural Science passage, in order of decreasing frequency:

1. Specific Detail
2. Inference
3. Cause-Effect
4. Comparison
5. Main Idea
6. Vocabulary
7. Point of View

Despite the scientific jargon that permeates this passage, in answering the questions you should treat the passage as you would the two other nonfiction passages. In this section, we'll give you examples of questions that could be asked on the sample passage above, so you can start getting familiar with the Natural Science section.

1. Specific Detail. Specific detail, the most common question type on the ACT Reading Test, is also a biggie on the Natural Science passage. For the previous passage, you could see questions like these:

The theory that describes God as the creator of all life is called:

A. creationism.
B. Lamarckism.
C. the theory of transformation.
D. the Book of Genesis.

According to the passage, the giraffe is a classic example of Lamarck's theory because of its:

F. webbed toes.
G. elongated neck.
H. small wings.
J. coloration.

According to the passage, Leclerc proposed the theory:

A. of the mechanisms of use and disuse.
B. of inherited traits.
C. that giraffes developed elongated necks over time.
D. that species changed over time from their original forms.

As we've mentioned, the best method for answering these questions correctly is simply to refer back to the passage. If you've made marginal notes and underlines, you'll have an easier time referring back to the passage and getting the right answer.

The correct answer to the first question, **A**, is conveniently located in the first three lines of the passage. For the second question, look to paragraph 5, where the author discusses the example of the giraffe. The first sentence of paragraph 5 reveals **G** to be correct. When answering the third question, you should refer to the discussion of Leclerc. In the first mention of him (in paragraph 3), you'll discover that **D** is the correct answer to the question.

2. Inference. Inference questions on the Natural Science passage are the same as they are elsewhere on the test. For example:

It is reasonable to infer from this passage that Lamarck's most lasting work on a theory of evolution is his hypothesis that:

A. species inherit traits acquired by their parents.
B. the forms of animals change over time.
C. giraffes develop long necks from straining to reach high tree branches.
D. species evolve gradually and constantly over time into more complex forms.

The answer to this question is in the first sentence of the last paragraph: "An extension of Lamarck's ideas of inheritance that has stood the test of time, however, is the idea that evolutionary change takes place gradually and constantly." The phrase "stood the test of time" indicates that this particular aspect of Lamarck's work is still relevant today. Thus the correct answer to this question is **D**.

3. **Cause-Effect.** Cause-effect questions appear pretty frequently on Natural Science passages because of the nature of their topics. Most Natural Science passages, including the sample one above, discuss cause-effect relationships that appear in nature. For example:

According to the passage, Lamarck proposed that the changing form of animals was a result of:

A. giraffes stretching their necks to reach high branches.
B. a natural tendency toward perfection and the inheritance of acquired traits.
C. organisms being created to fill specific roles.
D. hereditary genetics.

This particular cause-effect question also tests your understanding of one of the main points of the passage, as the main point happens to be a cause-effect relationship. If you understood the passage, you should be able to identify the correct answer as **B**. **A** deals specifically with Lamarck's example of giraffes, while the question calls for a general explanation for all animals. **C** is the belief of creationism, and **D** would not be discovered until after Lamarck's time.

4. **Comparison.** You will probably see one comparison question with the Natural Science passage. As we stated before, comparison questions usually accompany passages that contain a lot of factual information, and the Natural Science passage fits the bill.

According to the passage, the elongated neck of the giraffe is analogous to:

A. the small wings of the penguin.
B. the large wings of most birds.
C. the webbed toes of water birds.
D. the inheritance of elongated necks.

To answer this question, ask yourself what the giraffe's elongated neck can be compared to. In paragraph 5, the author names both the giraffe's neck and the water bird's toes as examples of the concept of use, so the best answer is **C**. To make sure, you can eliminate the other answers. **A** deals with the concept of disuse, so it is not analogous to the giraffe's neck. **B** is never discussed in the passage. **D** is not an analogous situation; it is a separate aspect of Lamarck's theory.

5. Main Idea. Main idea questions are always pretty straightforward. The tricky part is making sure that you read carefully enough to understand the main point of the passage or of a paragraph within it. Try this example:

The main point of the passage is to:

A. describe Lamarck's ideas on evolution and their relevance to modern theories of evolution.

B. explain how animals change through the mechanisms of use and disuse and through the inheritance of acquired traits.

C. discuss alternative theories to creationism.

D. show how Lamarck built upon the work of Leclerc.

If you read the passage carefully, you should be able to eliminate **C** and **D**, as they are clearly not the main focus of the passage. You may get stuck trying to decide between **A** and **B**, but you should remember that the question asks for *the passage's* main point, not for *Lamarck's* main point. Remembering that, you should be able to identify the correct answer, **A**.

6. Vocabulary. You will not see many vocabulary questions accompanying the Natural Science passage. The vocabulary questions that do appear on this passage may ask you to identify an unfamiliar scientific word from its context. You can employ the strategies described for vocabulary questions on the Humanities and Social Science passages to answer vocabulary questions here.

7. Point of View. Point-of-view questions are extremely rare on the Natural Science passage. If you see one, it will most likely ask you to identify the point of view of the passage's author. For example:

The main point of the passage is to:

A. describe Lamarck's ideas on evolution and their relevance to modern theories of evolution.

B. explain how animals change through the mechanisms of use and disuse and through the inheritance of acquired traits.

C. discuss alternative theories to creationism.

D. show how Lamarck built upon the work of Leclerc.

With which of the following statements would the author most likely agree?

A. Most scientists today believe in creationism.

B. Leclerc, not Lamarck, should be credited with taking the first step toward modern evolutionary theory.

C. Lamarck's theory that life evolves from simple to complex forms is still important today.

D. Today, giraffes have long necks because early giraffes did a lot of stretching.

The author of this sample passage does not seem to hold strong views on Lamarck, but it is still possible to eliminate wrong answers here and correctly answer the question. **A** and **B** are incorrect because there is little focus on them in the passage: Both creationism and Leclerc are mentioned, but only briefly. **C** looks like the right choice because the author states in the last paragraph that this aspect of Lamarck's theory "has stood the test of time." You can make sure that **C** is correct by eliminating **D**, which Lamarck, not the author, believes.

ACT READING PRACTICE SETS ANSWER SHEET

Set 1
1 Ⓐ Ⓑ Ⓒ Ⓓ
2 Ⓕ Ⓖ Ⓗ Ⓙ
3 Ⓐ Ⓑ Ⓒ Ⓓ
4 Ⓕ Ⓖ Ⓗ Ⓙ
5 Ⓐ Ⓑ Ⓒ Ⓓ
6 Ⓕ Ⓖ Ⓗ Ⓙ
7 Ⓐ Ⓑ Ⓒ Ⓓ
8 Ⓕ Ⓖ Ⓗ Ⓙ
9 Ⓐ Ⓑ Ⓒ Ⓓ
10 Ⓕ Ⓖ Ⓗ Ⓙ

Set 2
1 Ⓐ Ⓑ Ⓒ Ⓓ
2 Ⓕ Ⓖ Ⓗ Ⓙ
3 Ⓐ Ⓑ Ⓒ Ⓓ
4 Ⓕ Ⓖ Ⓗ Ⓙ
5 Ⓐ Ⓑ Ⓒ Ⓓ
6 Ⓕ Ⓖ Ⓗ Ⓙ
7 Ⓐ Ⓑ Ⓒ Ⓓ
8 Ⓕ Ⓖ Ⓗ Ⓙ
9 Ⓐ Ⓑ Ⓒ Ⓓ
10 Ⓕ Ⓖ Ⓗ Ⓙ

Set 3
1 Ⓐ Ⓑ Ⓒ Ⓓ
2 Ⓕ Ⓖ Ⓗ Ⓙ
3 Ⓐ Ⓑ Ⓒ Ⓓ
4 Ⓕ Ⓖ Ⓗ Ⓙ
5 Ⓐ Ⓑ Ⓒ Ⓓ
6 Ⓕ Ⓖ Ⓗ Ⓙ
7 Ⓐ Ⓑ Ⓒ Ⓓ
8 Ⓕ Ⓖ Ⓗ Ⓙ
9 Ⓐ Ⓑ Ⓒ Ⓓ
10 Ⓕ Ⓖ Ⓗ Ⓙ

Set 4
1 Ⓐ Ⓑ Ⓒ Ⓓ
2 Ⓕ Ⓖ Ⓗ Ⓙ
3 Ⓐ Ⓑ Ⓒ Ⓓ
4 Ⓕ Ⓖ Ⓗ Ⓙ
5 Ⓐ Ⓑ Ⓒ Ⓓ
6 Ⓕ Ⓖ Ⓗ Ⓙ
7 Ⓐ Ⓑ Ⓒ Ⓓ
8 Ⓕ Ⓖ Ⓗ Ⓙ
9 Ⓐ Ⓑ Ⓒ Ⓓ
10 Ⓕ Ⓖ Ⓗ Ⓙ

Set 5
1 Ⓐ Ⓑ Ⓒ Ⓓ
2 Ⓕ Ⓖ Ⓗ Ⓙ
3 Ⓐ Ⓑ Ⓒ Ⓓ
4 Ⓕ Ⓖ Ⓗ Ⓙ
5 Ⓐ Ⓑ Ⓒ Ⓓ
6 Ⓕ Ⓖ Ⓗ Ⓙ
7 Ⓐ Ⓑ Ⓒ Ⓓ
8 Ⓕ Ⓖ Ⓗ Ⓙ
9 Ⓐ Ⓑ Ⓒ Ⓓ
10 Ⓕ Ⓖ Ⓗ Ⓙ

Set 6
1 Ⓐ Ⓑ Ⓒ Ⓓ
2 Ⓕ Ⓖ Ⓗ Ⓙ
3 Ⓐ Ⓑ Ⓒ Ⓓ
4 Ⓕ Ⓖ Ⓗ Ⓙ
5 Ⓐ Ⓑ Ⓒ Ⓓ
6 Ⓕ Ⓖ Ⓗ Ⓙ
7 Ⓐ Ⓑ Ⓒ Ⓓ
8 Ⓕ Ⓖ Ⓗ Ⓙ
9 Ⓐ Ⓑ Ⓒ Ⓓ
10 Ⓕ Ⓖ Ⓗ Ⓙ

Set 7
1 Ⓐ Ⓑ Ⓒ Ⓓ
2 Ⓕ Ⓖ Ⓗ Ⓙ
3 Ⓐ Ⓑ Ⓒ Ⓓ
4 Ⓕ Ⓖ Ⓗ Ⓙ
5 Ⓐ Ⓑ Ⓒ Ⓓ
6 Ⓕ Ⓖ Ⓗ Ⓙ
7 Ⓐ Ⓑ Ⓒ Ⓓ
8 Ⓕ Ⓖ Ⓗ Ⓙ
9 Ⓐ Ⓑ Ⓒ Ⓓ
10 Ⓕ Ⓖ Ⓗ Ⓙ

Set 8
1 Ⓐ Ⓑ Ⓒ Ⓓ
2 Ⓕ Ⓖ Ⓗ Ⓙ
3 Ⓐ Ⓑ Ⓒ Ⓓ
4 Ⓕ Ⓖ Ⓗ Ⓙ
5 Ⓐ Ⓑ Ⓒ Ⓓ
6 Ⓕ Ⓖ Ⓗ Ⓙ
7 Ⓐ Ⓑ Ⓒ Ⓓ
8 Ⓕ Ⓖ Ⓗ Ⓙ
9 Ⓐ Ⓑ Ⓒ Ⓓ
10 Ⓕ Ⓖ Ⓗ Ⓙ

PRACTICE FOR THE ACT READING TEST

READING TEST

35 Minutes—40 Questions

DIRECTIONS: On this test, you will have 35 minutes to read four passages and answer 40 questions (ten questions on each passage). Each set of ten questions appears directly after the relevant passage. You should select the answer choice that best answers the question. There is no time limit for work on the individual passages, so you can move freely between the passages and refer to each as often as you'd like.

PRACTICE SET 1: PROSE FICTION

The following passage is adapted from the short story "A Wagner Matinée" by Willa Cather.

On the morning after her arrival, Aunt Georgiana was still exhausted from her lengthy train trip. She seemed not to realize that she was in the city where she had spent her youth, the place she had longed for hungrily half a lifetime ago.

I had planned a little pleasure for her that afternoon, to repay her for some
5 of the glorious moments she had given me when we used to milk together in the straw-thatched cowshed, and she would tell me of the splendid performances she had seen in Paris in her youth. At two o'clock the Symphony Orchestra was to give a Wagner program, and I intended to take my aunt; though as I talked with her, I grew doubtful about her enjoyment of it. Indeed, for her sake, I
10 hoped that her taste for such things was quite dead, and that the long struggle was mercifully ended at last. I suggested our visiting the Conservatory and the Common before lunch, but she seemed altogether too timid to venture out. She questioned me absently about various changes in the city, but she was chiefly concerned that she had forgotten to leave instructions about feeding half-
15 skimmed milk to a certain weakling calf, "old Maggie's calf, you know, Clark," she explained, evidently having forgotten how long I had been away.

From the time we entered the concert hall, however, she was slightly less passive, and for the first time seemed to recognize her surroundings. I had felt some apprehension that she might become aware of her absurd attire, or might
20 experience some painful embarrassment at stepping suddenly into the world to

which she had been lost for a quarter of a century. But, again, I found how su-
perficially I had judged her. She sat looking about her with eyes as impersonal,
almost as stony, as those with which the granite King Ramses in a museum
watches the ebb and flow of people about his pedestal—separated from them by
25   the lonely stretch of centuries.

When the musicians came out and took their places, she gave a little stir of
anticipation and looked with quickening interest down over the rail at that unchanging grouping, perhaps the first familiar thing that had greeted her eye since
she had left old Maggie and her weakling calf. I could feel how all those details
30   sank into her soul, for I had not forgotten how they had sunk into mine when I
came fresh from plowing between green aisles of corn, where one might walk from
daybreak to dusk without perceiving a shadow of change. The clean profiles of the
musicians, the gloss of their linen, the dull black of their coats, the beloved shapes
of the instruments, the patches of yellow light thrown by the green-shaded lamps
35   on the smooth, varnished bellies of the cellos and the bass viols in the rear, the
restless, wind-tossed forest of fiddle necks and bows—I recalled how, in the first
orchestra I ever heard, those long bow strokes seemed to draw the heart out of me,
as a magician's stick reels out yards of paper ribbon from a hat.

When the horns trumpeted the first strain from the *Tannhauser* overture, my
40   Aunt Georgiana clutched my sleeve, and at that moment I realized that for her
this broke a thirty-year silence.

When the overture finished, my aunt released my coat sleeve but said nothing,
while staring dully at the orchestra. Aunt Georgiana had been a good pianist
in her day, and her musical education had been broader than that of most music
45   teachers twenty-five years ago. My aunt had often spoken of Mozart's operas and
Meyerbeer's, and I could remember hearing her sing certain melodies of Verdi's.

I watched her closely throughout the prelude to *Tristan and Isolde,* trying
vainly to conjecture what that seething turmoil of strings and winds might
mean to her, but she sat mutely staring at the violin bows that drove diagonally
50   downward, like the pelting streaks of rain in a summer shower. I wondered if this
music had any message for her, and I was in a fever of curiosity, but Aunt Georgiana sat silent. She preserved this utter immobility throughout *The Flying Dutch-
man,* though her fingers worked mechanically upon her black dress, as though,
of themselves, they were recalling the piano score they had once played. Her poor
55   old hands had been stretched and twisted into mere tentacles to hold and lift
and knead with; the palms unduly swollen, the fingers bent and knotted—on one
of them a thin, worn band that had once been a wedding ring. As I pressed and
gently quieted one of those groping hands, I remembered with quivering eyelids
their comfort for me in other days.

60   Soon after the tenor began the "Prize Song," I heard a quick drawn breath and
turned to my aunt. Her eyes were closed, but the tears were glistening on her

cheeks, and I think, in a moment more, they were in my eyes as well. It never
really died, then—the soul that can suffer so excruciatingly and so interminably;
it withers to the outward eye only, like that strange moss which can lie on a dusty
65 shelf half a century and yet, if placed in water, grow green again.

1. The passage makes it clear that Aunt Georgiana:
   A. played violin in an orchestra.
   B. has not seen Clark for some time.
   C. often listens to music.
   D. grew up on a dairy farm.

2. It is reasonable to conclude from information provided in the passage that
   Clark's relationship with his aunt developed from:
   F. childhood trips to the symphony.
   G. recent family gatherings.
   H. childhood memories on a farm.
   J. summer vacation experiences.

3. In the second paragraph, lines 9–11, Clark expresses his hope that Aunt
   Georgiana's interest in music has subsided. Which of the following quotations
   from the passage suggests that his hope was misguided?
   A. "She was slightly less passive, and for the first time seemed to recognize her
      surroundings."
   B. "She gave a little stir of anticipation and looked with quickening interest down
      over the rail."
   C. "When the horns trumpeted the first strain from the Tannhauser overture, my
      Aunt Georgiana clutched my sleeve."
   D. "I heard a quick drawn breath . . . Her eyes were closed, but tears were glistening
      on her cheeks."

4. Lines 18–21 indicate that Clark's feelings about his aunt are best described as:
   F. tentative.
   G. disapproving.
   H. agonizing.
   J. compassionate.

5. Details of the passage suggest that Clark takes his aunt to the symphony
   because he has a sense of:
   A. guilt.
   B. responsibility.
   C. gratitude.
   D. indebtedness.

6. The idea that music is an emotional experience for the characters in this story
   is best exemplified by which of the following quotations from the passage?
   F. "Those long bow strokes seemed to draw the heart out of me."
   G. "I could feel how all those details sank into her soul."
   H. "It never really died, then—the soul that can suffer so excruciatingly."
   J. "I wondered if this music had any message for her."

7. The passage indicates that Aunt Georgiana once played:
    A. the *Tannhauser* overture.
    B. *Tristan and Isolde.*
    C. *The Flying Dutchman.*
    D. the "Prize Song."

8. According to the passage, Aunt Georgiana's hands are swollen from:
    F. a broken finger.
    G. manual labor.
    H. a recent illness.
    J. playing the piano.

9. Which of the following best describes Aunt Georgiana's nature as it is presented in the passage?
    A. Reserved
    B. Disinterested
    C. Considerate
    D. Nurturing

10. It can be reasonably inferred from the passage that the moss mentioned in the last paragraph is symbolic of Aunt Georgiana's:
    F. life.
    G. innocence.
    H. spirit.
    J. wisdom.

PRACTICE SET 1: ANSWERS & EXPLANATIONS

1. **B** Specific Detail
    In paragraph 2, Aunt Georgiana speaks to Clark about one of her cows, as if he should remember the cow. However, the last sentence of the paragraph states that Clark's aunt had forgotten how long he had been away. The correct answer is **B**. Although Georgiana appears to live on a farm, it is not clear whether she grew up on one, so **D** can be eliminated.

2. **H** Inference
    In the second paragraph, Clark explains that he wanted to repay his aunt for the fun times they had spent milking cows together in the cowshed. This indicates that Clark spent time with his aunt on a farm, and that is where their relationship developed. **H** is the correct answer. **J** is wrong because it is too much of a stretch. Clark visited Georgiana, but the text doesn't suggest that the visits happened during summer vacations.

3. **D** Inference
    When Clark's aunt cries during the "Prize Song," Clark realizes that his aunt's love for music has not gone away but was suppressed. The music revives the passion that she once felt before she left the city and the music. **C** is incorrect because it is not clear at this point in the story how the music is affecting Georgiana. The fact that she clutches Clark's coat sleeve indicates that the

music has some impact on her, but after the overture finishes, Georgiana does not appear moved. By the time the "Prize Song" is performed, Georgiana's emotions are strongly evident. **D** is the best choice.

4. **J**   Point of View
    G and **H** can be eliminated because they are too negative. Clark shows compassion for his aunt in this section of the passage. Clark is worried that his aunt will feel awkward because she does not fit in with the crowd, and he does not want her to feel any *painful embarrassment*. **J** is the correct answer.

5. **C**   Cause-Effect
    The first sentence of the second paragraph states that Clark planned the trip to the symphony to "repay" his aunt for her kindness to him in the past, so he wanted to express his gratitude. Clark does not feel indebted, which would imply that he owed her something. So, **D** can be eliminated. The correct answer is **C**.

6. **F**   Inference
    G and **H** describe the emotions of *feeling* and *suffering*, but these statements do not express the idea that music is emotional for the characters. Instead, the emotional release brought about by music is best exemplified by Clark's first symphony experience, as described in paragraph 4. Clark describes that the bow strokes drew "the heart" out of him, much like a magician draws ribbon from a hat. The correct answer is **F**.

7. **C**   Specific Detail
    In paragraph 7, the narrator indicates that when *The Flying Dutchman* is played, Aunt Georgiana moves her fingers as she remembers the notes of the piano piece she once played. The text doesn't mention her "playing along" with any of the other pieces, so **A**, **B**, and **D** are wrong. The correct answer is **C**.

8. **G**   Specific Detail
    In paragraph 7, the author describes Aunt Georgiana's hands as "stretched and twisted" because they have been used to "hold and lift and knead." The years Aunt Georgiana has spent working on the farm have affected her hands, which once only played the piano. **F** and **H** are incorrect because no mention is made of injury or illness. **J** is also wrong because Georgiana has not played the piano in many years. Therefore, **G** is correct.

9. **A**   Character
    Aunt Georgiana keeps her feelings inside, which leaves Clark wondering what his aunt thinks about the symphony. In the last paragraph, Aunt Georgiana finally releases some of her pent-up emotions, but even then she does so very quietly. While Clark's fondness for his aunt may be explained by the nurturing she gave him when he was young, in this passage she does not exhibit that characteristic. So, **C** is incorrect. The correct answer is **A**.

10. **H** Inference

Just as dry moss can be made green with water, Aunt Georgiana's love for music has been revived, despite the many years that have passed. Aunt Georgiana's water is music, which makes her soul or spirit "grow green again." Therefore, the answer is **H**. The word *soul* mentioned in the paragraph is closer in meaning to *spirit* than to *life*, so **F** is incorrect.

PRACTICE SET 2: PROSE FICTION

This passage is adapted from the short story "The Story of an Hour" by Kate Chopin.

Knowing that Mrs. Mallard was afflicted with heart trouble, extravagant care was taken to gently disclose the tragic news of her husband's death.

Her sister Josephine informed her through broken sentences and indirect hints. Her husband's friend Richards was there too, since he had been in the
5   newspaper office when reports of the railroad disaster were received, and Brently Mallard's name topped the register of victims killed. Richards verified the information with another telegram, before hurrying to Mrs. Mallard's residence to prevent a less careful and tender friend from bearing the unfortunate message.

Unlike other women, she did not react to the news with a paralyzed
10 inability to accept its significance, but instead she wept immediately, with sudden, wild abandonment, and once the storm of grief ended, she retreated upstairs to be alone.

A comfortable armchair faced the open window in her room, and she sank into it, pressed down by a physical exhaustion that haunted her body and reached her
15 soul. In the open square outside her house, the tops of trees were trembling with new spring life, and the delicious breath of rain was in the air. In the street, a peddler was selling his merchandise, while the notes of a distant song faintly reached her, and numerous sparrows were twittering in the branches.

With her head thrown back on the chair cushion, she sat motionless, except
20 when a sob emerged in her throat and shook her, much like a child who has cried itself to sleep continues to whimper in its dreams.

With a lackluster stare, she gazed outside, not with reflection, but with a glance that indicated a suspension of intelligent thought. She discerned the approach of something understated and mysterious, and she felt it creeping out
25 of the atmosphere and reaching toward her through the sounds, scents, and color in the air.

She was beginning to recognize what was attempting to possess her, and she was striving to beat it back with her willpower, which was as ineffective as her slender hands.

30 When she succumbed, a little whispered word escaped her slightly parted lips, and she repeated under her breath: "Free! Body and soul free!" The vacant stare and the terrified look left her eyes, which were now perceptive and bright, and her pulse beat rapidly, as coursing blood warmed and relaxed her entire body.

She did not consider whether or not it was a monstrous pleasure that had 35 overcome her, since an unmistakable and exalted perception enabled her to reject the suggestion as trivial.

She realized that she would weep again when she saw the caring, tender hands folded in death and her husband's loving face. Beyond that bitter moment though, she envisioned a lengthy procession of years to come that would belong to her abso-40 lutely, and she opened and extended her arms out in a welcoming gesture.

Josephine was kneeling before the closed door with her lips to the keyhole, imploring her sister for admission inside. "Louise, open the door. What are you doing, Louise? For heaven's sake, open the door."

Ignoring her sister's persistent requests, she swallowed the very elixir of life 45 through the open window and recklessly anticipated the solitary days ahead, and she breathed a momentary prayer that life might be prolonged.

Existence would be for her own pleasure in the upcoming years, and no one would impose either loving or cruel intentions. Although she had loved her husband at times, the unsolved mystery of love did not matter now during her 50 moment of illumination.

She arose and opened the door to her sister's unrelenting demands, and with a feverish triumph in her eyes, she carried herself unwittingly like a goddess of Victory. She embraced her sister's waist, and together they descended the stairs, as Richards stood waiting for them at the bottom.

55 Someone was opening the front door with a latchkey; Brently Mallard entered, somewhat unkempt and travel-stained, but composedly carrying his traveling bag and umbrella. Mr. Mallard, far from the accident scene, had not even realized a catastrophe had recently occurred, and he stood astonished at Josephine's piercing cry and Richards' unsuccessful attempt to conceal him 60 from his wife's view.

1. According to the narrator, Richards rushes to Mrs. Mallard's home to:
   A. inform Mrs. Mallard that the news report is incorrect.
   B. provide medical care to Mrs. Mallard.
   C. verify that the news he has learned is true.
   D. prevent others from telling Mrs. Mallard the news.

2. It can be reasonably inferred from the passage that Mrs. Mallard believes her new attitude is:
   F. improper.
   G. narcissistic.
   H. justified.
   J. empathetic.

3. Which of the following best describes Mrs. Mallard's nature as it is presented in the passage?
   A. Fragile
   B. Confident
   C. Tentative
   D. Complaisant

4. Considering the events of the entire passage, it is reasonable to infer that the relationship between Mr. and Mrs. Mallard would most accurately be described as:
   F. stimulating.
   G. vindictive.
   H. emotional.
   J. indifferent.

5. According to the passage, Josephine most likely implores her sister to open the door (lines 41–43) because Josephine:
   A. worries about Mrs. Mallard's health.
   B. wishes Mrs. Mallard would stop crying.
   C. wants her sister to plan the funeral.
   D. thinks her sister should be more upset.

6. According to the passage, at what point does Mrs. Mallard weep?
   F. After Richards tells her of the accident
   G. After she goes upstairs to her room
   H. After Josephine knocks on her door
   J. After she sees her husband downstairs

7. Mrs. Mallard would most likely agree with which characterization of her husband?
   A. Callous
   B. Affectionate
   C. Foolish
   D. Oppressive

8. It can be reasonably inferred from the passage that Mrs. Mallard says "Free! Body and soul free!" (line 31) because she is:
   F. inhibited.
   G. distraught.
   H. fulfilled.
   J. liberated.

9. It can be inferred from the passage that the "elixir of life" (line 44) represents Mrs. Mallard's:
   A. cure.
   B. faith.
   C. fear.
   D. hope.

10. The attitude of the narrator in this passage toward Mrs. Mallard is apparently one of:
    F. disapproval.
    G. pity.
    H. acceptance.
    J. reverence.

PRACTICE SET 2: ANSWERS & EXPLANATIONS

1. **D** Specific Detail
   Richards races to Mrs. Mallard's home so that he can gently break the news of Mr. Mallard's death. As stated in the last sentence of paragraph 2, Richards wants to tell her before a "less careful and tender friend" has the opportunity, since Mrs. Mallard has a heart condition. Richards is not *verifying* the information but rather *conveying* the news, so **C** can be eliminated. The correct answer is **D**.

2. **H** Inference
   Mrs. Mallard has an enlightening experience when she realizes life without her husband will mean freedom. In paragraph 9, Mrs. Mallard does not stop to "consider whether or not it was a monstrous pleasure that had overcome her," which suggests she feels justified in her happiness. **F** is the *opposite* of what the text suggests, since Mrs. Mallard doesn't stop to consider whether her feelings are inappropriate. Therefore, **H** is correct.

3. **B** Character
   From the beginning of the passage, the narrator makes it clear that Mrs. Mallard has a heart condition and that she is physically fragile; however, her nature and character reveal a strong and confident woman. So, **A** can be eliminated. Her reaction to the news is "unlike other women," and after spending time alone in her room she walks down the stairs with "feverish triumph." This description is far too strong for a *tentative* nature, so **C** is wrong. **B** is correct.

The ACT
English &
Reading
Workbook

4. **J** Inference
Mrs. Mallard's emotions reveal that she will not miss her husband, although the narrator suggests she loved him "at times." Mrs. Mallard's thoughts of her husband suggest he imposed his wishes upon her, which suggests a mutually indifferent relationship. **G** is too strongly negative, and **F** is the opposite of what the text suggests. So, **J** is correct.

5. **A** Cause-Effect
Josephine breaks the news to her sister with "broken sentences and indirect hints" because she worries Mrs. Mallard's heart condition will make her ill. Similarly, Josephine waits outside Mrs. Mallard's door because she is concerned for her sister's health during this time of stress. There is no suggestion that Josephine feels that Mrs. Mallard should be *more* upset, so **D** is wrong. **C** is also not discussed in the passage. Therefore, **A** is correct.

6. **F** Specific Detail
The only time in the passage that Mrs. Mallard weeps is immediately after Richards tells her Mr. Mallard died. While Mrs. Mallard is emotional and shaken in her room, she does not weep again, although she thinks she will at the funeral. So, **G** can be eliminated. The correct answer is **F**.

7. **D** Character
Mrs. Mallard would likely describe her husband as *oppressive*, which explains her feeling of freedom at the news of his death. In paragraph 13, the narrator states that now no one would "impose either loving or cruel intentions" on Mrs. Mallard. The word *impose* suggests Mr. Mallard dominated the marriage, even if sometimes his intentions were positive. **A** can be eliminated because it is the opposite of what the passage suggests. **C** is also wrong. The main issue that Mrs. Mallard appears to have with her husband is not that he was insensitive, or *callous*, but that she felt her freedom restrained by him. So, **D** is correct.

8. **J** Inference
Mrs. Mallard feels liberated as she realizes the death of her husband means freedom for herself. The second sentence of paragraph 8 reveals that her body relaxes and her pulse beats rapidly, suggesting she feels better knowing she is on her own. The word *fulfilled* is less accurate than the word *liberated* here, so **H** doesn't quite fit for describing her feelings. **J** is the correct answer.

9. **D** Inference
Mrs. Mallard's enlightenment gives her hope for her future. In paragraph 12, the narrator describes Mrs. Mallard's anticipation of the future, and she utters a quick "prayer that life might be prolonged." Therefore, the answer is **D**. There's no mention of a cure for her illness, so **A** is wrong. **B** is also incorrect because Mrs. Mallard *anticipated* a positive future rather than believing strongly in one.

10. **H** Point of View
The narrator accepts Mrs. Mallard's feelings and emotions without disapproval, pity, or reverence, and relays Mrs. Mallard's actions and emotions without judgment, so **F**, **G**, and **J** can be eliminated. **H** is the correct answer.

PRACTICE SET 3: SOCIAL SCIENCE

This passage is adapted from an article titled, "Autism: More Cases, But Why?" by Salif Bhatia.

A recent study by the Centers for Disease Control and Prevention (CDC) discovered that about 300,000 children in the United States have been diagnosed with autism, a complex disorder of the central nervous system. For every 1,000 school-age children, about 5.5 of them have been diagnosed with the
5   syndrome, which approximately equates to one case for every 166 people. According to the CDC, studies performed in the 1960s revealed that autism was fairly uncommon, affecting about one person for every 2,000 to 2,500. The reasons why autism cases have increased are a source of debate for both the medical community and the families of those who suffer from autism.

10   Some people may remember Dustin Hoffman playing an autistic savant in the 1988 movie, *Rainman*. Hoffman's character had exceptional mathematical aptitudes but no social skills. However, the complex world of autism cannot be captured in a two-hour movie, and while Hoffman brilliantly depicts an autistic man with an intellectual gift, severe autism is more often accompanied by
15   below average intelligence.

Autism affects brain function and ultimately impacts an individual's social development and communication abilities. Occurring in all racial, ethnic, and social groups, boys are four times more likely to be affected than girls. Typically, autistic individuals face difficulties with verbal and nonverbal communi-
20   cation and social interaction, which can hinder their ability to form relationships with others; they often show tendencies towards repetitive behaviors and maintain narrow, limited interests.

One possible reason for the higher number of autism cases may be that the syndrome is being diagnosed earlier, due to greater community awareness about
25   the symptoms of autism. Information abounds regarding children's developmental stages, so parents, educators, and physicians can keep abreast of a child's mental and physical progression to determine whether a child is reaching appropriate milestones. Early detection is critical for autistic children; autism begins before the age of three, and early intervention programs can significantly
30   improve an autistic child's social, language, cognitive, and motor skills.

In a multimedia age, the internet provides parents with resources, contacts, and guidelines to help them determine whether their child may have autism and to encourage them to seek early intervention from a physician. Many foundations, often touted by celebrities, have been established to raise aware-
35   ness about autism. Former NFL-player Doug Flutie, whose son is autistic, can be seen on commercials spreading the word about the foundation his family established, which supports autism research and education and provides services for families affected by the syndrome.

In the early 1990s, the government broadened the definition of autism to
40 include a wider range of levels from mild to severe, all with three common
characteristics: unusual behavior, communication difficulties, and relationship
problems. Initially, only individuals exhibiting severe autistic characteristics
were diagnosed with autism, while less severe cases were often diagnosed with
mental retardation or a learning disability.

45 Since the broadening of the syndrome's definition, reports indicate that
autism cases have increased, and there has been a corresponding decrease in
mental retardation and learning disability diagnoses. Some people believe this
shift in diagnoses may be because special education programs in schools did not
categorize students as autistic before the 1990s, while others suggest that
50 autism intervention programs have improved dramatically and are now
drawing younger students into the special education programs.

Genetics is believed to be another factor relating to the increased number of
autism cases; however, this relationship is based only on correlations and not on
hard evidence since no one knows the exact causes of autism. Studies indicate that
55 autistic elements may run in families, and relatives of an autistic person often show
some facet of the syndrome, such as language or social difficulties. Studies also
indicate that if one identical twin has autism, the other twin has a 60% chance of
having autism and a 75% chance of exhibiting some autistic characteristics.

California noticed an increase in the number of autistic children from less than
60 4,000 seeking social services in 1987 to nearly 18,000 in 2002, including a preva-
lence of Asperger's Syndrome, a type of high-functioning autism, in Silicon Valley.
One theory for the dramatic increase in California suggests that people with the
genes that determine autism are drawn toward technical professions such as
computer science because social interaction is limited. The theory contends that
65 men and women with these anti-social tendencies developed relationships, and
later, their offspring were diagnosed with full-blown autism and Asperger's.

However, the above theories are not necessarily the explanations for the rise
in autism. In fact, many experts think that while genetics may play a role in
autism, environmental, immunologic, and metabolic factors also increase the
70 likelihood of having the disorder.

Determined to discover a reason for the rise in autism cases, many parents
of autistic children believe a preservative found in some vaccines explains the
increase in autism cases; however, a recent study disproves this connection.
Other suspected environmental culprits include: diet, viruses, and medications.
75 For example, when taken during pregnancy, the prescription drug thalidomide
has been associated with an increased risk of autism.

That more children than ever are considered autistic is not in question, but
why. The increase may be due to increased awareness, a wider range of diagnoses, genetics, or external forces, such as the environment and medications. Are
80 there really more autistic children in the world, or is the world just recognizing
them more quickly?

1. According to the statistical data presented in the passage, how many people are currently diagnosed with autism in the United States?
    A. 166 out of 1,000
    B. 166 out of 300,000
    C. 5.5 out of every 1,000
    D. One out of every 2,000

2. The passage indicates that autism affects all of the following EXCEPT:
    F. physical development.
    G. cognitive abilities.
    H. social interaction.
    J. speech skills.

3. As it is used in line 56, the word *facet* most nearly means:
    A. surface.
    B. episode.
    C. expression.
    D. aspect.

4. The passage presents the information that "if one identical twin has autism, the other twin has a 60% chance of having autism and a 75% chance of exhibiting some autistic characteristics" (lines 57–58) primarily to make the point that:
    F. a connection is believed to exist between genetics and autism.
    G. doctors can predict autism based on family history.
    H. autism cases are increasing because of genetic mutations.
    J. all autism patients have relatives with autistic characteristics.

5. It can be reasonably inferred that twenty years ago autism cases:
    A. were not often detected before the age of three.
    B. were rarely diagnosed and never treated.
    C. primarily affected girls instead of boys.
    D. led physicians to review family histories.

6. According to information presented in the passage, which of the following is NOT a cause of autism?
    F. Genetics
    G. Viruses
    H. Vaccines
    J. Diet

7. One theory discussed in the passage indicates that autism rates in Silicon Valley, California, may have risen because of the:
    A. high number of young married professionals.
    B. technical workforce in the community.
    C. environmental issues surrounding computer chips.
    D. increased population in the area.

8. The author's tone in this passage can best be described as:
   F. skeptical.
   G. ambivalent.
   H. anxious.
   J. objective.

9. It can be inferred from the passage that current intervention programs for autistic children are:
   A. ineffective.
   B. successful.
   C. innovative.
   D. overcrowded.

10. According to the information presented in the passage, which of the following best describes the relationship between mental retardation and autism?
    F. They are the same syndrome but with different severity levels.
    G. Both have been linked to a medication often taken during pregnancy.
    H. Mental retardation cases have increased at a rate similar to autism cases.
    J. Mental retardation cases have decreased with the rise of autism cases.

PRACTICE SET 3: ANSWERS & EXPLANATIONS

1. **C** Specific Detail
   The opening paragraph provides the statistics for autism rates today and forty years ago. **D** is incorrect because it refers to the rate from the 1960s. The current rate is one case out of 166 people, which is the same as 5.5 out of 1,000 people. Therefore, the correct answer is **C**.

2. **F** Specific Detail
   Paragraph 3 outlines the difficulties faced by autistic individuals. Autism affects brain function, social interaction, and communication abilities but not physical development. **G**, **H**, and **J** can be eliminated. The correct answer is **F**.

3. **D** Words in Context
   The word *facet* as it is used in the sentence means an *aspect* or characteristic of autism. **A** and **B** are incorrect because language problems and social difficulties would not be considered *surfaces* or *episodes* of autism. The word *expression* in **C** is tempting, but *aspect*, **D**, is a more precise definition. The correct answer is **D**.

4. **F** Main Idea and Argument
   Autistic tendencies may run in families, according to studies discussed in paragraph 8. The statistics about twins supports the argument that genetics and autism are connected. **G** is incorrect because the paragraph does not argue that doctors can *predict* autism. It claims instead that autistic elements *may* run in families. **F** is the best choice.

5. **A** Inference

The theory presented in paragraph 4 suggests that there are more autism cases now because in the past doctors and parents were not closely monitoring children's developmental stages. Autism develops by the age of three, and many autism cases were not diagnosed because early detection did not occur. **B** is wrong because it goes too far. The passage never states that autism was *rarely* diagnosed, just that it wasn't diagnosed as early. So, **A** is correct.

6. **H** Specific Detail

Genetics, viruses, and diet are all mentioned in the passage as possible causes of autism. **F**, **G**, and **J** are therefore incorrect. Information presented in paragraph 11 states that a recent study disproves the connection between a preservative found in vaccines and the increase in autism cases. **H** is the correct answer.

7. **B** Cause-Effect

The theory presented in paragraph 9 suggests that Silicon Valley has seen an increase in autism because individuals with anti-social tendencies, which are a characteristic of autism, tend to work with computers to avoid social interaction. Numerous technical professionals live in Silicon Valley, so any autistic tendencies might show up in their children. **B** is therefore correct. **A**, **C**, and **D** aren't mentioned in the discussion of Silicon Valley, so they are incorrect.

8. **J** Point of View and Tone

F and **H** are too negative, so these can be eliminated. The author of the passage presents a variety of theories about the rise of autism cases, suggesting the author is objective. The correct answer is **J**.

9. **B** Inference

The last sentence of paragraph 7 states that autism programs have improved dramatically and are attracting younger students. If the programs have dramatically improved, it is reasonable to infer that they are successful. Although the programs may be innovative and overcrowded, no mention is made to support those ideas, so **C** and **D** are wrong. **B** is correct.

10. **J** Comparison

The connection between mental retardation cases and autism cases is explained in paragraphs 6 and 7. Prior to the 1990s, autism cases were often misdiagnosed as mental retardation. Since changes were made to the criteria for autism, more autism cases have been diagnosed, and there has been a corresponding decrease in mental retardation diagnoses. **H** is wrong because it reflects the *opposite* of what is stated in the passage. Therefore, **J** is correct.

PRACTICE SET 4: SOCIAL SCIENCE

The following passage is adapted from an essay titled, "The Irish Potato Famine: Causes and Effects" by Polly Hanson.

According to the most recent U.S. Census Report, more than 34 million American citizens claim Irish ancestry, a number that is almost nine times the current population of Ireland. One reason so many Americans have Irish blood is the fact that over 1 million people immigrated from Ireland to the United

5　States during the mid-1800s when they fled massive starvation in their homeland. The Irish Potato Famine was caused by a potato fungus that destroyed Ireland's primary food source. As a result of hunger or disease, the Famine killed nearly one million Irish men, women, and children. Many factors led to the devastation brought about by the Irish Potato Famine, including the British

10　government's rule over Ireland and a heavy dependence on potato crops.

Ireland's introduction to the potato in 1600 changed everything, and the vegetable remains a staple in the Irish diet even today. Although not indigenous to the country, the potato thrives in Ireland's cool, moist soil, and the crop caught on quickly with Ireland's farmers. Moreover, the potato worked well in

15　the tumultuous country because during times of peace the potato crop was a reliable food source, and during warfare, the root survived underground, unlike other crops. By the 1800s, more than three million Irish peasants depended solely on the sustenance of potatoes. Full of protein, carbohydrates, and vitamins, a diet of potatoes actually improved the health of Ireland's most

20　impoverished citizens. Thanks to the potato's abundance and its ability to keep people healthy and well fed, Ireland's population grew quickly—from less than three million in the 1500s to an astonishing eight million people in 1840.

While the potato proved to be a healthy and sought-after vegetable, many farmers could not grow the crop on their farms. Potatoes could only be grown on small

25　Irish farms. Under British law, Irish Catholics could not enter a profession or purchase their own land. As a result, many Irish Catholics rented small plots of land, usually less than five acres, and planted potatoes, which grew abundantly and required little labor. One acre of land could produce nearly twelve tons of potatoes, which was three times the amount of grain that could be grown on the

30　same plot of land. Irish tenant farmers produced nutritious food for their families and earned an income from the crops they sold—until the Potato Famine.

The ramifications of depending on one source of food became clear when the blight, *Phytophthora infestans*, appeared in Ireland in 1845. The airborne fungus revealed itself when leaves on healthy potato plants blackened and then rotted.

35　Cool breezes carried the fungal spores to nearby plants, and under perfect conditions, one infected plant could contaminate thousands more in a few days. Initially, when the potatoes were dug out of the ground they seemed edible, but within days they shriveled and rotted. The blight wiped out Ireland's potato crops between 1845 and 1848, leaving people with no food and no way to

40　support themselves.

Because the potato was the Irish's primary food source, the Potato Famine resulted in the loss of many lives. When the potato plants were destroyed, people begged for food or work, and diseases ran rampant across the countryside. Irish families who could afford to travel left the country on crowded ships. While estimates vary, it is believed that over the next decade, nearly one million Irish citizens died, and another two million fled the country to the United States, Canada, Great Britain, and Australia, causing the population of Ireland to shrink by one-fourth.

Repercussions from the famine lasted for years, due in part to the failure of the British government to appropriately provide relief. The British Prime Minister bought foreign grains and cancelled the tax on imported grains hoping that the price of bread would decrease enough so that the impoverished Irish could afford it. This repeal of the Corn Laws was politically controversial and slow to be enforced, which did not help the starving Irish. Nearly two years after the blight began, soup kitchens, emergency relief programs, and workhouses became available to the Irish victims, although the system of relief was too little and too late. The British government's insufficient response to the needs of Irish citizens caused further tension between the two countries.

In hindsight, depending on one crop seems imprudent, but at the time, Ireland saw no need for worry. While the phrase "luck of the Irish" is often used to describe the inexplicable good luck of a person of Irish descent, some suggest it is a sarcastic term referring to the lack of good fortune for the Irish during one of the worst times in their history.

1. According to the passage, before 1600 Irish farmers were unable to grow much food because:
    A. grain and seeds were not readily available.
    B. drought conditions destroyed harvests.
    C. battles damaged crops and farmland.
    D. Irish farms were too small for substantial crops.

2. The passage indicates that one reason for the popularity of the potato in Ireland was that it:
    F. made farmers prosperous.
    G. was drought-tolerant.
    H. required little land.
    J. could be stored for months.

3. It can be reasonably inferred that one of the factors that caused strife between the British and Irish was:
    A. politics.
    B. religion.
    C. farming practices.
    D. foreign imports.

4. As it is used in line 12, the word *staple* most nearly means a:
   F. fastener.
   G. necessary item.
   H. chief export.
   J. suitable material.

5. With which of the following statements would the author most likely agree?
   A. The effects of the Irish Potato Famine could have been lessened.
   B. Irish immigrants who fled the famine overburdened the U.S. economy.
   C. The British government responded appropriately to the needs of Irish citizens.
   D. Irish farmers should bear total responsibility for the effects of the famine.

6. As it is depicted in the passage, the blight can best be described as a:
   F. fungus.
   G. bug infestation.
   H. nutrient deficiency.
   J. soil disease.

7. It can be reasonably inferred from the passage that the British government was:
   A. prepared for Ireland's misfortune.
   B. unified in its approach for aiding the Irish.
   C. managed by corrupt government officials.
   D. ill equipped for a disaster in Ireland.

8. According to the passage, the repeal of the Corn Laws was intended to:
   F. decrease the export of grain.
   G. provide relief to British farmers.
   H. raise funds for workhouses.
   J. increase foreign grain imports.

9. According to the information presented in the passage, what is the relationship between the potato crop and the population of Ireland?
   A. The population was cut in half after the blight and the ensuing famine.
   B. The number of Irish-Americans decreased once Ireland's farmers began harvesting potatoes again.
   C. The population nearly tripled after potatoes became the dominant food source prior to the blight.
   D. While the potato is historically connected to Ireland, there is no corresponding relationship with the country's population.

10. One of the main points made in paragraph 3 is that potatoes:
    F. improved the physical health of citizens.
    G. encouraged laziness among farmers.
    H. prevented illness and disease.
    J. allowed tenant farmers to buy their own land.

PRACTICE SET 4: ANSWERS & EXPLANATIONS

1. **C** Cause-Effect
    The second paragraph of the passage explains that battles between the Irish and English erupted in the countryside. As a result, farmers could not grow enough food, and their land was destroyed. The correct answer is **C**. Although paragraph 4 does mention that Irish farms were small, it does not state that farms were *too small* for substantial crops. **D** is therefore incorrect.

2. **H** Specific Detail
    Paragraph 4 states that the potato was successful in Ireland because it grew abundantly even on small plots of land. Drought and storage are not mentioned in the paragraph, so **G** and **J** are incorrect. **H** is the correct answer.

3. **B** Inference
    As discussed in paragraph 4, Irish Catholics could not own land under British law. Since the law applied specifically to Catholics, it can be inferred that religion was a controversial issue. The Irish would have used the land for farming, but farming practices aren't suggested as an issue, so **C** is incorrect. **B** is the correct answer.

4. **G** Words in Context
    F and **H** can be eliminated because they do not fit the context here. As used in this sentence, an item that is a *staple* is essential, basic, and necessary. The potato was a staple in the diets of the Irish in the 1800s, and it remains a staple today. Therefore, the answer is **G**.

5. **A** Inference
    Throughout the passage, the author notes that both the Irish and the British government made mistakes that could have lessened the effects of the famine. The Irish farmers only planted one crop, and its destruction led to their own. In addition, the government's delayed and inappropriate response to the crisis increased the number of deaths. Because both parties were responsible, **D** can be eliminated. **A** is the best choice.

6. **F** Specific Detail
    The fifth paragraph describes the blight, an airborne fungus, and its effects on the potato crop. **G**, **H**, and **J** aren't mentioned in the description of the blight. So, **F** is correct.

7. **D** Inference
    The information found in paragraph 7 states that it took the government two years to begin offering relief programs and soup kitchens to the Irish, suggesting the government was not prepared for a catastrophe. **B** is incorrect because the repeal of the Corn Laws was controversial. This suggests a divided, not unified, government. **D** is the correct answer.

8. **J** Specific Detail

The purpose of repealing the Corn Laws, as explained in paragraph 7, was to cancel the tax on imported grains, so Irish farmers would be able to purchase foreign grain. Relief was provided to Irish, not British, farmers, so **G** is incorrect. If the prices were low enough, the government hoped the Irish would be able to buy affordable bread and keep from starving. The correct answer is **J**.

9. **C** Comparison

The last sentence of the third paragraph states that the abundant potato crop led the population to expand from less than three million citizens in the 1500s to eight million in 1840, which is nearly a triple increase. **C** is correct. **D** is incorrect because it contradicts information given in the passage.

10. **F** Main Idea and Argument

A diet of purely potatoes provided enough nutrients and vitamins to improve the health of Irish citizens. So, **F** is correct. **H** is incorrect because it is too exaggerated. Potatoes improved the health of the Irish but did not necessarily *prevent* illness.

PRACTICE SET 5: HUMANITIES

The following passage is adapted from an article by Joseph Maxwell titled, "Mail-Order Homes of the Early 20th Century."

With the click of a button, people around the world order clothes, books, furniture, and nearly anything else on the internet without thinking twice about it. A century ago, the Sears Roebuck catalogue was the closest equivalent to internet shopping, albeit a more leisurely version. While consumers today
5 might use the internet to investigate home prices and availability, most people would probably not purchase a residence without at least walking through it, but that is exactly what homebuyers often did at the turn of the 20th century.

Americans flipping through their Sears Roebuck catalogue in the early part of the 20th century found build-it-yourself house kits advertised in between
10 pages featuring farm equipment, baby bottles, and dresses. Prices for kit homes ranged from $450 to $5,000, depending on the size and features. In 1908, the first year Sears offered home-kits for sale, the building plans and materials for Sears' "Modern Home Number 159," a two-story house complete with three bedrooms and one bathroom, could be purchased for $652 (about $13,000 in
15 today's dollars). This price was far more affordable than the cost of standard home construction. For the next thirty years, approximately 500,000 working- and middle-class Americans purchased do-it-yourself homes from a dozen different manufacturers and achieved the Great American Dream.

During the early 1900s, home ownership was a top priority for middle class
20 Americans, who had grown weary of living in noisy tenements or run-down

farmhouses. With a strong American economy and a fast-growing population, many people wanted new and better homes with modern conveniences, such as indoor plumbing and electricity. While the economy was surging, that did not necessarily mean the average American had the funds or skills to build a house from scratch, which involved cutting every piece of lumber with a hand saw.

Since 1895, Sears had been offering building supplies and house plans through its mail-order catalogue, but sales for these items were extremely poor and the company considered closing down the unprofitable division. Instead, in 1906, new management suggested a revolutionary idea of delivering building materials directly from the factory to the customer, which would eliminate storage and shipping costs for Sears and reduce prices for customers. In 1908, Sears introduced its "Modern Homes" division to the public through a special catalogue offering 22 house kits of moderate size, a number which eventually grew to over 400 available models as the dwellings increased in popularity. Other companies, such as Montgomery Ward and Aladdin, followed the approach Sears took and began selling kit-built homes, although Sears' popular catalog and name recognition gave the company a solid lead in the prefabricated housing market.

Convenience, affordability, and the flexibility of design drove the sales of kit homes, which came in a variety of styles, designs, and prices. Because professional architects were working for manufacturers, purchasers of prefabricated dwellings could customize their homes if a particular model did not meet their needs or desires. This allowed owners to become designers. With the assistance of architects, and for an additional cost, more windows could be added, bathroom fixtures changed, additional cabinetry included, and roofs raised to provide more space for additional bedrooms. Kits could also be purchased in stages, allowing people to add on to their homes as they saved more money or as their needs changed.

Kit home manufacturers utilized the expanding railway system to deliver their goods to homebuyers, enabling people in rural Kansas to own a home as fancy as one owned by a family in urban Chicago. After a customer had chosen a model from a catalogue and placed an order, two railcars containing 30,000 pieces—lumber, doorknobs, light fixtures, nails, paint, shingles, and the kitchen sink—would arrive at the depot nearest the building site. Transporting the materials from the station to the site involved numerous trips by truck or horse cart between the two locations for the homeowner. Prefabricated homes are more often found in cities than in rural areas due to the difficulty of transporting the construction pieces. However, in some cases, railways were amenable to helping rural homeowners take delivery of their materials by stopping miles from a depot and as close as possible to the construction site.

The kits from Sears touted the notion that "a man of average abilities" could assemble his own home. Every kit included a leather-bound instruction book with precise directions, precut lumber, and numbered pieces to make assembling the puzzle as simple as possible. Knowing some homeowners would not want to tackle such a large project, Sears provided estimates for what carpenters, painters, and other skilled laborers would most likely charge for their

65   services. Masonry and plaster were not included in the package, but sugges-
tions were provided in the instruction book regarding how many bricks would
be required for specific models. While some wary homeowners employed
professional carpenters, other families viewed the event as a fun family project
that lasted weeks and months.

70   Although all kit-built homes were assembled in virtually the same manner,
in no way were they architecturally identical. Mail-order houses ranged from
modest two-room bungalows to ten-room abodes in various architectural styles,
including New England Colonial, Craftsman, Cape Cod, Spanish, and Prairie.
Climate and location often determined the popularity of a house style. For
75   example, Spanish style houses and bungalows dominate the California landscape, while the one-story, thatch-roofed Craftsman bungalow style houses
prevail in Milwaukee.

In addition to architectural differences, most kit-home manufacturers differen-
tiated styles by quality level, offering a standard level and a top of the line for the
80   more discerning customer. Higher quality kit homes included heavy-duty shingles
and thicker walls for colder climates, while the standard homes used fewer
materials and were meant for warmer climates. While kit homes were inexpensive, both the standard level and premium level models included superior materials and shared similar features. High quality wood was used in all models for
85   structural support, flooring, and trim. As extra premium components, kit home
manufacturers often incorporated exterior features such as double-hung windows,
half-moon doors, and sun porches, while large moldings, decorative archways, and
built-in nooks and niches added to the interior quality of the homes.

To thousands of families one hundred years ago, mail-order homes provided
90   affordable, quality mass housing, something that contemporary families still
aim to find. Today, these old Sears homes are considered collectable because of
their high quality construction and materials; the homes are as solid today as
they were when they were first assembled. A modern-day Sears homeowner has
not only a well-built house, but a piece of Americana as well. Mail-order homes
95   reflect a time in the United States when quality counted and when innovations
were intended to help people achieve their dream of home ownership.

1. According to the passage, which of the following factors influenced the
popularity of kit homes?
     I. Strong economy
     II. Home design features
     III. Tax incentives
A. II only
B. III only
C. I and II only
D. I, II, and III

2. It can be reasonably inferred from the name "Modern Home Number 159," that early kit homes could be described as:
   F. ornamental.
   G. multi-functional.
   H. unassuming.
   J. unconventional.

3. As it is used in line 29, the word *revolutionary* most nearly means:
   A. drastic.
   B. innovative.
   C. rebellious.
   D. elaborate.

4. One of the main points made in the passage is that kit homes:
   F. will last throughout the next several decades.
   G. helped many Americans realize their dreams.
   H. represent American quality and creativity.
   J. offered middle-class citizens financial security.

5. The passage indicates that premium and standard level kit homes were alike in that they both:
   A. included high quality hardwood floors.
   B. featured extra thick walls for insulation.
   C. included bricks and mortar in the kits.
   D. had sun porches and large moldings.

6. The passage indicates that the expansion of the railroad:
   F. allowed people in rural areas to build kit homes.
   G. lowered costs for kit home manufacturers.
   H. negatively affected sales at local lumberyards.
   J. allowed for direct delivery to any building site.

7. One of the main points made in the seventh paragraph is that:
   A. the construction of kit homes always took months to complete.
   B. many different styles were available to customers.
   C. not every homebuyer was willing or able to assemble his or her house.
   D. manufacturers strived to make assembling homes easy for homeowners.

8. The passage indicates that the style a homeowner selected depended heavily on:
   F. lot size.
   G. local trends.
   H. building permits.
   J. environment.

9. It can be reasonably inferred from the fifth paragraph that one reason companies such as Sears and Montgomery Ward kept architects on their staff was to:
   A. satisfy safety and building requirements.
   B. influence worldwide housing trends and designs.
   C. encourage customers to buy extra features.
   D. reassure first-time homebuyers.

10. It can be reasonably inferred from the last paragraph that people who currently own early 20th-century kit homes regard them as:
    F. obsolete.
    G. invaluable.
    H. lucrative.
    J. commonplace.

PRACTICE SET 5: ANSWERS & EXPLANATIONS

1. **C** Specific Detail
   The second sentence of paragraph 3 states that the American economy was strong, and as a result people wanted to build new homes. The first sentence of paragraph 5 points out that kit homes were affordable and had flexible designs. No mention is made in the passage about tax incentives, so **B** and **D** are incorrect. The correct answer is **C**.

2. **H** Inference
   The name "Modern Home Number 159" seems unassuming because it is merely a number in a series, as opposed to a pretentious, fancy name. **F**, *ornamental*, is the opposite of what the name suggests. So, **H** is correct.

3. **B** Words in Context
   Sears was on the verge of closing its home division, until someone developed an innovative idea to deliver materials directly to customers. The concept was revolutionary because it had never been done before. The correct answer is **B**. There's no indication that the idea was *drastic* or *rebellious*, so **A** and **C** can be eliminated.

4. **G** Main Idea and Argument
   The last sentence of paragraph 2 states that 500,000 Americans achieved their dream of home ownership. The same point is repeated in the final sentence of the essay. Therefore, **G** is the correct answer.

5. **A** Comparison
   Paragraph 9 discusses the similarities and differences between standard and premium level homes. All homes included high quality wood flooring, while porches, molding, and thick walls were extra features. **D** and **B** are therefore incorrect. As noted in paragraph 7, masonry and plaster were not included in any kits. **C** can be eliminated. **A** is the best choice.

6. **F** Specific Detail
The first sentence of paragraph 6 states that railroad expansion allowed for the delivery of mail-order homes to rural areas of the United States. Deliveries could be made as close as the railroad tracks came to a building site, but not directly to a site, so **J** is wrong. Shipping costs and local lumberyards are not discussed, so **G** and **H** are out. Therefore, the correct answer is **F**.

7. **D** Main Idea and Argument
The seventh paragraph focuses on what manufacturers did to make construction simple. They included instructions, precut lumber, and numbered pieces to simplify the process for homeowners. While it is mentioned in the paragraph that not all homeowners assembled their own homes, that is not the focus of the paragraph. **C** is therefore wrong. The correct answer is **D**.

8. **J** Specific Detail
Paragraph 8 states that climate and location determined which house styles were popular in certain parts of the country. Paragraph 9 then states that models with thicker walls were built in colder climates, and standard level homes, which had fewer materials, were intended for warmer environments. **J** is the correct answer. Although location is mentioned, local trends are not, nor are building permits or lot size, so **G**, **H**, and **F** are incorrect.

9. **C** Inference
Sears and other kit home companies allowed buyers to customize their homes with the assistance of staff architects. Since alterations and additions cost extra money for customers, they were most likely profitable for kit home manufacturers. The correct answer is **C**. There is no suggestion that architects met a need to satisfy safety or building requirements, so **A** is incorrect.

10. **G** Inference
The author points out in the final paragraph that Sears homes are now collector's items, which would make them invaluable. While they are old houses, they would not be considered obsolete because they are still useful and of good quality. **F** can therefore be eliminated. The correct answer is **G**.

PRACTICE SET 6: HUMANITIES

The following passage is adapted from an article about Philo T. Farnsworth by Mark Edmunds titled, "There You Are, Electronic Television."

Connecting an Idaho potato field and modern telecommunication may seem like a stretch, but only because the inventor of the latter remains nameless to most of the world. Philo Taylor Farnsworth, the unheard of father of television, began and ended his life in virtual anonymity despite his enormous contribu-
5   tion to the world.

In 1906, Farnsworth was born in a log cabin in Beaver City, Utah, a community settled by his grandfather fifty years earlier under the instructions of Brigham Young, the Mormon leader. *Popular Science* and science books intrigued the young Farnsworth, who moved with his family to a ranch in Idaho when he was twelve years old, the same year he built an electric motor. The following year, Farnsworth won his first national science contest with a thief-proof automobile ignition switch.

Farnsworth's interests leaned toward molecular theory, electricity, and motors, as well as such newly available devices as the Bell telephone and the Edison gramophone. Farnsworth convinced his chemistry teacher, Justin Tolman, to tutor him and allow him to audit a senior level class. Farnsworth later credited Tolman for inspiring him to learn and experiment and for providing him with a solid background of scientific knowledge.

Tolman, who recognized the brilliance of his student, encouraged Farnsworth to produce sketches and prototypes of a vacuum tube that would later revolutionize television. As the story goes, Farnsworth's inspiration for the tube came while leading a horse-drawn plow during the summer of 1921 when he was only 15 years old. Turning back to evaluate his fieldwork, Farnsworth had an epiphany: he realized that he could scan an image in parallel rows, just as he was plowing the field row by row. Farnsworth imagined that he might be able to transmit an image to a screen one line at a time, firing electrons in a beam through the vacuum in a glass tube.

However, before Farnsworth followed up on his idea, he enrolled at Brigham Young University in 1924, with only two years of high school to his credit. In 1926, two years into college, Farnsworth's father died, so he returned home to help support his mother by taking a public works job in Salt Lake City.

Despite being away from the scientific community for a time, Farnsworth never relinquished his dreams of invention. With the encouragement of his wife, Pem, and the financial support of friends, Farnsworth moved to San Francisco and set up a laboratory. On September 7, 1927, Farnsworth scratched a straight line down the center of a piece of black painted glass to make a slide. As Farnsworth, Pem, and George Everson, an investor, watched from one room, Cliff Gardner dropped the glass slide between a carbon arc lamp and a camera tube, which Farnsworth had invented earlier that year. Watching the receiver, the Farnsworths and Everson saw the straight-line image, and then they saw the image move when Gardner rotated the slide. Farnsworth had just demonstrated a transmission from the first all-electronic television, and with what could probably be called the understatement of the century, he simply remarked, "There you are, electronic television." Farnsworth's successful presentation earned him more funding, but it also placed him in the middle of an electronics industry race that he had not expected.

Farnsworth continued making improvements to his television for the next few years, and in 1930 Farnsworth earned a patent for his all-electronic television.

While Farnsworth may have been the first to invent the all-electronic television, Vladimir Zworykin, an electrical engineer at RCA, had invented a television that used a cathode ray tube and an all-electric camera tube. David Sarnoff, the RCA chief, offered to purchase Farnsworth's patents for $100,000, but the engineer refused and joined the Philco Company instead.

A patent battle eventually ensued over who invented television, Zworykin and RCA, or Farnsworth. During the legal battle, Farnsworth's high school teacher testified for his former student, stating that Farnsworth had conceived of the television idea in high school, and Tolman produced the original sketch as evidence. In 1934, the U.S. Patent Office decided in favor of Farnsworth, and after RCA lost court appeals, the company finally agreed to pay Farnsworth royalties.

The television was featured at the New York World's Fair in 1939 and soon after went on sale to the public. Unfortunately, Farnsworth did not earn many royalties from RCA because the government suspended sales of television sets during World War II, and by the time the war ended, Farnsworth's patents were near expiration. RCA took advantage of the situation by increasing television production and sales, and the company also publicized Zworykin and Sarnoff as the inventors of television.

Farnsworth could not battle such a large corporation, so he moved forward by working on other projects, including radar systems, the first simple electronic microscope, the first baby incubator, and nuclear fusion. Farnsworth remained relatively unknown as the chief creator of the world's most prevalent electronic invention, despite the fact that when he died in 1971 the average television set contained approximately 100 items he had patented.

Ironically, Farnsworth disliked his primary invention because he saw how it led people to waste their lives. In the mid 1950s, the inventor appeared as Dr. X on the television program "What's My Line." Trying to determine the identity of the mystery guest, one of the panelists asked Dr. X if he had invented a machine that causes pain, to which Farnsworth replied, "Yes. Sometimes it's most painful."

1. According to the passage, which of the following inspired Farnsworth to be an inventor?
   A. The telephone
   B. His biology teacher
   C. His grandfather
   D. The telegraph

2. It can be reasonably inferred from the passage that the relationship between Farnsworth and Tolman was based on:
   F. fierce competitiveness.
   G. absolute confidence.
   H. mutual admiration.
   J. family connections.

3. According to the passage, Farnsworth's vacuum tube involved images being scanned in:
    A. high frequency waves.
    B. magnetic waves.
    C. parallel rows.
    D. perpendicular rows.

4. As it is used in line 24, the word *epiphany* most nearly means:
    F. unexpected appearance.
    G. sudden insight.
    H. gradual understanding.
    J. meaningful experience.

5. One of the main points made in the passage is that Philo Farnsworth:
    A. was an outcast of the scientific community.
    B. received little recognition for his work.
    C. was ruined by corporate legal battles.
    D. became discouraged when his ideas failed.

6. As it is used in line 8, the word *intrigued* most nearly means:
    F. captivated.
    G. entangled.
    H. obscured.
    J. manipulated.

7. It can be reasonably inferred from the passage that the relationship between Zworykin and Farnsworth was:
    A. controversial.
    B. systematic.
    C. complementary.
    D. adversarial.

8. According to the passage, in what order, from earliest to latest, did Farnsworth invent the following devices?
    F. Electronic television, camera tube, radar
    G. Radar, camera tube, electronic television
    H. Camera tube, electronic television, radar
    J. Camera tube, radar, electronic television

9. It can be inferred from the passage that Farnsworth's television invention left him with feelings of:
    A. remorse.
    B. satisfaction.
    C. indifference.
    D. bitterness.

10. One of the main points of the eighth paragraph is that:
   F. RCA wanted control of Zworykin's cathode ray tube patent.
   G. RCA attempted to purchase all of Farnsworth's patents.
   H. Farnsworth contended that RCA had withheld television profits from him.
   J. RCA and Farnsworth disagreed about who owned the television patent.

PRACTICE SET 6: ANSWERS & EXPLANATIONS

1. **A** Specific Detail
   In the third paragraph, the information states that Farnsworth was interested in the newly available telephone and gramophone. Justin Tolman was an inspiration to him, but Tolman taught chemistry, not biology. So, **B** can be ruled out. The correct answer is **A**.

2. **H** Inference
   Tolman and Farnsworth admired each other greatly. Farnsworth took his prototypes and sketches to Tolman for advice, and Tolman testified for Farnsworth during his legal battles. Therefore, the correct answer is **H**. **F** can be eliminated because it is too negative. And **G** is too strong because of the word *absolute*, so **G** is also incorrect.

3. **C** Specific Detail
   In the fourth paragraph, the author discusses Farnsworth's inspiration for the vacuum tube. After plowing a field, Farnsworth realized he could scan an image in parallel rows, which makes **C** correct.

4. **G** Words in Context
   Farnsworth had a sudden insight about electronic television after plowing a field, as suggested by the word *realized*. The fact that Farnsworth came up with the idea after turning back to look at his field suggests that his insight occurred suddenly during the process of his work. Therefore, the correct answer is **G**. The insight was not gradual, so **H** is incorrect. The experience may have been meaningful for Farnsworth, but the word *epiphany* relates to the suddenness of the insight, so **J** can also be eliminated.

5. **B** Main Idea and Argument
   The opening paragraph refers to Farnsworth as "the unheard of father of television." Farnsworth was set back by his legal battles, but he managed to continue inventing many important devices. **C** and **D** can therefore be eliminated. So, **B** is correct.

6. **F** Words in Context
   Science books and magazines captivated Farnsworth from an early age. Farnsworth found science interesting enough to build electric motors and enter science contests at a very young age. **F** is the correct answer. **G**, *entangled*, and **J**, *manipulated*, have negative meanings that do not fit the context here.

7. **D**   Inference
Paragraphs 7, 8, and 9 describe the legal battle between Zworykin's employer, RCA, and Farnsworth. The two engineers were in a race to patent television, and their relationship was adversarial. **C** is the opposite of what is stated in the passage, and although the two men certainly had a controversy between them, there is no suggestion that their *relationship* itself was something that others disagreed over. **A** can therefore be eliminated as well. The correct answer is **D**.

8. **H**   Specific Detail
In paragraph 6, the information states that Farnsworth invented a camera tube earlier in the year. The camera tube was used in the demonstration of electronic television, so the television came after the camera tube. That means **F** is out. Later in life, Farnsworth invented a radar system, as noted in paragraph 10. Therefore, **G** and **J** can be eliminated. This makes **H** correct.

9. **A**   Inference
The last paragraph of the essay describes Farnsworth's attitude about television and his experience on a game show. When asked if his invention caused pain, Farnsworth replied, "Sometimes it's most painful." Farnsworth's response suggests regret and remorse. **B**, *satisfaction*, is too positive, and **D**, *bitterness*, is too negative. **C**, *indifference*, is too neutral, so the correct answer is **A**.

10. **J**   Main Idea and Argument
Paragraph 8 focuses on the legal battle between RCA and Farnsworth about who invented television. RCA did attempt to purchase Farnsworth's patents, but this is not the subject of the eighth paragraph, so **G** is incorrect. The correct answer is **J**.

PRACTICE SET 7: NATURAL SCIENCE

The following passage is adapted from an article by Gordon Jacobs titled, "Are You Getting Enough Sleep?"

Sleeping in class. Loading up on caffeine. Staying up late on the computer. For many teenagers, these are the activities that fill a typical day, but at what cost? Doctors and sleep experts recommend teens sleep nine hours a night, but reports show only 20 percent of them actually get that much shuteye. To make matters
5   worse, as adolescents age, they often sleep less: sixth-graders report sleeping an average of 8.4 hours, while high school seniors sleep only 6.9 hours a night, a loss of almost 12 hours of sleep every week. Sleepy teenagers pay the price for poor slumber habits because sleep deprivation decreases cognitive abilities, increases emotional problems, and raises the risk of physical health issues.

10   Sleeping during class may instigate laughs from friends and irritation from teachers, but it is an indication of sleep deprivation, which decreases mental activity. When the brain does not get enough rest, it fails to function efficiently because it is working so hard to counteract the negative effects of sleep loss. As a

result, concentration difficulties arise and an individual's problem-solving skills
become impaired, both of which directly impact an adolescent's ability to succeed
in school. A survey of over 3,000 high school students discovered that teenagers
receiving Cs, Ds, and Fs in school slept about 25 minutes less and went to bed
about 40 minutes later than their counterparts did who earned better grades.

Much of a student's school day is spent learning unfamiliar concepts and
tasks, and sleep deprivation hinders a teenager's ability to retain new information. Research indicates that individuals who sleep the recommended amount
the night after learning new material perform better on the next day's assessment than their peers who sleep less. After an individual learns new information, that night during sleep, activity occurs in the area of the brain that
processed that information earlier in the day, which improves retention during
tests the following day. Sleeping well is critical to the brain's ability to organize
and memorize new information.

Adolescents having trouble focusing in school and completing assignments are
often diagnosed with Attention Deficit Hyperactivity Disorder (ADHD). Recent
research draws an interesting connection between sleep deprivation and ADHD.
Some people have actually been misdiagnosed with ADHD, when a lack of
sufficient sleep due to a sleeping disorder such as sleep apnea or insomnia was
their actual problem. The similarity in symptoms—irritability, defiance, and
problems in school—makes it easy to understand why an improper diagnosis
might occur. In some cases, people have a sleep disorder in addition to ADHD, and
once the sleep issues are treated, improvements are seen in the ADHD symptoms.

No one who has stayed out late and gotten up early the next day can doubt
that sleep deprivation causes irritability. While caffeine may improve the
situation temporarily, long-term lack of sleep can cause a teenager's emotional
health to deteriorate drastically. Insufficient sleep leads to stress and anxiety,
the primary causes of insomnia. Insomnia and depression are interrelated
because insomniacs grow depressed from insufficient sleep, while people who
are depressed often have difficulties sleeping. Teenagers today are busier than
ever, and when sleep deprivation interferes with their ability to think, work,
and socialize, they are at risk for emotional problems, including depression.

Depression and sleep deprivation share some common symptoms including a
loss of interest in activities, a lack of energy, and moodiness. Certain areas of the
brain monitor emotions, determine social interactions, and facilitate decision-
making processes. During deep sleep, the activity in these areas is greatly reduced,
which suggests that deep sleep enables people to maintain appropriate emotional
and social functioning levels while they are awake. Much like a toddler who has
missed a nap acts out through temper tantrums, a teenager lacking enough sleep
may exhibit emotional sensitivity during ordinary activities and interactions.

Besides cognitive and emotional problems related to a lack of sleep, a teenager's
physical health can be negatively affected as well. Just as mothers and doctors
have been saying for years, it turns out that proper rest is needed for a healthy

body. Sleep deprivation increases the chance for infections by changing the blood levels of particular immune cells and proteins, thus putting sleepy adolescents at a greater risk for getting sick than their peers who get a good night's rest.

60   In addition to becoming ill, people who lack the recommended amount of sleep may gain weight. Research indicates that sleeping for only short durations may increase the likelihood of obesity because sleep deprivation increases the body's production of Ghrelin, an appetite-stimulating hormone, and reduces the production of the counterpart hormone, leptin, which suppresses appetite. A person's
65   appetite tends to increase with the decrease of sleep, and this may lead to obesity.

The nature of a typical teenager is to stay up late, especially in today's society with video games and computers keeping them entertained at all hours. While getting nine hours of sleep may seem impossible to some adolescents, their cognitive abilities, emotions, and health are being sacrificed. So perhaps the old adage was
70   right—"Early to bed, early to rise, makes a person healthy, wealthy, and "wise."

1. According to the passage, sleep deprivation:
    A. affects mostly middle school students.
    B. is caused by a sleeping disorder.
    C. stems from a hormonal imbalance.
    D. increases the likelihood of illness.

2. The passage suggests that if teenagers improved their sleep habits they would:
    F. not be diagnosed with ADHD.
    G. improve their social relationships.
    H. recover from illnesses quickly.
    J. improve their grades in school.

3. According to the passage, in order for the brain to function efficiently, adolescents should sleep how many hours each night?
    A. Six hours
    B. Nine hours
    C. Twelve hours
    D. Seven hours

4. It may be reasonably inferred from the passage that poor sleep habits partially explain:
    F. school attendance problems.
    G. adolescent indifference.
    H. teenage mood swings.
    J. increased information retention.

5. The passage indicates that deep sleep helps people maintain emotional stability because:
    A. the area of the brain that controls emotions slows down.
    B. people forget about their problems while they sleep.
    C. the brain's cognitive activity increases during sleep.
    D. the body's hormone activity decreases during sleep.

6. According to the passage, which of the following is NOT a symptom shared by both ADHD and sleep deprivation?
   F. Excess activity
   G. Disobedience
   H. School problems
   J. Irritability

   7, 30

7. The passage indicates that sleep deprivation may result in weight gain because the body:
   A. produces less Ghrelin and more leptin.
   B. decreases the levels of both Ghrelin and leptin.
   C. produces more Ghrelin and less leptin.
   D. increases the levels of both Ghrelin and leptin.

8. One of the main points made in the passage is that getting the suggested amount of sleep:
   F. is too difficult for most teenagers.
   G. improves a teenager's cognitive functioning.
   H. enhances an adolescent's confidence.
   J. becomes easier to accomplish in adulthood.

9. With which of the following statements would the author most likely agree?
   A. Sleep deprivation causes only short-term problems.
   B. The sleep habits of today's teenagers are harmful.
   C. School behavior problems are rising because of sleep problems.
   D. Sleep deprivation explains the increase of obesity in the United States.

   10/10!

10. The author suggests teenagers could perform better in school if they:
    F. slept longer on weekends to catch up on lost sleep.
    G. took naps before finishing homework.
    H. slept the recommended amount on school nights.
    J. played fewer video games and watched less television.

PRACTICE SET 7: ANSWERS & EXPLANATIONS

1. **D** Specific Detail
   The last sentence of paragraph 7 states that sleep deprived teens have a higher risk of getting sick than adolescents who sleep more. So, **D** is correct. Paragraph 8 points out that sleep deprivation can affect hormone levels. However, the text does not suggest that sleep deprivation is *caused* by hormone imbalance, so **C** is incorrect.

2. **J** Inference
   The second paragraph explains that the brain does not work well when sleep loss has occurred. The brain has to work harder to make up for the "negative effects" brought about by sleep deprivation, so when it is time to solve problems, remember information, or concentrate, the brain cannot function as well as it

would with more rest. Therefore, if teenagers improved their sleep habits, their grades would improve as well. This makes **J** correct.

3. **B** Specific Detail
Information in the first paragraph states that sleep experts and doctors recommend nine hours of sleep for teenagers. The rest of the paragraph discusses the actual amount of sleep that most teens get, which is less than what is recommended. **A** and **D** are too low, so they can be eliminated. The correct answer is **B**.

4. **H** Inference
In the sixth paragraph, the negative effect of sleep loss for a teenager is compared to that for a toddler. Both a toddler and a teenager display moodiness and emotional sensitivity as a result of sleep deprivation. **J** represents the *opposite* of what happens due to sleep deprivation. Therefore, **H** is correct.

5. **A** Cause-Effect
A cause-effect relationship between deep sleep and emotions is discussed in paragraph 6. The areas of the brain that control emotions rest during deep sleep; people are able to control their emotions better when that part of the brain has rested well overnight. **A** is the correct answer. Decision-making brain activity *decreases* during sleep, so **C** is incorrect.

6. **F** Specific Detail
Paragraph 4 explains the connection between ADHD and sleep deprivation. Misdiagnosis occurs because the symptoms of both conditions include irritability, defiance, and school problems. **J**, **G**, and **H** are therefore incorrect. Excess activity is a symptom of ADHD, not sleep deprivation. This makes **F** the best answer.

7. **C** Cause-Effect
The information in paragraph 8 states that sleep deprivation increases Ghrelin and decreases leptin, which may lead to weight gain. **C** is correct. **A** represents the *opposite* of the information given in the text.

8. **G** Main Idea and Argument
Paragraphs 2 and 3 discuss the negative cognitive effects of poor sleep habits. Sleep deprivation prohibits the brain from functioning at its best. Therefore, if teenagers sleep more, they will concentrate better and retain more information. So, **G** is correct. **F** is wrong because it is an exaggeration. Teenagers do not tend to get enough sleep, but the text never suggests that getting enough sleep is *too* difficult for teenagers.

9. **B** Point of View and Tone
Throughout the essay, the harmful effects of sleep deprivation are discussed. Sleep deprivation lowers cognitive abilities, increases emotional problems, and causes some physical problems. The correct answer is therefore **B**. School behavior problems are also related to other issues, such as ADHD, so eliminate

C. And while the passage notes that sleep deprivation may lead to obesity, it doesn't go so far as to suggest that sleep deprivation alone *explains* the increase in obesity in the U.S. **D** can also be eliminated.

10. **H** Inference
F and **G** are wrong because sleeping more on the weekends and taking naps are not mentioned in this passage. Although less TV and video games might improve study skills and sleeping habits, not participating in these activities is never suggested. So, eliminate **J**. Paragraph 3 discusses how sleeping well the night after learning new information improves test scores because it allows the brain to process the new material. Therefore, **H** is correct.

PRACTICE SET 8: NATURAL SCIENCE

The following passage is adapted from an essay by Stephanie Pierce titled, "The Technology Behind 3-D Films."

For most people, the classic image of 3-D films involves a dark 1950s movie theater filled with people wearing cardboard glasses watching a horror movie. Theatre patrons feel more like participants than mere observers when creepy characters seemingly reach out of the screen. Three-dimensional technology
5   reconstructs the way people normally see and create a sense of depth.

Three-dimensional technology has evolved since its early beginnings. Despite popular belief, the 1950s was not the first time audiences watched 3-D movies. *The Power of Love* premiered in 1922 and required audience members to wear anaglyph glasses, with one red lens and one green lens. Most 3-D films today use improved
10   methods, although Producer Robert Rodriguez chose to use anaglyph glasses for his films *Spy Kids 3-D:Game Over* and *The Adventures of Sharkboy and Lavagirl*.

The anaglyph method for producing 3-D films involves filming images from two slightly different viewpoints, one from the perspective of each eye. The two images are then projected onto the movie screen, one in red and one in blue, using two
15   different projectors. Anaglyph images, also known as stereoscopic images, must be viewed through glasses fitted with a red filter for one eye, and a blue or green filter for the other eye. The eye covered by the red filter sees only the red parts of the image, while the eye covered with the contrasting color sees only blue or green parts. The illusion of a 3-D image occurs because of the subtle separation of light
20   that provides a slightly different perspective to each eye. The brain combines the two colored images and interprets the mixed messages as being a result of different distances. However, discoloration often distorted early films that were made using the anaglyphic process because colors were the tools used to create the 3-D effect. As a result, the image quality of the early anaglyph films was poor.

25   During the heyday of the 3-D movie, which was 1952 through 1955, very few studios used the anaglyphic process, but instead turned to Polaroid filters because

they allowed color viewing. In the theater, two synchronized projectors carry two film prints, one for the left eye and one for the right eye. The projectors are placed at different angles and with different polarizations, and the two images are
30 superimposed onto the screen. Polarizing filters work by only allowing light of a specific direction through a lens, which for 3-D filmmakers meant improved film quality because polarized glasses were nearly clear unlike their colored predecessors. Moviegoers' 3-D glasses, which have lenses with different polarizations, separate the two different images, so that only one image is projected to each eye,
35 much like looking through binoculars or a View-Master. Although each eye is presented with a slightly different image, the brain manages to reassemble the two pictures resulting in meteors and monsters careening toward moviegoers.

Filmgoers first recognized the benefits of polarization at the 1939 New York World's Fair. The short film, *In Tune with Tomorrow*, was the first 3-D movie to
40 be filmed in color and shown using Polaroid filters. Created at the request of Chrysler Motor Company to boost sales, the extremely popular movie showed a 1939 Chrysler Plymouth being assembled, with music in the background. A few other short 3-D films were produced over the next decade, but the medium exploded during the 1950s.

45 During the early 1950s, the film industry faced stiff competition from the growing popularity and easy access of television. Movie ticket sales plummeted, and film industry executives needed something new to draw consumers away from their TVs and back into theaters. The answer to the studios' financial troubles was the 3-D movie. The gimmick was a hit with moviegoers, who
50 flocked to see movies such as *Bwana Devil*, *House of Wax*, *The Mad Magician*, and *Robot Monster*. While science fiction and horror movies were the preferred genres for 3-D special effects, movie studios also produced westerns and a few comedies using the polarization technique.

While polarization is still the preferred method used for 3-D films, other
55 options exist for studios and videogame-makers. With alternate-frame sequencing, two cameras are used to film a movie, like the other 3-D methods. When the images are printed onto one filmstrip, left-eye images are alternated with right-eye images. During viewing, the film is run at twice the normal speed, and the audience wears special shutter glasses with lenses that rapidly open
60 and close as the corresponding frames appear on the screen. While this method would be too cost prohibitive for movie studios to use for the public, some home 3-D systems are equipped with the technology.

Another 3-D method available to filmmakers, but not often used, involves a concept known as the Pulfrich effect. It uses the eye's tendency to equate distance with motion, which results in a 3-D effect. The problem with using this
65 method is it cannot show stationary objects jumping out of the screen because of its dependence on movement. The Pulfrich effect has been used occasionally on special television episodes, and viewers with Pulfrich glasses are able to see the effect, while other viewers do not notice it.

70   Although the present technology for 3-D video has never achieved the same widespread success as its audio cousins, stereo and surround-sound, many believe the future for video will be 3-D. Holographic projection and other new technology that once seemed like science fiction will be the needed break-through that will appeal to mass audiences. Presently, the future for video is

75 high-definition, but to quote the catch phrase from the campy 1952 3-D film, *Bwana Devil,* "What do you want? A good picture, or a lion in your lap?"

1. The passage indicates that another term for the anaglyph method of 3-D film production is:
    A. polarization.
    B. Pulfrich effect.
    C. alternate-frame sequencing.
    D. stereoscopic.

2. According to the passage, why was the anaglyph method not often used by movie studios during the 1950s?
    F. It was too expensive for public theaters.
    G. It did not allow for viewing a film in color.
    H. The glasses were unpopular with moviegoers.
    J. Film production was too time consuming.

3. The passage indicates that film studios began producing 3-D films in the 1950s because:
    A. improved technology lowered the costs of filming.
    B. horror film directors wanted special effects.
    C. the Pulfrich effect had been so popular on television.
    D. television was a competitor for moviegoers.

4. It may be reasonably inferred from the information in paragraph 5 that *In Tune with Tomorrow* was:
    F. a documentary.
    G. a newsreel.
    H. an advertisement.
    J. a propaganda film.

5. The passage suggests that the themes of many 1950s 3-D movies were:
    A. evocative.
    B. absurd.
    C. insightful.
    D. exotic.

6. The passage indicates that Polaroid filters improved film quality because the filters only allow light to pass through that is:
    F. first filtered by a projector.
    G. of a precise brightness.
    H. tinted red or blue.
    J. of a single direction.

7. According to the information presented in the passage, which of the following best describes the relationship between the anaglyph method and polarization?
   A. They are different names for the same method of creating 3-D films.
   B. Discoloration occurs as a result of both methods.
   C. They both involve dual film projection.
   D. Both require viewers to wear red and blue glasses.

8. As it is used in line 20, the word *perspective* most nearly means:
   F. mental outlook.
   G. vista.
   H. expectation.
   J. visual appearance.

9. One of the main points made in paragraphs 7 and 8 is that:
   A. polarization is the only technique used by modern 3-D film producers.
   B. 3-D methods other than polarization exist but are rarely utilized.
   C. the Pulfrich effect is a concept used frequently in science fiction films.
   D. holographic images are a 3-D technology often used in video games.

10. As it is used in line 22, the word *distorted* most nearly means:
    F. inaccurately reproduced.
    G. changed the meaning of.
    H. made crooked.
    J. misrepresented.

PRACTICE SET 8: ANSWERS & EXPLANATIONS

1. **D** Specific Detail
   In paragraph 3, the passage states that anaglyphic images are also called stereoscopic images. So, **D** is correct. **A**, **B**, and **C** refer to different methods for making 3-D films, not the anaglyph method.

2. **G** Specific Detail
   The opening sentence of paragraph 4 states that studios used polarization because it allowed for color viewing. Studios did not use anaglyphs because the film results were better with polarization. Poor film quality is mentioned in paragraph 3 as a drawback of anaglyph films, but **F**, **H**, and **J** are not mentioned as problems. This makes **G** the best choice.

3. **D** Cause-Effect
   The first two sentences of paragraph 6 explain that movie studios were being hurt by television. More people were staying home to watch TV, which was free, and they were not going to the movies. As a result, the studios began using 3-D films as a way to entice people to go to the movies. Horror films did use 3-D technology for special effects, but this was not the *motivation* for producing 3-D films in the 1950s. **B** can be eliminated. Therefore, **D** is correct.

4.   **H**   Inference

As explained in paragraph 5, *In Tune with Tomorrow* was a film created for Chrysler showing a Chrysler car being assembled. The film was developed to boost sales. It can be inferred that Chrysler hoped the film would inspire people to buy their car, so the film can be considered an advertisement. **J**, *propaganda*, is too strong. The correct answer is **H**.

5.   **B**   Inference

The names of the 1950s 3-D films, *The Mad Magician* and *Robot Monster*, imply the films were absurd and possibly ridiculous. The names do not suggest films with deep, meaningful messages, so **A** and **C** are incorrect. So, **B** is correct.

6.   **J**   Specific Detail

The description in paragraph 4 explains that polarizing filters allow light to come through in only one direction. **F**, **G**, and **H** aren't mentioned in paragraph 4. This makes **J** correct.

7.   **C**   Comparison

Anaglyph and polarization are two different methods of creating 3-D films, so **A** is incorrect. Although both methods require viewers to wear glasses, only anaglyph involves red and blue filters, so **D** is wrong. Early anaglyph films distorted images, but polarization produced improved film quality, so **B** can be eliminated. Both methods do involve the use of two projectors. Therefore, the answer is **C**.

8.   **J**   Words in Context

Perspective in this sentence relates to the visual appearance of the 3-D image. Each eye receives a different picture, or perspective, and then the brain combines the two images to create a 3-D effect. **F**, **G**, and **H** do not fit within the context here. So, **J** is correct.

9.   **B**   Main Idea and Argument

Paragraphs 7 and 8 do not discuss polarization but instead the other available types of 3-D technology. So, **A** is incorrect. Alternate-frame sequencing is too expensive to be used much, and the Pulfrich effect has only been used on occasion. **C** is therefore wrong as well. The correct answer is **B**.

10.   **F**   Words in Context

Distorted in this sentence refers to the poor image results of the film. The technique caused the visual appearance of the film to be very low quality, as stated in the last sentence of paragraph 3. **G** and **J** do not fit the context here. **H** is too much of a stretch; the passage explains that the films were poor quality, not that they were crooked. The correct answer is **F**.

OVERVIEW OF THE ACT WRITING TEST

A "great ACT essay" and a "great essay" are *not* the same thing. Truly great essays can take hours or even days to plan, research, and write. The ACT essay can't take more than 30 minutes. That means you've got to write an essay that reflects your genius in less time than it takes to watch your favorite sitcom, right? Wrong.

The ACT creators know that 30 minutes isn't enough time for anyone, anywhere, to write a genius essay. Forget genius. Forget about trying to write an essay that changes the world. When the ACT says to you, "Here's 30 minutes, write an essay," what they mean is: "Write a *standard* essay that does exactly what we want."

To give the ACT essay graders what they want, you need to have a very firm essay-writing strategy in place before you sit down to take the test. You then need to apply that strategy to whatever question the ACT essay poses. In this chapter, we'll teach you a strategy for writing a great ACT essay that will work every time, on any topic. It all starts with fast food.

THE FAST FOOD ESSAY

One of the best things about fast food is not just that it's quick, it's *consistent*. Walk into a McDonald's in Tosserdorf, Germany, and a Big Mac is still a robust, comforting Big Mac, just like at home. What makes fast food so consistent? Restaurants like McDonald's use the same ingredients and preparation methods at every location.

In this chapter, we'll show you how to apply the concept behind fast food to the process of writing the ACT essay. Practice with the two sample essay prompts provided in this workbook. With practice, you'll be able to write a top-notch ACT essay every time. To make it happen, you need to know three key things that all the fast food chains know:

1. Your Customers
2. Your Ingredients
3. How to Put the Ingredients Together

KNOW YOUR CUSTOMERS

After you finish taking the ACT, two "raters" will score your essay. These raters are trained and certified specifically for grading the ACT essay. Each rater is instructed to give every essay a score on a scale of 1–6. The two grades are then added together to make up your entire essay subscore, which will range from 2–12. If the two raters come to wildly different scores for an essay, like a 2 and a 5, a third rater will be brought in.

The essay-rater are your *customers*, and you want to give them an essay that tastes just like what they're expecting. How are *you* supposed to know what *they're* expecting? You can learn exactly what ACT essay-raters expect by looking at the actual ACT essay directions.

The ACT Essay Directions

Read the directions now and make sure you understand them:

> You have 30 minutes to construct an essay based on the above question. Think about your position on the question and make sure you have supporting reasons and examples to back up your opinion. Write an essay based on one of the two points provided, or you may choose to write on a different point of view.

We've expanded upon these directions and created a list of Do's and Don'ts in order to make the rules of great ACT writing easy to grasp:

DO	DON'T
Write only on the given topic.	Write on a topic that relates vaguely to the one given.
Take a clear position on the topic.	Take a wishy-washy position or try to argue two sides.
Write persuasively to convince the rater.	Write creatively or ornately just to show off.
Include reasons and examples that support your position.	Include examples not directly related to your position.
Write with correct grammar and spelling.	Forget to proof your work for spelling and grammar mistakes.
Write as clearly as possible.	Use too many fancy vocabulary words or overly long sentences.
Write specifically and concretely.	Be vague or use generalizations.
Write about five paragraphs.	Put more importance on length than on quality.
Write only on the given lined paper.	Make your handwriting too large (or you'll sacrifice space).
Write as neatly as possible in print.	Write in cursive. Print is much easier to read.

The Rater's Instructions

The raters must refer to a set-in-stone list of criteria when evaluating each essay and deciding what grade (1 through 6) it deserves. We thought you might appreciate having the scoring criteria spelled out and explained by the ACT right before your very eyes. They address a student's ability:

- To take and articulate a perspective on an issue
- To maintain a clear focus on the perspective throughout the essay
- To explain a position by using supportive evidence and logical reasoning
- To organize ideas logically
- To communicate clearly in writing

And here's how they separate the good from the bad:

SCORE	CHARACTERISTICS
4–6	Writers will show a clear understanding of the purpose of the essay by articulating their perspective and developing their ideas.
	Most generalizations will be developed with specific examples to support the writer's perspective.
	A clear focus will be maintained throughout the paper.
	The paper will show competent use of language.
	Although there may be some errors, these will only occasionally distract the rater and will not interfere with the rater's ability to understand the writer's meaning.
1–3	Writers will not clearly articulate a perspective on the issue.
	The writing will usually demonstrate some development of ideas, but the development may be very general or repetitious.
	Most papers will maintain focus on the general topic identified in the prompt, but they may not maintain focus on the specific issue.
	Except for the weakest papers, the essay will use a clear but simple organizational structure.
	The language will be understandable for the most part, but errors will distract the rater and possibly interfere with understanding.

Now you know your customers, and you know what they want. We'll spend the rest of this chapter teaching you precisely how to give it to them.

KNOW YOUR INGREDIENTS

To write a tasty ACT essay, you've got to know the necessary ingredients. The different grades of 1–6 are based on the quality of your essay in four fundamental categories:

1. **Positioning:** The strength and clarity of your stance on the given topic
2. **Examples:** The relevance and development of the examples you use to support your argument
3. **Organization:** The organization of each of your paragraphs and of your essay overall
4. **Command of Language:** Sentence construction, grammar, and word choice

1. Positioning

ACT essay topics will address issues that pertain to high school students. A typical ACT topic will give you a statement that addresses ideas like *dress codes*, *block scheduling*, *justice*, *the definition of success*, or *the importance of learning from mistakes*. Though this list may sound overwhelming at first, the broadness of the topics means that with a little thought you can come up with plenty of examples to support your position on the topic.

Philosophers take years to write volumes on the topics of *justice* or *success*. On the ACT, you get 30 minutes. Given these time constraints, the key to writing a great ACT essay is taking a strong position on an extremely broad topic. A solid position requires you to employ two strategies:

*   Rephrase the Prompt
*   Choose Your Position

Here's a sample prompt with the directions you will find on the test:

Many successful adults recall a time in their life when they were considered a failure at one pursuit or another. Some of these people feel strongly that their previous failures taught them valuable lessons and led to their later successes. Others maintain that they went on to achieve success for entirely different reasons. In your opinion, can failure lead to success? Or is failure simply its own experience?

You have 30 minutes to construct an essay based on the above question. Think about your position on the question and make sure you have supporting reasons and examples to back up your opinion. Write an essay based on one of the two points provided, or you may choose to write on a different point of view.

Rephrase the Prompt

Rephrase the prompt in your own words and make it more specific. If you rephrase the question:

"In your opinion, can failure lead to success?"

You might come up with a sentence like:

"Failure can lead to success by teaching important lessons that help us avoid repeating mistakes in the future."

Putting the ACT essay question in your own words makes it easier for you to take a position confidently since you'll be proving your own statement, rather than the more obscure version put forth by the ACT.

Choose Your Position

Agree or disagree. When you choose an argument for a paper in school, you often have to strain yourself to look for something original, something subtle. Not here. Not on the 30-minute, fast food essay. Once you've rephrased the topic, agree or disagree with it. It's that simple.

At this point, you may be thinking, "I could argue the 'agree' side pretty well, but I'm not sure that I totally believe in the agree side because . . ." Drop those thoughts. Remember, you're not going to have a week to write this essay. You need to keep it simple. Agree or disagree, then come up with the examples that support your simple stand. And don't take a position that straddles both sides of the issue.

2. Examples

To make an ACT essay really shine, you've got to include excellent examples. There are two things that make excellent ACT examples stand out from the crowd:

- Specific Examples
- Variety of Examples

Specific Examples

Strong examples discuss specific events, dates, or measurable changes over time. You must write about things that have happened in detail.

Let's say you're trying to come up with examples in support of the position that "Learning the lessons taught by failure is a sure route to success." Perhaps you come up with the example of the American army during the Revolutionary War, which learned from its failures in the early years of the war how it needed to fight the British. Awesome! That's a *potentially* great example. To make it *actually* great, though, you have to be able to say more than just, "The American army learned from its mistakes and then defeated the British Redcoats." You need to be specific: Give dates, mention people, battles, tactics. If you use the experience of the American army in the Revolutionary War as an example, you might mention the signing of the Treaty of Paris in 1783, which officially granted the Americans independence and gave the United States all lands east of the Mississippi River.

Don't be intimidated if you can't instantly recall the dates of pivotal historical events. Any descriptive details that you *can* provide will strengthen your argument, whether they are personal examples or historical facts. Just make sure to choose examples that you know a lot about in order to be specific. Knowing that the Americans defeated the British is the start of a great example, but you need to show specifically how the American victory answers the question, "In your opinion, can failure lead to success?" What failures on the part of the British government and army led to the Americans' success? (Morale issues, leadership differences, inadequate soldiers and supplies, the Battle of Yorktown, and so on.) The one-two punch of a solid example and details that use the example to prove your argument make the difference between a good ACT example and a great one.

Variety of Examples

The other crucial thing about ACT essay examples is how much ground they cover. Sure, you could come up with three examples from your personal life about how you learned from failure. But you're much more likely to impress the raters and write a better essay if you use a broad range of examples from different areas: history, art, politics, literature, and science, as well as your own life. That means when you're thinking up examples, you should consider as wide a variety as possible, as long as all of your examples work to prove your argument.

To answer the question, "In your opinion, can failure lead to success?" you might choose one example from history, literature, and business or current events. Here are three examples that you might choose from those three areas:

- History: The Americans' victory over the British in the Revolutionary War.
- Literature: In spite of David Copperfield's difficult childhood, he eventually found personal and professional happiness.
- Business or Current Events: The JetBlue airline succeeding by learning from the mistakes of its competitors.

A broad array of examples like those will provide a more solid and defensible position than three examples drawn from just one or two areas.

3. Organization

No matter what topic you end up writing about, the organization of your essay should be the same. Whether you're asked to answer, "Can failure lead to success?" or "Does progress always come at a cost?" the *structure* of your essay should be almost identical. The ACT is looking for those standard ingredients, and the structure we're about to explain will make sure those ingredients stand out in your essay.

So what's this magical essay structure? Well, it's back to the trusty fast food analogy: A good ACT essay is a lot like a triple-decker burger.

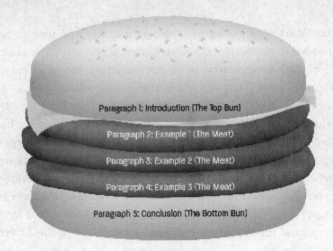

Paragraph 1: Introduction (The Top Bun)

Paragraph 2: Example 1 (The Meat)

Paragraph 3: Example 2 (The Meat)

Paragraph 4: Example 3 (The Meat)

Paragraph 5: Conclusion (The Bottom Bun)

No matter what the topic is, how you feel about it, or which examples you choose, you should always follow this five-paragraph structure on your ACT essay. The first and last paragraphs are your essay's introduction and conclusion; each of the middle three paragraphs discuss an example that supports and illustrates your argument. That's it.

Just as important as the organization of your entire essay is the organization within each of the five paragraphs. Let's take a closer look at each paragraph next.

The Top Bun: Introduction

The introduction to an ACT essay has to do three things:

* Grab the rater's attention
* Explain your position on the topic clearly and concisely
* Transition the rater smoothly into your three examples

To accomplish these three goals, you need three to four sentences in your introduction. These three to four sentences will convey your thesis statement and the overall map of your essay to the raters.

The Thesis Statement

The thesis statement is the first sentence of your essay. It identifies where you stand on the topic and should pull the raters into the essay. A good thesis statement is strong, clear, and definitive. A good thesis statement for the essay prompt, "In your opinion, can failure lead to success?" is:

> Learning from the lessons taught by failure is a sure route to success.

This thesis statement conveys the writer's position on the topic boldly and clearly. In only a few words, it carves out the position that the essay will take on the very broad, vague topic: learning from failure yields success.

The Essay Summary

After the thesis statement, the rest of the first paragraph should serve as a kind of summary of the examples you will use to support your position on the topic. Explain and describe your three examples to make it clear how they fit into your argument. It's usually best to give each example its own sentence. Here's an example:

> The United States of America can be seen as a success that emerged from failure: By learning from the weaknesses of the Articles of Confederation, the founding fathers were able to create the Constitution, the document on which America is built. Google Inc., the popular internet search engine, is another example of a success that arose from learning from failure, though in this case Google learned from the failures of its competitors. Another example that shows how success can arise from failure is the story of Rod Johnson, who started a recruiting firm that rose out of the ashes of Johnson's personal experience of being laid off.

Three sentences, three examples. The rater knows exactly what to expect from your essay now and is ready to dive in.

The Meat: Three Example Paragraphs

Each of your 3 example paragraphs should follow this basic format:

- 4–5 sentences long
- The first sentence should be the topic sentence, which serves as the thesis statement of the paragraph. It explains what your example is and places it within the context of your argument.
- The next 3–4 sentences are for developing your example. In these sentences you show through specific, concrete discussion of facts and situations just how your example supports your essay thesis statement.

Below we've given you an example of a strong meat paragraph:

> The United States, the first great democracy of the modern world, is also one of the best examples of a success achieved by studying and learning from earlier failures. After just five years of living under the Articles of Confederation, which established the United States of America as a single country for the first time, the states realized that they needed a new document and a stronger government. In 1786, the Annapolis Convention was convened. The result, three years later, was the Constitution, which created a more powerful central government while also maintaining the integrity of the states. By learning from the failure of the Articles, the founding fathers created the pivotal document of a country that has become both the most powerful country in the world and a beacon of democracy.

The best meat paragraphs on the ACT essay are specific. The ACT's essay directions say to make sure you provide examples to back up your opinion. In its topic sentence, this paragraph states that the United States is one of the great examples of "a success achieved by studying and learning from earlier failures." It then uses the specific example of the Articles of Confederation, the Annapolis Convention, and the Constitution to prove its position. It's specific throughout and even includes a few dates.

Transitions Between Meat Paragraphs

Your first meat paragraph dives right into its topic sentence, but the second and third meat paragraphs need transitions. The simplest way to build these transitions is to use words like *another* and *finally*. That means your second meat paragraph should start off with a transitional phrase such as, "Another example . . ."

A slightly more sophisticated way to build transitions is to choose examples from different sources, such as history and business. If the first paragraph is about a political instance of learning from failure and the second is from business, make that fact your transition: "As in politics, learning from failure is a means to gaining success in business as well. Take the case of . . ."

The Bottom Bun: Conclusion

The conclusion of your essay should accomplish two main goals:

- Recap your argument, while broadening it a bit.
- Expand on your position and look to the future.

To accomplish these two goals, your conclusion should contain three to four sentences.

The Recap

The recap is a one-sentence summary of what you've already argued. As in the thesis statement, the recap should be straightforward, bold, and declarative. By "broadening" your argument, we mean that you should attempt to link your specific examples to other fields, such as politics, business, and art. Here's a recap example:

> The examples of the Constitution, Google, and Rod Johnson make it clear that in the realms of politics and business, the greatest successes arise from careful considerations of the lessons of failure.

Expand on Your Position

The last two or three sentences of the essay should take the argument you just recapped and push it a little further. One of the best ways to push your argument further is to look to the future and think about what would happen if the position that you've taken in your essay could be applied on a broader scale. Here's an example:

> Failure is often seen as embarrassing, something to be denied and hidden. But as the examples of the U.S. Constitution, Google, and Rod Johnson prove, if an individual, organization, or even a nation is strong enough to face and study its failure, then that failure can become a powerful teacher. The examples of history and business demonstrate that if everyone had the courage and insight to view failure as a surefire way to learn from mistakes, success would be easier to achieve.

The Bottom Bun wraps up the entire ACT essay. And there you have it! If you follow the template we have just provided, and break down the essay into its core ingredients, your ACT essay will be strong, clear, and easy to write.

The Universal ACT Essay Template

To make sure you really get the essay organization we're suggesting, we'll sum it all up. Here's the ACT essay outline you should use, no matter what topic you get or what position you take:

Length		Purpose
The Introduction		
Thesis Statement	1 sentence	Describe your position clearly and concisely.
The Essay Summary	3 sentences	Lay out the three examples you will use to support your thesis statement.
Example Paragraph #1		
Topic Sentence	1 sentence	Describe your example and fit it into the context of your overall thesis statement.
Example Development	3–4 sentences	Show how your example supports your argument. Be as specific as possible.
Example Paragraph #2		
Topic Sentence	1 sentence	Describe your example and fit it into the context of your overall thesis. Provide a transition from the previous example paragraph.
Example Development	3–4 sentences	Show how your example supports your argument. Be as specific as possible.
Example Paragraph #3		
Topic Sentence	1 sentence	Describe your example and fit it into the context of your overall thesis. Provide a transition from the previous paragraph.
Example Development	3–4 sentences	Use specific facts to show how your example supports your argument. Be as specific as possible.

The Conclusion

Recap	1 sentence	Summarize your argument and examples, and link the examples to broader things like politics, history, art, business, etc.
Broaden Your Argument	2–3 sentences	Expand your position by contemplating what would happen in the world if other groups followed the argument you make in your essay.

4. Command of Language

Taking a clear position and defending it with solid detailed examples is a strong start to a successful ACT essay. But the ACT raters also care about the mechanics of your writing, which we call your "command of language." Think of your command of language as your fast food essay's Special Sauce—it's the coating of perfect word choice, grammar, sentence structure, and spelling that oozes through your entire essay. An ACT essay with a clear position and strong examples won't get a perfect score without the Special Sauce, so pay close attention to these three facets of your essay:

- Variation in Sentence Structure
- Word Choice
- Grammar and Spelling

Variation in Sentence Structure

Sentence structure is very important. Sentence structure, if done well, can keep your readers engaged and help make your essay exciting and easier to read. Sentence structure, if it is monotonous and unchanging, can make your essay sound boring and unsophisticated. Sentence structure is important on the ACT essay. Sentence structure is also important in essays you write for school.

Did you notice how dull that entire last paragraph became after the first two sentences? That's because every one of those sentences not only started in the same way but also all had the same predictable, plodding rhythm.

Now go back and look at the earlier sample meat paragraph on the U.S. Constitution. Notice how the various sentences start differently and also have different internal rhythms. These variations in sentence structure keep the writing vibrant and interesting. Focus on changing the structure of your sentences as you write the essay. You don't have to invert every clause, but you should be careful not to let a few sentences in a row follow the same exact structure. You've got to mix it up. Here's the boring first paragraph of this section rewritten with varied sentence structure:

Sentence structure is very important. Varying the structure of your sentences keeps your reader engaged and makes your writing easier to read and more exciting. Monotonous and repetitive sentence structure can make your essay sound boring and unsophisticated. Mixing up your sentence structure is crucial on the ACT essay—it's also important to consider when writing essays for school.

Much easier to read and far less repetitive, right?

Transitions Between Sentences

One great way to vary your sentence structure while increasing the logical flow of your essay is to use transitions. Transitions provide the context necessary to help readers understand the flow of your argument. They're words, phrases, or sentences that take readers gently by the hand, leading them through your essay. Here are some examples of different kinds of transitions you can use to spice up your sentence structure:

- Showing Contrast: Katie likes pink nail polish. *In contrast,* she thinks red nail polish looks trashy.
- Elaborating: I love staying up late. *Even more than that,* I love sleeping in until noon.
- Providing an Example: If you save up your money, you can afford pricey items. *For example,* Patrick saved up his allowance and years later purchased a sports car.
- Showing Results: Manuel ingested nothing but soda and burgers every day for a month. *As a result,* he gained ten pounds.
- Showing Sequence: The police arrested Bob at the party. *Soon after,* his college applications were all rejected, and *eventually* Bob drifted into a life of crime.

Overly Complex Sentences

Sometimes students think writing long, complicated sentences will impress teachers. Maybe, but it won't impress ACT essay-raters. Keep your sentences short and simple. Complex sentences are difficult to understand, and your ACT essays should be as clear and easy to read as possible.

We could fill an entire book with guidelines for creating simple and succinct prose. Instead, we'll give you two handy rules to simplify the sentences that you write on the ACT essay:

1. Never write a sentence that contains more than three commas. Try to avoid sentences with more than two commas. (Unless you need to include a list.)
2. Never write a sentence that takes up more than three lines of ACT-essay paper.

Those rules are certainly not foolproof, but abiding by them will keep you from filling your ACT essay with overly complex sentences and will ultimately make your essay easier to understand.

Word Choice

When students see that "word choice" plays a part in their essay score, they often think they have to use tons of sophisticated vocabulary words in order to score well. That belief is wrong and potentially damaging to your ACT essay score. If you're straining to put fancy words into your essay, you're bound to end up misusing those words. And misusing a sophisticated word is a worse offense than not using one at all.

Word choice doesn't mean that you have to go for the big word every time. It means you should go for the *proper* word, the best word, the word that makes your essay as clear as possible. Let's look at part of the paragraph about the U.S. Constitution:

> The United States, the first great democracy of the modern world, is also one of the best examples of a success achieved by studying and learning from earlier failures. After just five years of living under the Articles of Confederation, which established the United States of America as a single country for the first time, the states realized that they needed a new document and a stronger government. In 1786, the Annapolis Convention was convened. The result, three years later, was the Constitution, which created a more powerful central government while also maintaining the integrity of the states. By learning from the failure of the Articles, the founding fathers created the pivotal document of a country that has become both the most powerful country in the world and a beacon of democracy.

This is 6-level writing, but it isn't teeming with five-syllable words. What the passage does do is use every single word correctly. When it includes an uncommon word, like *beacon*, it uses the word appropriately and effectively. Now *that's* good word choice.

So don't try to use a word unless you know what it means. Don't go throwing around tough words in the hope that you'll impress your rater. The likelihood is that you're going to use the word incorrectly and give the rater a bad impression. Instead, keep it simple, and stick to words you know well.

Grammar and Spelling

A few grammar or spelling mistakes throughout your essay will not destroy your score. The ACT understands that you're bound to make minor mistakes in a rushed 30-minute essay.

Raters are instructed to look for *patterns* of errors. If a rater sees that your punctuation is consistently wrong, that your spelling of familiar words is often incorrect, or that you write run-on sentences again and again, your score will suffer.

You need to be able to write solid grammatical sentences to score well on the essay. As for learning the grammar, well, you're in luck. We cover all the rules of basic grammar and usage in the Usage/Mechanics Questions on the English Test section of this book.

KNOW HOW TO PUT THE INGREDIENTS TOGETHER

By now you know all of the ingredients you should use and the template you should follow to write a great ACT essay. Next you need to learn the writing process. Follow the five steps we describe below and you'll be on your way to a "6."

Five Steps to a "6"

STEP 1:	Understand the prompt and take a position.	1 Minute
STEP 2:	Brainstorm examples.	4–5 Minutes
STEP 3:	Create an outline.	5–6 Minutes
STEP 4:	Write the essay.	15 Minutes
STEP 5:	Proof the essay.	3 Minutes

Step 1. Understand the prompt and take a position. (1 minute)

The first thing you must do before you can even start to think about your essay is read the prompt very carefully. Here's the sample topic we are using throughout this section:

> Many successful adults recall a time in their life when they were considered a failure at one pursuit or another. Some of these people feel strongly that their previous failures taught them valuable lessons and led to their later successes. Others maintain that they went on to achieve success for entirely different reasons. In your opinion, can failure lead to success? Or is failure simply its own experience?
>
> You have 30 minutes to construct an essay based on the above question. Think about your position on the question and make sure you have supporting reasons and examples to back up your opinion. Write an essay based on one of the two points provided, or you may choose to write on a different point of view.

Make sure you understand the topic thoroughly by making it your own. To do that, use the two steps we discussed in the Positioning section:

- Rephrase the prompt. "Failure can lead to success by teaching important lessons that help us avoid repeating mistakes in the future."
- Choose your position. (In our example, we agree with the first question in the prompt.)

You believe the answer to the question, "In your opinion, can failure lead to success?" is yes. Terrific.

That's it. One step down, four to go.

Step 2. Brainstorm examples. (4–5 minutes)

Brainstorming, or thinking up, examples to support your position is the crucial next step. Plenty of ACT test-takers will succumb to the temptation to plunge straight from understanding the topic (Step 1) into writing the essay (Step 4). Skipping the brainstorming session will leave you with an opinion on the topic but with no clearly thought-out examples to prove your point. You'll write the first thing that comes to mind, and your essay will probably derail. So even though you feel the time pressure, don't skip brainstorming.

Brainstorming seems simple. You just close your eyes and scrunch up your face and THINK REALLY HARD until you come up with some examples. But, in practice, staring at a blank page under time pressure can be intimidating and frustrating. To make brainstorming less daunting and more productive, we've got two strategies for you:

Brainstorm by Category

The best examples you can generate to support your ACT essay topic will come from a variety of sources, such as science, history, politics, art, literature, business, and personal experience. So, brainstorm a list split up by category in order to organize your thoughts. Here's the list we brainstormed for your agreement with the question, "In your opinion, can failure lead to success?"

Current Events	failure of 9/11 security led to heightened security at airports
Science	babies learn to walk only after trying and failing time and time again
History	can't think of one
Politics	the U.S. Constitution was only written after the failure of the Articles of Confederation
Art	can't think of one
Literature	James Joyce became a writer only after failing as a singer
Personal Experience	Rod Johnson (your uncle), realized the need for a placement agency in South Carolina after getting laid off
Business	through watching the failures of its competitors, Google learned how to create a successful search engine

Let's say you took four minutes and came up with a list of eight categories like ours, and got examples for six of them. That's still great. That means your next step is to choose the top three of your six potential examples.

Prepare Ahead of Time

Brainstorming ahead of time can be a great method because it gives you time to do more than just brainstorm. You can actually prepare examples for each of the eight categories we've brainstormed above in our chart. You could, for instance, read about various scientists, learning about their successes, their failures, the impact of their discoveries (positive and negative), and memorizing dates, events, and other facts.

The risk inherent in planning ahead is that you can get stuck with a topic on the ACT in which all your knowledge about scientists just isn't applicable. But while this is somewhat of a risk, since the ACT essay topics are so broad, you can often massage your examples to fit. Still, if you don't want to risk wasting your time with advance preparation, don't.

Choose Your Top Three

When you go through your brainstormed and preprepared examples to decide which three you should actually use, you need to keep three things in mind:

1. Which examples can you be most specific about?
2. Which examples will give your essay the broadest range?
3. Which examples are not controversial?

The first two reasons are pretty straightforward: Specificity and variety in your examples will help you write the strongest essay. The point about controversy is a bit more subtle. Staying away from very controversial examples ensures that you won't accidentally offend or annoy your rater, who might then be more inclined to lower your grade. For instance, the 9/11 example from our brainstormed list should be cut. The event just is too full of unresolved issues to serve as a suitable essay topic, and the last thing you want to do is upset anyone.

Here's another example. Let's say that you're not so certain if that story about James Joyce being a singer is even really true, and you think lots of people might select the babies walking example. That would mean you decide to keep the examples about the U.S. Constitution, Google, and the story of Rod Johnson.

Now that you've narrowed down your brainstormed topics to the top three, it's time to move on. Next up: Outlining.

Step 3. Create an outline. (5–6 minutes)

After brainstorming comes the essay-writing step that students tend to dread most—writing an outline. We're here to encourage you to embrace the outline. Love the outline! Live the outline! At the very least, *write* the outline. Organizing your ideas in outline form and then sticking to that outline is crucial. Though you may feel that you're wasting your time, the five or six minutes that you invest in writing out an outline will *definitely* be paid back when you write the essay.

Writing the Outline

Since your outline is a kind of bare-bones "map" of your essay, the outline should follow our Universal ACT Essay Template. Here's a summary of the template:

PARAGRAPH #	PURPOSE	WHAT IT SHOULD CONTAIN
1	Introduction	Thesis Statement; State 3 Examples
2	Example 1	Topic Sentence for Example 1; Explain Example 1
3	Example 2	Topic Sentence for Example 2; Explain Example 2
4	Example 3	Topic Sentence for Example 3; Explain Example 3
5	Conclusion	Thesis rephrased in a broader way; a look into the future

As you write the outline, remember that conveying your ideas clearly is what matters most. Your outline need not be articulate or even comprehensible to anyone other than you. However, it must contain all the essential raw material that will become your thesis statement, topic sentences, and your concluding statement when you write your essay.

As you sketch out your outline, consider where you want each example to go. We suggest that you put what you consider to be your strongest example first, followed by the second strongest, and then the least strong. We suggest this because the essay is a timed section, and if you run out of time and can only fit two example paragraphs between your intro and conclusion, they should be your best two examples. Here's a sample outline we've written based on the topic and examples we have already discussed. Notice that we've placed our examples in strongest to weakest order starting in paragraph 2.

PARAGRAPH 1: INTRODUCTION	Failure can lead to success teaching lessons, learning mistakes. Three examples: 1) U.S. Constitution and Articles failure 2) failed dot coms lead to better, more successful online businesses 3) guy who started successful recruiting business after getting laid off.
PARAGRAPH 2: EXAMPLE 1 (BEST)	U.S. Constitution developed by studying the failures of previous document, Articles of Confederation. By studying failures the U.S. became true revolutionary democracy.
PARAGRAPH 3: EXAMPLE 2 (NEXT BEST)	Google studied competitors' struggles, then came up with better technological solution and better business model. Since failure is good teacher, intelligent companies look for failure everywhere, even in rivals, to learn and evolve.
PARAGRAPH 4: EXAMPLE 3 (NEXT BEST)	Johnson founded job placement agency based on difficulties finding a new job after getting laid off. Studied his failure; found problems lay with system, not with him.
PARAGRAPH 5: CONCLUSION	Failure often seen as embarrassing. People try to hide it. But if you or society take responsibility for it and study it, history shows failure leads to success for everyone.

Your outline does not have to be written in complete sentences. Notice how in the example above we drop articles and pronouns and write in a note-taking style. Write just enough to convey to yourself what you need to be able to follow during the actual writing of your essay. Once you have the outline down on paper, writing the essay becomes simply a job of polishing language and ideas, rather than creating them from scratch.

Step 4. Write the essay. (15 minutes)

Writing the essay consists of following your outline and plugging in what's missing. Your outline should already contain a basic version of your thesis statement, one topic sentence for each of your three examples, and a conclusion statement that ties everything together. The final product will be about ten more sentences than what you've jotted down in your outline. So, all together your essay should be about fifteen to twenty sentences long.

As you write, keep these three facets of your essay in mind:

- Organization
- Development
- Clarity

Following your outline will make sure you stick to the Universal ACT Essay template. That means *organization* shouldn't be a problem.

As far as *development* goes, you should make sure that every sentence in the essay serves the greater goal of proving your thesis statement, as well as the more immediate purpose of building on the supporting examples you present in the introduction and in each example paragraph's topic sentence. You should also make sure that you are being *specific* with your examples: give dates, describe events in detail, and so on.

By *clarity*, we mean the simplicity of the language that you use. That involves spelling and grammar, but it also means focussing on varying sentence length and structure, as well as including a few well-placed vocabulary words that you definitely know how to use correctly.

Do not break from your outline. Never pause for a digression or drop in a fact or detail that's not entirely relevant to your essay's thesis statement. You're serving fast food, and fast food always sticks to the core ingredients and the universal recipe.

If You Run Out of Time

If you're running out of time before finishing the introduction, all three example paragraphs, and the conclusion, there's still hope. Here's what you should do: Drop one of your example paragraphs. You can still get a decent score, possibly a 4 or 5, with just two. It is more important that you provide two well-written examples than three poorly written examples. Just be sure to include an introduction and a conclusion in every ACT essay.

The Finished Essay—Our Example

Here is an example of a complete ACT essay. It's based strictly on the outline we built in Step 3 of our Five Steps to a "6" with a focus on clear, simple language and the occasional drop of Special Sauce.

Learning the lessons taught by failure is a sure route to success. The United States of America can be seen as a success that emerged from failure: by learning from the weaknesses of the Articles of Confederation, the founding fathers were able to create the Constitution, the document on which America is built. Google Inc., the popular internet search engine, is another example of a success that arose from learning from failure, though in this case Google learned from the failures of its competitors. Another example that shows how success can arise from failure is the story of Rod Johnson, who started a recruiting firm that rose out of the ashes of Johnson's personal experience of being laid off.

The United States, the first great democracy of the modern world, is also one of the best examples of a success achieved by studying and learning from earlier failures. After just five years of living under the Articles of Confederation, which established the United States of America as a single country for the first time, the states realized that they needed a new document and a stronger government. In 1786, the Annapolis Convention was convened. The result, three years later, was the Constitution, which created a more powerful central government while also maintaining the integrity of the states. By learning from the failure of the Articles, the founding fathers created the pivotal document of a country that has become both the most powerful country in the world and a beacon of democracy.

Unlike the United States, which had its fair share of ups and downs over the years, the internet search engine company, Google, has suffered few setbacks since it went into business in the late 1990s. Google has succeeded by studying the failures of other companies in order to help it innovate its technology and business model. Google identified and solved the problem of assessing the quality of search results by using the number of links pointing to a page as an indicator of the number of people who find the page valuable. Suddenly, Google's search results became far more accurate and reliable than those from other companies, and now Google's dominance in the field of internet search is almost absolute.

The example of Rod Johnson's success also show how effective learning from mistakes and failure can be. Rather than accept his failure after being laid off, Johnson decided to study it. After a month of research, Johnson realized that his failure to find a new job resulted primarily from the inefficiency of the local job placement agencies, not from his own deficiencies. A month later, Johnson created Johnson Staffing to correct this weakness in the job placement sector. Today Johnson Staffing is the largest job placement agency in South Carolina, and is in the process of expanding into a national corporation.

Failure is often seen as embarrassing, something to be denied and hidden. But as the examples of the U.S. Constitution, Google, and Rod Johnson prove, if an individual, organization, or even a nation is strong enough to face and study its failure, then that failure can become a powerful teacher. The examples of history and business demonstrate that failure can be the best catalyst of success, but only if people have the courage to face it head on.

In the Sample ACT Essay section at the end of this chapter, we'll provide analysis to explain more fully why we think this essay deserves a "6." For now, it's time to move on to the final step of our Five Steps to a "6"—proofing your essay.

Step 5. Proof the essay. (3 minutes)

Proofing your essay means reading through your finished essay to correct mistakes or to clear up words that are difficult to read. If you don't have three minutes after you've finished writing the essay (Step 4), spend whatever time you do have left proofing. Read over your essay and search for rough writing, bad transitions, grammatical errors, repetitive sentence structure, and all that Special Sauce stuff. You should also be on the lookout for instances in which bad handwriting makes it look as if you've made a grammatical or spelling mistake.

If you're running out of time and you have to skip a step, proofing is the step to drop. Proofing is important, but it's the only one of the Five Steps to a "6" that isn't absolutely crucial.

SAMPLE ACT ESSAY—UP CLOSE

Here's the sample prompt again:

> Many successful adults recall a time in their life when they were considered a failure at one pursuit or another. Some of these people feel strongly that their previous failures taught them valuable lessons and led to their later successes. Others maintain that they went on to achieve success for entirely different reasons. In your opinion, can failure lead to success? Or is failure simply its own experience?
>
> You have 30 minutes to construct an essay based on the above question. Think about your position on the question and make sure you have supporting reasons and examples to back up your opinion. Write an essay based on one of the two points provided, or you may choose to write on a different point of view.

Below is our example of the "6" essay. As you read, note that we have marked certain sentences and paragraphs to illustrate where and how the essay abides by our Universal ACT Essay Template.

A "6" Essay

Learning the lessons taught by failure is a sure route to success. (THESIS STATEMENT) The United States of America can be seen as a success that emerged from failure: by learning from the weaknesses of the Articles of Confederation, the founding fathers were able to create the Constitution, the document on which America is built. (BEST SUPPORTING EXAMPLE [#1]) Google Inc., the popular internet search engine, is another example of a success that arose from learning from failure, though in this case Google learned from the failures of its competitors. (NEXT BEST SUPPORTING EXAMPLE [#2]) Another example that shows how success can arise from failure is the story of Rod Johnson, who started a recruiting firm that rose out of the ashes of Johnson's personal experience of being laid off. (NEXT BEST SUPPORTING EXAMPLE [#3])

The United States, the first great democracy of the modern world, is also one of the best examples of a success achieved by studying and learning from earlier failures.

(TOPIC SENTENCE FOR EXAMPLE #1) After just five years of living under the Articles of Confederation, which established the United States of America as a single country for the first time, the states realized that they needed a new document and a stronger government. In 1786, the Annapolis Convention was convened. The result, three years later, was the Constitution, which created a more powerful central government while also maintaining the integrity of the states. By learning from the failure of the Articles, the founding fathers created the pivotal document of a country that has become both the most powerful country in the world and a beacon of democracy. (FOUR DEVELOPMENT SENTENCES TO SUPPORT EXAMPLE #1)

Unlike the United States, which had its fair share of ups and downs over the years, the internet search engine company, Google Inc., has suffered few setbacks since it went into business in the late 1990s. (TOPIC SENTENCE FOR EXAMPLE #2) Google has succeeded by studying the failures of other companies in order to help it innovate its technology and business model. Google identified and solved the problem of assessing the quality of search results by using the number of links pointing to a page as an indicator of the number of people who find the page valuable. Suddenly, Google's search results became far more accurate and reliable than those from other companies, and now Google's dominance in the field of internet search is almost absolute. (THREE DEVELOPMENT SENTENCES TO SUPPORT EXAMPLE #2)

The example of Rod Johnson's success as an entrepreneur in the recruiting field also shows how effective learning from mistakes and failure can be. (TOPIC SENTENCE FOR EXAMPLE #3) Rather than accept his failure after being laid off, Johnson decided to study it. After a month of research, Johnson realized that his failure to find a new job resulted primarily from the inefficiency of the local job placement agencies, not from his own deficiencies. A month later, Johnson created Johnson Staffing to correct this weakness in the job placement sector. Today Johnson Staffing is the largest job placement agency in South Carolina, and is in the process of expanding into a national corporation. (FOUR DEVELOPMENT SENTENCES TO SUPPORT EXAMPLE #3)

Failure is often seen as embarrassing, something to be denied and hidden. But as the examples of the U.S. Constitution, Google, and Rod Johnson prove, if an individual, organization, or even a nation is strong enough to face and study its failure, then that failure can become a powerful teacher. (THESIS STATEMENT REPHRASED IN BROADER WAY THAT PUSHES IT FURTHER) The examples of history and business demonstrate that failure can be the best catalyst of success, but only if people have the courage to face it head on.

Why This Essay Deserves a "6"

First, we need to assess whether this essay contains the four essential ingredients of a great ACT essay. Here they are, just to refresh your memory:

1. **Positioning:** The strength and clarity of the position on the given topic
2. **Examples:** The relevance and development of the examples used to support the argument
3. **Organization:** The organization of each paragraph and of the essay overall
4. **Command of Language:** Sentence construction, grammar, and word choice

This essay serves up all four ACT essay ingredients. It takes a strong and clear stance on the topic in the first sentence and sticks to it from start to finish. It uses three examples from a diverse array of disciplines—internet technology to history and politics to a profile of an entrepreneur—and it never veers from using these examples to support the thesis statement's position. The organization of the essay follows our Universal ACT Essay Template perfectly, both at the paragraph level (topic sentences and development sentences) and at the overall essay level (intro, three meaty example paragraphs, a strong conclusion). The command of language remains solid throughout. The writer does not take risks with unfamiliar vocabulary but instead chooses a few out of the ordinary words like *beacon*, *deficiencies*, and *innovate* that spread just the right amount of Special Sauce throughout the essay. Sentence structure varies often, making the entire essay more interesting and engaging to the rater. Finally, no significant grammar errors disrupt the overall excellence of this ACT essay.

Here's a quick-reference chart that takes a closer look at this "6" essay based on the ACT's evaluation criteria for raters and based on our Universal ACT Essay Template.

ACT CRITERIA FOR "6" ESSAYS	YES OR NO?
Takes and articulates a perspective on an issue	YES
Maintains a clear focus on the perspective throughout the essay	YES
Explains a position by using supportive evidence and logical reasoning	YES
Organizes ideas logically	YES
Communicates clearly in writing	YES

OUR UNIVERSAL ACT ESSAY TEMPLATE CRITERIA	YES OR NO?
Thesis statement in first sentence of paragraph 1	YES
Three examples listed in paragraph 1 in order from best to worst	YES
Topic Sentence for example in paragraph 2	YES
3-4 development sentences to support paragraph 2's example	YES
Topic Sentence for example in paragraph 3	YES
3-4 development sentences to support paragraph 3's example	YES
Topic Sentence for example in paragraph 4	YES
3-4 development sentences to support paragraph 4's example	YES
Conclusion paragraph contains rephrased thesis statement	YES
About 15 sentences total	YES

Now that you know to how to construct a "6" essay, practice with the two sample essay prompts in the practice sets section. We'll show you "3" and "4" sample responses and explain how to rework them into "6" essays.

PRACTICE FOR THE ACT WRITING TEST

WRITING TEST

30 Minutes—1 Essay

DIRECTIONS: This section will test your writing skills. You will have thirty (30) minutes to construct an essay. Before starting your essay, read the essay prompt closely to understand exactly what you are supposed to do. Your essay will be graded on how well it conveys opinions on the stance taken on the question in the prompt, provides supportive evidence, focuses on the writing prompt's topic, creates a position through logical reasoning, and uses proper and clear language based on the standards of written English.

You may choose to use the unlined pages on the next page to outline your essay. Your work in this space will not be graded, but your writing on the lined pages that follow will be graded. Do not skip lines when writing your essay, even if you think you may not need all the lines. Corrections and additions may be written neatly between the lines, but do not write in the margins. Make sure you write clearly because illegible essays will not be graded.

You may review your work if you finish writing in under thirty minutes. When time is called, lay your pencil down immediately.

DO NOT START THE TEST UNTIL TOLD TO DO SO.

WRITING SAMPLE PROMPT 1

With enough advanced placement credits, college students may have the option of completing a four-year college degree in three years. Some people think that completing college in three years is a good idea because it helps students and their parents save money. Other people think that students should not complete college in three years because students on the fast track may lose the benefits of a four-year education, including graduating with their entering class. In your opinion, should students complete college in three years if this option is available to them?

You have 30 minutes to construct an essay based on the above question. Think about your position on the question and make sure you have supporting reasons and examples to back up your opinion. Write an essay based on one of the two points provided, or you may choose to write on a different point of view.

Plan your essay in the space below. When you are ready, you may begin writing on the lined pages that follow.

Start WRITING TEST Here.

If you need more space, please continue on the next page.

WRITING TEST

WRITING TEST

If you need more space, please continue on the next page.

WRITING TEST

STOP here with the WRITING TEST.

SAMPLE RESPONSES WITH EXPLANATIONS

A "3" Essay

Completing college in three years if you have the credits can sometimes be a good idea. But you have to keep your goals in mind and make sure your getting a good education.

Some people have to complete college in less years to save money. College is expensive, a fourth year adds to the cost. It is good for students to be responsible by "spending less". Because the money can be used for other important things.

College students sometimes get tired of going to school for so many years. After four years of high school, another four years is a long time. With classes and extra activities, you are on the go all the time. All of this work can make you just want to slow down. Your grades may suffer also.

In the end its really up to each person. I say don't spend four years if you can help it. Use your credits to finish college early and save money. It may help you have a better education than if you spent all four years.

Why This Essay Deserves a "3"

This essay would receive a score of 3 because the writer shows some skill in completing the task. The writer does take a position on the issue (*Completing college in three years if you have the credits can sometimes be a good idea*) and also offers some reasons to support the view (*Some people have to complete college in less years to save money. College students sometimes get tired of going to school for so many years*). The writer provides some evidence to support these reasons (*A fourth year adds to the cost. Another four years is a long time.*) The ideas are ordered logically and are grouped together in coherent paragraphs. The introduction reveals the writer's position, and the conclusion restates that position. The essay also shows a basic command of language and grammar.

However, the essay has several drawbacks. The writer's position is expressed somewhat ambiguously, stating only that completing college in three years can "sometimes be a good idea." In the introduction, the writer also provides a contrasting point of view (*But you have to keep your goal in mind*), which makes the writer's point less forceful. The details provided are general, not specific. For instance, paragraph 2 states that students' money "can be used for other important things," but it doesn't describe these details. The essay contains very few transitions, and the transitions that do exist are very simple, such as "in the end." The introduction and conclusion are not well developed, and the essay contains distracting grammar errors. The writer chooses words that are basic (*a good idea*) and not very descriptive.

This essay could be significantly improved by focusing on all four ingredients that make a strong essay: Positioning, Examples, Organization, and Command of Language. First, the positioning of the essay could be improved with a more forceful thesis statement. Second, the examples in the essay could be more specific and varied. Third, the organization of the essay could be revised to follow the Universal ACT Essay Template, which would involve developing each part of the essay more fully. Fourth, the essay could show greater command of language by correcting grammar mistakes, developing sentence structure, and including appropriate descriptive words.

A "6" Essay

Students should gain the most from their advanced placement credits by taking advantage of the option to complete college in three years. Financial savings provide one obvious benefit of a shorter college program: Students who complete college in three years cut their college costs by 25 percent. A three-year program also allows students a much-needed year of rest from school, which is important for reducing burnout. Another motivation for finishing college early is the freedom gained from an additional year to pursue personal interests.

The most significant reason for completing college in less time concerns financial savings. With expenses exceeding $20,000 per year for some private institutions, the cost of a four-year education can be a true burden. Financial aid helps to reduce costs to some degree, but many families still wind up with huge loans if their incomes don't qualify them for grant aid. Students who complete college in three years save themselves a full year of tuition and living expenses, in some cases eliminating the need for loans all together. Even a reduced-rate federal Perkins Loan can be costly when 5 percent interest is added each year, so the financial savings of a three-year degree program are considerable.

In addition to saving students money, the choice to complete college in three years can help prevent burnout. Students who are admitted to competitive colleges usually owe this achievement to perfect grades and impressive high school resumes. Many students hold multiple leadership positions for four years of high school, all while excelling at challenging advanced placement courses. After graduating, these students are faced with four more years of difficult coursework, social commitments, and possibly part-time jobs. This unending activity can cause college students to burn out over time. Three-year programs offer students a way to shorten their college stays and reduce stress.

Armed with savings and a renewed outlook, students who complete college in three years can also benefit from the flexibility that a "free" fourth year provides. Without the requirement of a fourth year of schooling, students can use their freed-up time in whichever way suits them best. For example, John Stoddard graduated from Harvard University in three years using his AP credits. He went on to spend the next year in France studying European business culture, which helped him choose a career in global business development. Other students might start jobs early or simply use their "free" year for mastering a hobby such as skiing. Regardless of the path chosen, completing college early provides students additional time to meet personal goals.

Early college completion programs are sometimes criticized for reducing the social support that students gain from graduating with their peers. But as the financial savings, stress reduction, and increased freedom show, completing college early offers clear advantages to students. Eligible students can boost their "lifelong learning" by moving through educational requirements quickly when given the option. A three-year degree enables them to use their resources to better explore what life has to offer beyond the structured school environment.

Why This Essay Deserves a "6"

This sample is strong on all four ingredients of a successful ACT essay. First, the essay presents a forceful position on the topic in its thesis statement: *Students should gain the most from their advanced placement credits by taking advantage of the option to complete college in three years.* Second, the essay supports this forceful position by providing three clear reasons, which are each developed with specific details. The initial reason, financial savings, is supported with details that show why college is expensive and how a three-year program can save costs. The second reason, preventing burnout, is supported by an in-depth explanation of college stress, which shorter programs can help alleviate. The final reason, *increased freedom*, is upheld with an example from personal experience based on an individual that the writer knows.

The third ingredient of the essay, organization, is also strong. This essay follows the Universal ACT Essay Template, including an introduction, three body paragraphs, and a conclusion. The "meaty" example paragraphs all have clear topic sentences that are developed in the body of that paragraph. The essay is well developed and fits within the 15–20 sentence range. The essay also stands out in terms of the fourth ingredient, command of language. Sentences are varied in structure and contain no significant errors. The author's choice of wording is descriptive and clear, adding just the right touch of Special Sauce to earn this essay a score of 6.

WRITING SAMPLE PROMPT 2

Educators debate adding financial classes, which teach students the basic principles of money management, to high school curricula. Some educators support including financial classes because they think that high school students will benefit from learning how to handle money from an early age. Other educators do not support including financial classes because they think that limited classroom time should be focused on academic subjects, such as math and reading. In your opinion, should financial classes be offered at high schools?

You have 30 minutes to construct an essay based on the above question. Think about your position on the question and make sure you have supporting reasons and examples to back up your opinion. Write an essay based on one of the two points provided, or you may choose to write on a different point of view.

Plan your essay in the space below. When you are ready, you may begin writing on the lined pages that follow.

Start WRITING TEST Here.

If you need more space, please continue on the next page.

The ACT
English &
Reading
Workbook

202

WRITING TEST

If you need more space, please continue on the next page.

If you need more space, please continue on the next page.

WRITING TEST

STOP here with the WRITING TEST.

SAMPLE RESPONSES WITH EXPLANATIONS

A "4" ESSAY

Many educators debate weather or not financial classes should be included in high schools to teach students the basic principles of money management. This is the individual school's choice and should be decided through weighing the pros and cons carefully. In my opinion, financial classes should be offered in high schools because they will help students better manage their money.

Even though it is true that time in the classroom is needed for other subjects, learning about finances is important because today's students don't know a lot about money. Also, the only way that many students learn about money is through their parents, who sometimes aren't very knowledgeable either.

Another reason is that classes may help students avoid making mistakes in handling money, such as getting into debt and ruining their credit. Students often receive a lot of credit card offers from companies that might charge them high interest rates. Learning about money could help students avoid the debt trap.

In addition, you will learn to be successful at a younger age. If you are older, you have less time to put away money toward achieving your dreams. Most people wait and wait to do anything about finances until they have some sort of wake up call. They spend their money and don't think about saving and then something happens one day to make them realize that they haven't achieved what they hoped for.

In conclusion, I think that offering financial classes in high school is the right choice because of the need for more knowledge and earlier success. Learning about finances is as important as learning academic subjects because it will help students in real life, but every school has to make it's own choice.

Why This Essay Deserves a "4"

This essay would receive a score of 4 because it shows adequate skill in responding to the task. The writer takes a position on the essay issue (*In my opinion, financial classes should be offered in high schools because they will help students better manage their money*). The writer also provides evidence to support his position in the three body paragraphs. Three reasons are given, one in each paragraph. Each paragraph sticks to the point made in its topic sentence. The introduction and conclusion are clear, and the writer's command of language is sufficient with only a few errors.

Though this essay completes the writing task adequately, the essay could be improved with greater depth in two areas. First, the writer could provide more specific and varied examples to illustrate the points. The three body paragraphs are very general in their support of the thesis. Specific details would help elaborate on the writer's points and make the essay more persuasive. Second, the writer could express a stronger command of the language by choosing more precise, descriptive words to convey detail. For instance, in the conclusion the writer states that offering classes is "the right choice." A better phrasing might state that financial classes "are a necessity." The word *necessity* is more precise than the word *right* because it conveys more meaning.

A "6" Essay

Financial classes should be offered at the high school level to teach students how to effectively manage their money. The need to improve students' financial knowledge is one strong reason for offering such courses early. Financial courses can also help students steer clear of mistakes that arise out of ignorance, including credit problems and poor investments. A third reason for offering the courses in high school is to help students establish financial security earlier in life.

The most important reason to teach financial classes in high school is because American students need to improve their financial knowledge. In 2002, a group known as the JumpStart Coalition gave a nationwide exam to determine the financial savvy of U.S. high school students. On average, the students answered only 50 percent of the questions correctly, which was considered a failing grade. Without formal classes, most students learn about finances from their families. If families aren't financially successful, students may have no way of learning how to manage money effectively. This situation could be improved with training at the high school level.

In addition to increasing students' knowledge, high school financial training is vital for helping students avoid costly mistakes. Students are bombarded with credit card offers in college or even earlier. With credit card rates skyrocketing as high as 29 percent, those who don't understand credit are vulnerable to making poor decisions. These bad decisions aren't limited to people of modest income: the bankruptcies of celebrities like Mike Tyson and MC Hammer show that even millionaires can mismanage their money by maintaining lavish lifestyles and spending beyond their means. Financial classes offered in high school could minimize these types of problems by teaching students balance and frugality.

Offering financial classes in high school can also set people on the road to financial success much earlier in life. Not everyone has the discipline of J. C. Penney, who started his first business at age 8 when his father informed him that he'd have to buy his own clothes. Though raised by poor farmers, Penney was determined to succeed in business and opened his first store at the age of 27. The typical individual is more likely to resemble Harland Sanders, who founded Kentucky Fried Chicken. He received his first Social Security check for $105 at age 65 and realized that he had to do something to change his fortune. Teaching finance principles in school is one way to help people achieve success at an earlier age.

Non-academic classes are sometimes criticized for tying up precious classroom time needed for core learning subjects. However, the benefits of financial programs—including increased knowledge, better decision-making, and earlier financial success—make the classes a necessity for high school students. Even if students don't have the resources of a celebrity, they can still benefit from learning to live within their means and develop conscious money management skills. However, if schools believe that adding a class in finance would take up too much time, a section on finance might be added to another course, such as health. In summary, high school finance classes are one step toward educating students how to effectively manage their money.

Why This Essay Deserves a "6"

This essay is markedly better than the "4" essay in all four ingredients necessary for ACT writing. The "4" essay expressed a clear position, but this essay goes further to provide a well-written, carefully worded thesis: *Financial classes should be offered at the high school level to teach students how to effectively manage their money.* The essay then develops the thesis in detail with specific and varied examples. In paragraph 2, the writer mentions a survey that shows how students are lacking in knowledge. In paragraph 3, the writer discusses high credit card rates and the spending habits of certain celebrities. The writer then compares two successful businessmen in paragraph 4.

Both essays follow the organization of the Universal ACT Essay Template, but the "6" essay develops each component in more depth. In the introduction, the essay lays out each of the three reasons that will be discussed in the body paragraphs. Each body paragraph is developed with four sentences, not just one or two. The conclusion also expands upon the writer's point by stating that finance classes can help students to reach their dreams.

Finally, the "6" essay shows a much stronger command of language. Phrases such as *financial savvy* (paragraph 2) and *mismanage* (paragraph 3) express the writer's ideas very descriptively. The word choice and sentence structure are sophisticated but still clear. This improved version therefore earns a score of 6.

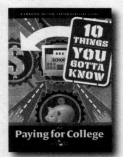